Outside Mental Health Voices and Visions of Madness

Books by Will Hall

Outside Mental Health: Voices and Visions of Madness

Harm Reduction Guide to Coming Off Psychiatric Drugs
(Available in 15 languages)

Outside
Mental Health
Voices and Visions
of Madness

Will Hall

"Will Hall's *Madness Radio* has long been for many a refuge and an oasis from the overblown claims and corporate interests of American psychiatry and Big Pharma. This collection of interviews and writings—bold, fearless, and compellingly readable—captures *Madness Radio*'s importance and fierce independence, urging us to think differently and anew about the 'thought disorders' involved in illness and wellness, sanity and recovery. Required reading."

Christopher Lane
author of *Shyness: How Normal Behavior Became a Sickness*

"This is a brilliant book... Nicely written, and wonderfully grand and big-hearted in its exploration of the world of mental health and much more. Remarkable in scope, *Outside Mental Health* delves into autobiography, psychology, sociology, philosophy, and spirituality. Will Hall elevates the radio interview format into an art."

Robert Whitaker
author of *Anatomy of an Epidemic: Magic Bullets, Psychiatric Drugs, and the Astonishing Rise of Mental Illness in America*

"Will Hall's gentle wisdom shines through in this diverse collection of intimate interviews. *Outside Mental Health* adds to our collective understanding of the complexity of human suffering, and offers new opportunities for compassion and healing."

Yana Jacobs. LMFT
former Chief of Adult Mental Health Services, Santa Cruz County, California, and current Senior Program Officer, Foundation for Excellence in Mental Health Care

"It is an exhilarating challenge and a great pleasure to be interviewed by Will Hall—a widely knowledgeable and widely explorative interviewer."

Maxine Sheets-Johnstone PhD
author of *Phenomenology of Dance*, University of Oregon Department of Philosophy

"An intelligent, thought-provoking, and rare concept...These are voices worth listening to."

Mary O'Hara
The Guardian newspaper columnist, and author of *Austerity Bites: A Journey to the Sharp End of Cuts in the UK*

"*Outside Mental Health* is a must-read, not only for those in the mental health field, family members, and those who experience extreme or altered states, but for anyone interested in creating a more just and compassionate world. Hall's lyric, authentic voice, woven throughout, speaks powerfully to the dominant narrative about mental illness, and provides hope for transformational change in our approach to emotional distress."

Alison Hillman
Open Society Foundation Human Rights Initiative, past Program Director for Disability Rights International, and 2011 appointee to the Presidential Committee for People with Intellectual Disabilities

"There are few books that I come across that make me want to drop everything I am doing and immediately read it on the spot. *Outside Mental Health* is such a book. Will Hall has given us a real gift: this book offers us a new, helpful, liberating—and dare I say, sane—way of re-envisioning our ideas of the nature of mental health and mental illness in a world gone mad. Truly an inspired, and inspiring, work."

Paul Levy
author of *Dispelling Wetiko: Breaking the Curse of Evil* and Director of the Padmasambhava Buddhist Center, Portland Oregon

"Will Hall has done an extraordinary job bringing together a wide-ranging and diverse collection, all united by a concern with empowerment. These voices challenge current orthodoxy and constitute a fantastic resource for those who are seeking change."

Dr. Pat Bracken MD
psychiatrist, philosopher, and Clinical Director of Mental Health Services, West Cork, Ireland

"This extraordinary book will make a difference for therapists and 'patients' alike. Interviews and essays acknowledge the overuse of medication and hospitalization, but don't demonize these treatments... *Outside Mental Health* reads with fierce emotional intensity: journeys shaped by forced commitments, homelessness, and soul-crushing family conflicts, as well as extraordinary triumphs, creativity, and originality."

Stanley Siegel
author, *The Patient who Cured His Therapist and Other Tales of Therapy*, and publisher, *Psychology Tomorrow* web magazine

"A terrific conversation partner."

Joshua Wolf Shenk
author of *Lincoln's Melancholy: How Depression Challenged a President and Fueled His Greatness*

"Phenomenal... a tome of treasures, filled with great findings for all kinds of seekers. And it begins with Will Hall's story, bravely and lovingly told. This outstanding book has brought together a rich trove of fascinating interviews with survivors, philosophers, researchers, artists, psychiatrists, journalists and scientists, all of whom illuminate the darkness and plot innovative strategies for survival and recovery."

Susan McKeown
Grammy award winning singer-songwriter

"*Outside Mental Health* explores the lived experience of psychosis and psychiatric treatments with openness and curiosity. Will Hall brings lessons learned from his own altered states and work as a therapist to offer fresh perspectives on madness and how to respond to it."

Arnold Mindell PhD
Jungian therapist, founder of Process Oriented Psychology, and author of *Processmind: A User's Guide to Connecting with the Mind of God*

Published in the United States by Madness Radio
Funded with Kickstarter

ISBN 978-0-9965143-0-9
eBook ISBN 978-0-9965143-1-6

Grateful acknowledgment is made to the following
for permission to reprint previously published material:

Brooks Permissions: *The Crazy Woman* © Gwendolyn Brooks

Hibernian Music: *Singing In The Dark* © Susan McKeown

Deviant Type Press: *Inbetweenland* © Jacks McNamara

Houghton Mifflin Harcourt Publishing Company:
Her Kind © Anne Sexton

Penguin USA: *Autobiography of a Schizophrenic Girl:
The True Story of "Renee"* © Marguerite Sechehaye

Selections from *Old New York City Where I Lay My Head*
© Eddie Bartók-Baratta

www.madnessradio.net
www.outsidementalhealth.com
www.willhall.net

Cover & text design by Alex Harris, www.alex-harris.co

Contents

Contents

Contents

Preface

WHAT DOES IT MEAN TO BE CALLED "CRAZY" IN A CRAZY WORLD?

Before I began to work as a community advocate and therapist, and before this book was conceived, I was a psychiatric patient. At age 26 my file from San Francisco's Langley Porter Psychiatric Institute read schizoaffective disorder schizophrenia, I carried a bus pass with the word DISCOUNT above my photo, and each month Social Security deposited $700 in my bank account to live on. "You have a thought disorder," the team of doctors told me in the locked ward. "Symptoms can be managed with medications, but there is no cure."

For many months before I was first hospitalized, there no sun was shining in my world. I barely spoke. I walked through the city all night, afraid of people watching me, unable to escape the loud, angry voice telling me I should die. I climbed out my apartment window to hide from my roommates, I watched for a demon to come at me through a postcard, through phone calls with no one on the other end. Then, on a cold January night, desperate for a way out, I wandered to the Golden Gate Bridge, dragging my bloodied hand against a chain-link fence. As the dawn broke, I stood by the roadside and held up an orange scrap of plastic sign debris, a riddle displayed for the rush-hour traffic. I was trying to say something, but I didn't know what it was. I made my way to the Divisadero Street clinic. Maybe they could tell me.

Staff put me under observation, then tied me down in restraints. They drove me in a dark van to San Francisco General Hospital, where, terrified, I was admitted as a psychiatric patient. And after more hospitalizations and stays in mental health residences, more tests and observation, I was pronounced schizophrenic.

Should I believe doctors who said my mind was unreliable and my only hope medications? Was this my new life, with no possibility of something more? Or should I start asking questions?

Today I no longer have a prescription for antipsychotic medications, Social Security deposits no money in my account, and I haven't been in a mental health facility in fifteen years. How did I get from there to here? How did I prove a team of psychiatric medical experts completely wrong about me?

Outside Mental Health is part of the answer.

For three years, I trusted doctors. I only got worse. In the hospital I was asked about a "family history of mental illness." I was never asked about a family history of trauma. My father was a foot soldier in the Korean War, and my mother is a sexual abuse survivor; I endured neglect and bullying at home and at school; I grew up amid the racial conflict of the South. I began to ask if war and social oppression could be part of why I was so terrified, why I fell into frozen states and couldn't move or speak. What if my "catatonia" was a way to protect myself, not just a proof of a diseased brain? Doctors asked me if I had "auditory hallucinations." But what if I was having spiritual experiences, what if I was hearing the tormented echoes of my ancestors? Maybe the visions I saw really were coded messages, messages about the world I live in. And what does it mean to be told you have a "thought disorder" in a world that is so disordered by violence, consumerism, and fear?

The diagnosis of incurable mental illness is not something you just leave behind when the hospital discharges you: the bracelet can be cut off, but the identity remains. As I began to ask questions, I realized I had to regain trust, not just in other people, but in my own mind. I desperately wanted to get better, but at each step my schizophrenia diagnosis blocked the way, making me doubt myself. If I didn't find my own voice, the doctors' verdict could become a self-fulfilling prophecy. Thinking for myself meant unlearning what the hospital said, and defying the relentless narratives of hopelessness that saturate our media culture.

We consider people with a severe mental disorder to be incapable of taking charge of their own destiny by exploring, learning, and finding a way. But this is a stereotype. There are growing numbers of people around the world who have survived psychosis and hospitalization and moved on, all kinds of people, from all kinds of backgrounds, with privilege and without, using many different strategies and all sharing one commonality: we are human. And like all living creatures, human beings have an innate capacity, even if it is just a potential, for survival, growth, and healing. Finding a life beyond madness, like finding a way out of any human suffering, is possible for anyone.

When I found friendship in the psychiatric survivor movement, my recovery picked up momentum. Drawing on my past training in journalism, I started the community radio program *Madness Radio*, seeking out conversations with people in the "mad movement" whom I learned about in support groups, gatherings, and workshops. Those interviews sustained me, gave me clues, and unlocked doors, reinforcing what I had learned and inspiring me to continue my search. A different understanding of my madness and "psychosis" emerged. I had nearly lost everything, and the stories on *Madness Radio* and now in these pages were making it possible to re-create a life for myself.

I interviewed more than 150 people, all of them excluded from usual mental health media coverage. Patients described how, like I was, they were abused in the name of care, even as they also soared to extraordinary spiritual and creative heights. Journalists helped me understand Big Pharma's corruption of science in the name of profits, and explained a more honest approach to what is known and not known about the mind. Researchers overturned conventional wisdom about medications and supported my choice not to take psychiatric drugs. Spiritual seekers conjured connections between mysticism, meditation, and psychosis. My own religious sensibility and indigenous heritage as mixed-race Choctaw Indian were reawakened, and I taught myself to listen for messages and purpose in what were labeled my delusions, paranoia, and voices.

With each *Madness Radio* conversation, I became more convinced: to find out who I was after being told I was schizophrenic, I would have to keep going outside "mental health." As I met fear and discrimination around my diagnosis, it became clear that the term "schizophrenic" stood in the way of my being a full human being. And it became clear that a world that would label anyone schizophrenic, even in the name of help, is a world that itself is crazy.

So I was left with the question: What place outside mental health could possibly be "outside" enough? More and more, I shed my identity as a mental patient and got closer to a new vantage point on myself. I expanded my support group work and began leading trainings and classes, earned a degree, and started working with individuals and their families as a counselor.

But I also faced a growing, and surprising, paradox.

The stronger I became in reality, and the more I became capable and my "functioning" improved, the more something unexpected happened. My altered states and different mental experiences that got called "psychosis" did not go away. They became *more* real. I found more and more reason to believe in the truth of my "symptoms." I wasn't recovering from "madness." Something far more mysterious was happening.

The hospitals and the threat of my label have faded. Today I am less isolated, more in control, and less terrified than I was that day when a team of doctors gathered around a consulting table to pronounce me schizophrenic. But my most "florid" symptoms of that time, my unusual beliefs, my conversations with voices, my paranoia, my contemplation of suicide, my silent inward withdrawal, my perception of prophetic omens... all of that remains. Professionals made their case for my severe mental illness diagnosis by presenting symptoms as evidence, but that evidence is all still part of me today, even as I live outside any psychiatric care or treatment.

I am doing something completely different from what medical and mass media narratives say I should be doing: I am regaining my wellbeing in the world while at the same time losing touch more and more with "reality." My madness is leading me somewhere that is *more* real than what everyone seems to say is real. I'm leaving behind not just the doctors' diagnosis, but also the mechanistic, soulless, and "objective" reality that gave rise to it.

I have begun to arrive somewhere very far outside mental health indeed.

"WHO'S THAT COMING IN THROUGH THE BACK DOOR?" When I was a kid, every Sunday we visited my grandparents' small family home on "the Boulevard," and every Sunday we passed by the front door. My father led us instead up the narrow side stairway to the kitchen, and when we rang the doorbell it wasn't my grandmother or grandfather who greeted us. The door opened and we were welcomed and hugged first by the cook and housekeeper, who were black, or "colored," as was still said at my grandparents' home in South Carolina in 1973.

I thought everyone who came to visit passed the front door and walked up the back steps like we did, until one day I saw my uncle's family arrive: they rang the front doorbell, and then gave a proper greeting to my grandparents. They did not hug the housekeeper first.

I didn't understand it, but each time my father led us up the back steps we were somehow at odds with the normal reality of my grandparents' house. This mysterious ritual was never mentioned, but I do remember a few times hearing my grandmother, with a strange tone in her voice, shout from the middle bedroom, "Who's that coming in through the back door?"

My grandmother knew, after so many Sundays, who was there. So why the question? And why did I hear a hint of something in her raised voice, a disguised satisfaction? She was, after all, calling loud attention to my father's unusual act, which was perhaps better passed over in silence.

The odd sound of that satisfaction resounded deep within me. My family fought again and again; growing up I lived in a frightening, ongoing tumult. But the fights were strange and incomplete, exploding out of tension that never eased and then suspended by obedience that was never talked about. And while this obedience was at times brutally physical, it was not total. In defiance of my grandfather's loud bigotry, my father had black friends and chose to marry my mother, a woman with mixed racial ancestry. So was my father's herding us through the back door another, subtle act of opposition? And was my grandmother's raised voice and "Who's that coming in through the back door?" a disguised act of allegiance with her son against my grandfather?

And why were the silver and crystal locked away in the mirrored cabinet, never taken out, for any occasion?

Social change in the South, like change everywhere, takes place in the quiet, tense gestures, as well as the grand dramas. My father was by no means anti-racist and my grandmother was by no means feminist. But the rise of Civil Rights, the challenge to Jim Crow, and the stirrings of the women's movement all played out along the fault lines of torn families and micro-conflicts, not just in the clamor of protests on the television news. When I heard my grandmother call out, "Who's that coming in through the back door?" I heard more in what was not said than in what was said.

Before I knew much about life, I was terrified by complex and confusing patterns of obedience and resistance that went along with the violence around me. There was raging abuse at home, and then my father, mother, brother and I would cross town for a polite dinner with our grandparents, as if nothing had happened. I listened to whites and blacks converse warmly with each other face-to-face, then heard, when they thought I was too young to understand, bitterness and rage spill out behind each other's backs. I saw my father screaming at my mother one moment and then smiling at her the next. I was bullied at the same school where I was praised for my success. Conversations avoided what everyone felt: code switching and caricature swirled unnoticed through the language, as if everyone were performing a dance choreographed in trance. Mysterious allegiances puzzled me, exchanges of secret conflicts and unspoken truths. And for some reason when others looked the other way, I found these knots of communication uncannily irresistible: they hinted at a reality much more compelling than the one openly acknowledged and spoken about, a reality calling to me.

Many fathers bring their sons into a world of violence and give them no guidance to navigate it. And some fathers are themselves lost in a phantasmagorical maze of complicity and dissimulation, both victim and perpetrator, a self-denial that can be far more oppressive than cruder forms of coercion. For violence to continue in the structural fabric of day-to-day life, as racism in the South (and the rest of the US) has since slavery time and as domestic violence continues, it must be wrapped in silence, in mute assent and carefully negotiated acceptance. The simple act of a Sunday visit becomes strange and incomprehensible to a young boy. Something was reaching me for in all those messages that I heard and felt. And so maybe to find my way to "reality," I had to leave behind what other people claimed was real.

TODAY I WILL MEET SOMEONE FOR THE FIRST TIME. I make breakfast, and last night's dream rings in my imagination: I was with my brother, we were playing together outside.

As I recall the strange atmosphere of the dream, I break a single egg into a bowl, and look down. I see two yolks there, fused together, both from the same shell.

I arrive at my counseling office, and the woman I meet says why she has come to see me. She tells me her birth was traumatic. She tells me that her twin sister died when she was born, and, she says, her sister is still haunting her.

Psychiatrists haven't helped; they labeled her delusional.

I sit listening to this anguished woman talk about her twin sister. I recall the dream about my brother from the night before, and I remember the egg I broke this morning. I know that it is only the habit of what we call "real" that makes us think there are two people in this room, instead of there being one person here, meeting themselves for the first time.

I REMEMBER THE DAY MY FATHER FIRST ENDED HIS SILENCE about his mental hospitalizations. He had never before told me of his own psychiatric diagnosis, had never told me about the shock therapy, the confinement, the beatings, or the drugging. There had been unspoken signs, comments overheard or tones of voice exchanged in strange moments between my mother and father, but it was all hidden, carried quietly underneath his grim, traumatic scars. It was too shameful, too painful, despite the fact that, if I had learned about it sooner, it might have helped me make sense of the chaotic and often terrifying way he treated us.

The day my father first spoke to me about his past as a psychiatric patient was just after the first time I myself had been hospitalized, and he never spoke about it again. This is how he said it: He looked at me with his eyes and face set in a subtle grimace, struggling not to speak and also forcing himself to speak. "I was in mental hospitals," he said. And then, with restrained fury, daring me to defy his command, he stared even more closely. "You knew that."

No, I didn't know that.

Or maybe I did, in that other reality, the reality that was there but we acted as if wasn't. In that moment of revelation about his hospitalizations, he was domineering and brutal, and he was familiar, repeating an established pattern of abuse towards me, turning my own beliefs and reality inside out, inducing me with a false truth. I was to believe that I already knew what I knew I didn't know, but now I did know it, because he commanded it. He was, in a way, driving me crazy. But there was also something more.

That moment was, for my father, also a rare act of trust and vulnerability. Just to have said that much, or that little, was a risk of love. I do wish that, instead of demanding that I join in his lying to himself and join the lies about psychiatric abuse that pass for normal, my father had apologized for not speaking with me sooner. I do wish my father had put more faith in our bond, had relied on me more and trusted me more with his emotional honesty. But, just as he never defied his own father in front of me, at the same time he did marry the woman he loved and did guide us through the back door on Sundays to greet the black staff first. My father's decision to remain silent about his own psychiatric traumas was a complex negotiation of survival. It was his way between the violence of normalcy and the imagined greater violence of that other reality. Maybe the openness I wanted would have let something in, something between him and his father, or something in between him and me, something unspeakable and unimaginable, something that might have been too much.

And so in these and many other small gestures and silent conversations, there was a teaching for me, and some answers to the question of what does it means to be called crazy in a crazy world. Because there is no world more crazy than a world of violence accepted as normal.

THIS WEEK IS BAD. I carry a physical object stuck in my heart, pinched and weighted, sharp edges. I am short of breath, I keep thinking of killing myself. Isn't there an expiration date on this? Numb, for days now I've been numb, can't work, just sleeping, can't talk to anyone. Now I'm in crisis.

In the late afternoon, I realize my stomach is aching, so I drive to a restaurant. I can't leave the car. I sit staring at the dust on the windshield. And there is a familiar stranger sitting with me, a terrifying stranger, and I want to leave the car but can't, I'm a hostage. A demon is there and wants to kill me. No, there is no demon, demons aren't real. I can convince myself. No, I can't convince myself. But if there is no demon, then also there are no kind spirits to protect me, there is only the truth that I deserve to die. I am between worlds. Yes. There is something in the car with me.

And then all I can think to do is apologize, to myself, to the demon, to my parents. An apology to the spirits that aren't really there? Just imagination. Nothing but death and wanting to die. But I keep apologizing; I plead, I yell, the windows rolled up, the hood of my sweatshirt hiding my tears from anyone in the parking lot. The demon roars at me, the dead are talking. I start to scream. I scream until I am hoarse. I start to weep. *I'm sorry. I'm sorry.*

Darkness, and it's cold outside, but even though I've been sitting in a car with the engine off I'm warm, inside I am warm. I take a breath, and my breath opens and opens more. I'm not gasping, and I'm calmer. No pinched, sharp stone in my heart. I look around in the car, there is no one here. No demon. For now, I don't want to die. Face wet from tears, I'm done with my apology. I'm not sorry. I'm just hungry.

There is no light in the car and no streetlamp in the parking lot. I sent several text messages an hour ago, *please, I don't want to be alone,* but got no reply. Saturday night, no one available. But now, in the car, breathing deeply and done with apologies, my phone lights up, and my friend is calling me.

He tells me he just got my message. He is on the road, in Oklahoma, driving across the state, and he had an impulse to stop at a roadside shop with a sign offering healing. He didn't call me back sooner, because he was still in the session with the healer.

My mother grew up in Oklahoma, and my friend is driving through Oklahoma. He says he is on Indian land. "Wait," he asks, "what tribe did you say your mother has ancestry from?" I tell him the Choctaw nation. And he says the land he is driving through, where he stopped for healing a thousand miles away, is the Choctaw nation. He was there at the same time I was screaming in my car, with a healing of my own.

Either it's just a coincidence, or it's a meaningful way of being in the world. It could be a reality just as true as any culture's reality. A different reality. And it could be a reality where I am not a schizophrenic with a thought disorder, a reality where it all means something else.

JUST BEFORE MY FIRST HOSPITALIZATION, in 1992, I was writing an academic journal essay about the history and future of the environmental movement. Lifelong patterns of emotional extremes and traumatic events, family violence, and school bullying were catching up with me, now combined with sleepless nights in a room strewn with stacks of photocopies and library books. As I wrote, my essay started to take on enormous weight. Was I onto some great discovery or vital insight? Could I unlock human liberation and impact our survival as a species? I felt uncanny inspiration, a force propelling me forward with each word I put down on the page.

There on my desk beside my research was a copy of the old photography news magazine *Life*. On the cover was an image of the planet Mars, with the large headline, "OUR NEXT HOME?" The cover began to haunt me. A message. Psychosis is often described as a "break" with reality, but this was the dawning of a different reality. There was an approaching presence, as I stared at the photo of Mars on the cover of *Life,* and the three words there, over and over.

"OUR NEXT HOME?"

That headline, and the god of war. The Scottish critical psychiatrist R.D. Laing, whose writing shaped the psychiatric survivor movement, tells this story in his autobiography, *Wisdom, Madness and Folly*: When he was in Glasgow medical school, a physiology lecturer showed the class X-ray films of people eating and digesting food. The film struck Laing as odd, and then he realized why. How, he asked the lecturer, was such a film possible, since X-rays are deadly and the prolonged exposure needed to create movie images would certainly kill the person being filmed? The lecturer looked at him and replied, simply: the films were made during World War II, created by doctors working for the military. They were from concentration camps. They were films of Jewish prisoners experimented on, and killed. And then, to Laing's horror and with the quiet assent of the classroom full of students, the lecturer continued the class.

I didn't understand it at the time, but as I looked at the cover of *Life* magazine in the middle of the night, alone in my room and spiraling deeper into an altered state, I felt some of the same horror that Laing must have felt. The normal, the ordinary, a medical school lecture, the cover of a popular magazine, was also a grotesque testimony to barbarous violence. One of the worst crimes of World War II, medical torture, became a convenient instrument of graduate instruction without any acknowledgment, without any pause. And here, on my desk, was the mass extinction of life on Earth as just a reason to relocate to other planets, a headline in a magazine. Was I, like Laing, discovering that "reality" is violence called normal? Was this realization pointing to somewhere else, to a different reality, a place where people who get called "crazy" might actually know more than the "normal" people do, know more about the violent truths of the world we live in?

What is that place? Can we go there, instead of abandoning Earth for the barren planet of the god of war? Instead of living in the reality of normalized violence, not just the South, under Jim Crow, not just medical torturers, not just families torn by fighting, but everywhere?

"I was puzzled, and uneasy," Laing writes. "Hardly any of my psychiatric colleagues seemed puzzled or uneasy. This made me even more puzzled and uneasy."

Years later, I realized what had awakened within me that terrifying night. That night was a crisis, a culmination of years of wrenching inner conflict, and a fall into deep pain. It was a break with reality. And something horrifying seized me: I am human in an inhuman world. I cannot choose to leave behind this heart or its truth, and there may be a price. It may mean being taken to a place where everyone says I am crazy, it may mean going mad.

ON THE HOSPITAL'S LOCKED FOURTH FLOOR, I drew an elaborate map in colored pencil, and each imaginary location had a rhyme alongside it. *A swampy bit / to hike around / watch out or sink / into the ground.* One drawing was pinned on a bulletin board by the dining area, like they do in children's classrooms. After dinner one night, I noticed two of the staff interested in what I had created, pointing to my words with enjoyment and reading the little poems I had written. I walked up behind them. "I made that," I said, in a rare moment of reaching out for contact. They both stopped talking and froze. Neither of them had noticed me there, and now they didn't respond. They turned to me but didn't look me in the eye or say a word. And while I stood there in shock, they walked away, as if they hadn't heard me, as if I were invisible.

What institutionalized, normalized violence could make them act like that?

WHEN I WAS A KID GROWING UP IN SOUTH CAROLINA the reality of violence and power that impacted me so deeply was not spoken about. This reality made its way in through coded messages, and through subtle defiances. Through the back door. And so this book is full of back doors. The contributors gathered here hold the possibility that the way we have been shown, the way of normalizing violence and telling people that madness is in their heads, is not the way we have to go.

I am not among those who see mental illness as a myth, or think the only problem is with doctors and their treatments. *Outside Mental Health* is a call to rethink madness and our responses to it, not to neglect those in pain. Human suffering and madness are real. People do lose touch. During my time of deepest torment, I was so incapacitated and impaired that a disability check and housing subsidy were lifelines to survival. As much as I want to change the mental health system, I am grateful for the support it did give me. Nor do I demonize medications, as harmful as they can be. I have seen meds help a wide diversity of people, and I embrace a harm reduction view, advocating for each person to find their own way.

At the same time, *Outside Mental Health*, like the *Madness Radio* interviews it's based on, emphasizes what has been missing. This book doesn't try to be balanced; it tries to be *balancing*. These are voices left out by other media, voices that helped me and others find our way past a medical diagnosis and towards a more human understanding of ourselves. And because each chapter represents a moment in my own learning, I'm certainly limited by my own background and experience. There are many things that this book doesn't do, many perspectives that I wish I had been able to include. *Outside Mental Health* is a snapshot, not an overview, and offers new visions of madness, not a single new vision of what madness is.

As you explore these interviews, guest essays, and some of my own writing all gathered from ten years of *Madness Radio*, I invite you to join a conversation, a conversation that is much broader, and more honest, than the one we have been having. I became who I am by listening to these voices and learning from these different visions. I hope *Outside Mental Health* takes you to new places and opens up new questions, for you, for the people you care about, and for us all.

"Who's that coming in through the back door?" ■

Outside Mental Health Voices and Visions of Madness

Voices

The Muse's Call
Bonfire Madigan

Bonfire Madigan Shive is a visionary cellist, vocalist, healing activist, and touring musician. A key figure in riot grrrl, queercore, and chamber punk, she was a founding collective member of The Icarus Project.

At night I'd be making up little magical worlds at four in the morning. I still believe there was a spirit in the wall behind where the doorknob hit, a portal to many worlds.

WILL HALL You've always been a visionary outsider, tell us about that.

BONFIRE MADIGAN My parents were counter-culture young people in the late '70s. My mother was a heavy trauma survivor who was in a car accident that so badly damaged her left brain she had to learn basic motor skills again. She was told it was unlikely that she could have kids. My father was a long-haired hippie who fell in love with my mom when she was sixteen. He would sit outside her hospital room and do all the physical therapy with her. My grandparents were going to put her in a nursing home, they couldn't figure out what to do. So my father said "Well I want to marry her." She was underage, and my father became her legal custodian. A year and a half later I was born, conceived in a cranberry bog shack they were squatting in.

WH **This was in the Pacific Northwest?**

BM Washington State. I lived in tipis, in cars, and cabins with no running water or electricity. I was raised by a radical counterculture tribe of indigenous people and back-to-the-land people and farmer communities. I was renamed Running Pony by a woman named Horse Woman. She gave us a part quarter horse, part Shetland pony, and I named it Co-Pony. It would wake me up in the morning and I would ride through the trails down to where the breakfast nook was. I was about two and a half years old at the time. Before I could run in a straight line I could pull myself up onto Co-Pony.

That was such a different world; we treat our children so precious now.

WH **Your mom was partly in this reality and partly in other realities?**

BM She was so different and an amazing force, an intense anti-authoritarian. She had to deal with being ostracized and pathologized and being told she wasn't smart. I dealt with that a lot, that people like us just weren't as smart as other people.

We moved around frequently, and there was always dread of our housing being taken away or even me and my sister being taken away by Child Protective Services. When the school became concerned that I was malnourished at the age of seven or eight, I had to perform for their assessment. I learned "Ok, I see the role they want me to play." So that is how I fell in love with being a performer. I became a story-teller and moved into different roles and shoes. It was a healing possibility for me, and freed me from some of the persecution and judgment.

WH **Your family ran into conflict with the system and police?**

BM That threat was always there, often because of my mother's behaviors. She just wasn't going to conform. She would do a lot of really bizarre things that would confuse and enrage people. She was also always dealing with addiction, and I trace that back to the hospital telling her she needed something from outside to heal her, whether it was drugs, vocational schools, or whatever. She tried to work but she got fired from fast food restaurants, she got kicked out of programs because she just wouldn't behave. They would say she had an IQ of 30-something, and that would of course break her spirit. But she was so childlike and so positive most of the time, she was a real healer. She just naturally carried around this non-judgmental healing energy that made you feel heard and listened to. She believed in each person's own healing capacity. She worked with kids with disabilities, and older people, and was a private nurse for a few years. It exposed me to people who were experiencing reality in different ways, friends with cerebral palsy she was taking care of, a young boy with Huntington's disease. I found myself attracted to these kids and the way that they were experiencing the world and how we could learn things from each other. So I think even at the age of nine I was involved with disability rights.

WH Did you yourself ever end up in the system?

BM Mom lived with the constant threat of Washington State Hospital, in Skagit Valley where she grew up. She had uncles who worked there, and they had thrown her brothers and sisters in when they were on acid trips they couldn't come down from. After she was in the coma my mom had so much fear, paranoia and rage about her own hospital experience. She would say "I would rather die or be in jail or on the streets than in a psych ward." That's such a young age for me to hear that she would rather die.

Once the school sent a child psychiatrist to our house to see if I was malnourished. He was completely the stereotype: a white guy with a beard and a little turtleneck sweater. I felt all this shame, I remember looking at my dad like "I'm so sorry, I'm so sorry." There was nothing wrong, but I knew "Ok, I have to perform this role to make the psychiatrist go away." My mother used heroin, it was her way of self-soothing, so there would be a lot of altercations with police. I would often get persecuted under this guise of concern.

Then the principal pulled me into her office wanting to know if I was a drug dealer or doing drugs. By this time I was into Riot Grrl, feminism, music, and I was a vegan, I was going to Earth First! and Queer Nation meetings, getting totally radicalized. I felt so much shame when my dad looked at the principal and said "It isn't Madigan, it's her mother who is the heroin addict." It was the first time I heard my dad say that to somebody outside of our family, and I had so much shame I started with tears. I couldn't look at the principal in

My mom lived with the constant threat of Washington State Hospital. She would say "I would rather die or be in jail or on the streets than end up in a psych ward."

the face but I wanted to throttle her, it was just so insensitive. And then she looked at me and put her hand on my shoulder and said, "I know what you're going through, my husband is a chain smoker." My dad and I looked at each other and we had a little chuckle, "Ok, you upper middle class liberal." But we knew the principal meant well. But it was like, "Thanks, and... can we go now?"

WH When did art become part of who you are?

BM My mother made me a Raggedy Anne doll, and it was like my best friend. I would talk with it, we'd swap clothes, it was my companion that I would tell my deepest secrets to. And as I got older my mom would go through many different states, there was a lot of rage and a lot of pain, dishes flying across the kitchen, things like that. And I remember feeling "I don't know what love is unless it's things smashing around me."

I had a little room with a hole in the wall exactly the size of the doorknob from the door being slammed so much. At night I'd be up making little magical worlds at four in the morning. I still believe there was a spirit in the wall behind where the doorknob hit, a portal to many worlds. I called the spirit Whisper, it was very androgynous and childlike, and I would put my mouth up to that hole and we would talk.

A few years later I found the cello, my life-long amulet and friend. I connected to a dialogue beyond text and dominant languages.

WH How did you discover the cello?

BM I was nine for "meet the instruments day" at school, and they paraded all of us into the cafeteria with instruments set up. At first I went right for the trumpet, but a woman intervened and said, "Oh, no. Your mouth is all wrong for the trumpet." So I went to another line, and out of the corner of my eye I saw a big violin. Something clicked in me and I started thinking, "That's what I want." So I said "What's that big violin, can I play that, can I try that?" And the woman said, "Oh, no, we decided we're not getting it out, but there's these flutes over here..." I was usually the smallest girl in the room, I was very small for my age, and I felt like she was sending me to this little petite thing, the flute. So I lost it. I think because I felt shut down by that woman, I threw a tantrum and started screaming, "I want the big violin! That's what I want! The big violin!"

I threw a tantrum and said "I want the big violin! I want the big violin!

Finally they handed it to me, and I put my arms around it and it was just like the Raggedy Anne doll my mom made. It was like hearing Whisper in the door. Just running my hands on it felt like a woman's body, or my body, so human yet wooden, it took me back to living in tipis and the trees and the forest. And when I held that bow... that's horsehair in the bow, you know... it connected everything up to that point together. And I said, "What is this? What is this?" She said, "It's a cello."

I ran home, and my mom was doing bong hits or something, really loaded. I said, "Mom! I know what I'm going to do. I'm going to play the cello!" And she looked at me and smiled because I was so happy. But then she just said, "What the heck is a cello?" And in that moment I thought, "This amazing wooden thing I just had my arm around, I'm going to make it about us, about my mom and me, I'm going to make it about who we are." And that's what I set out to do.

WH Beautiful. How did you bring the cello into punk rock and Riot Grrl? No one had done that before.

BM I was in Seattle in the early '90s and we would drive down to Olympia for the all-ages shows, and I got exposed to punk, which was an ideology of "find your creative voice and share it with us." I was seeing performances and music and words that I had never heard on the radio or TV. I started to realize I could use what I had, acoustic instruments, and instead of an outward explosion of energy and rage and voicing, I could draw people closer and have them lean in. I started the band Tattle Tale

Sometimes I had to say things no one wanted to say, and then people would get scared of me. I didn't know how to express things in a way that was compassionate.

with Jen Wood, and next thing you know we're playing at these hardcore punk boys' shows where they've got their shirts off, and when it was our turn we would play right in the middle of the mosh pit where all that energy was, without any mics or anything, and we would play our songs. And these teenage, shirtless, sweaty boys would sit down and lean in and kind of touch each other and they're listening to us, and people were crying. Jen was fifteen at the time I had just turned seventeen.

WH How do you create songs?

BM Every day to me is alive, an electric moment that I am conversing with. This is what keeps me excited about being in this reality right now, and keeps me away from what I call my "deep-pressing-end," and my relationship to my suicidal feelings. It's almost like there's always something waiting there to reveal itself to me, and I am in a position to hear it and absorb it, and then I can sculpt with it.

Every day to me is alive, an electric moment I am conversing with.

WH You mentioned being a livewire for the present moment. Can that vulnerability be difficult?

BM Sometimes I had to say things no one wanted to say, and then people would get scared of me. I didn't know how to express things in a way that was compassionate, so it alienated me from a lot of people. And I had so much of my own trauma. After my mom died people close to me couldn't handle it, they didn't know she was using heroin. A lot of people died in my family and my life, so that was really hard, the isolation. After burning out my lovers and friends, I became aware that I needed to put my healing in my own hands. Now I create a life and a schedule that is healing to me, and I don't feel judged for it. If I need to sleep from 6am to noon, this is where I'm at, and people have to support that.

Punk was an ideology of "find your creative voice, and share it with us."

WH Did that lead you to become a mental health activist?

BM I felt so sensitive that I was collecting a lot of stuff around my home, so much that my partner said "I think you should go to this meeting." So I started going to groups for people with hoarding issues. Then I became facilitator, and then was hired as an advocate around harm reduction, homelessness, and accommodations for people with mental health "disabilities."

Today I feel safe sharing all this publicly because I have a whole community around me of people who talk about states of consciousness and mood extremes. We are the web we weave together to save our own lives. I want to create a world not only worth living in but worth thriving in, a world we can all be excited about contributing to. That is something my mother didn't get in her lifetime, and it definitely fuels me. For me this is a very exciting time, a kind of, as the Zapatistas of Mexico like to say, global-awakening for the humble, simple people. A time for all of us to heal. ■

The Golden Heart of Contamination
David M. Burns

David Burns was one of the original organizers with Freedom Center and a leading architect of Freedom Center's first activist campaigns. This essay was written in 1992.

OCD is a solitary encounter with the raw power of the psyche. It is a great burden, but I see no reason to call it an abnormality or a sickness.

I woke up one morning to discover that some of the small bones in both my feet were fractured. I could not walk. I learned later that the night before, in an alcoholic blackout, I had jumped from the window of my second story room, landed on the concrete sidewalk, and then gone inside and returned to bed. I was not badly hurt, but I was frightened. So I quit drinking for the first time.

After an initial exhilaration I found myself in an intolerable state: a problem with consciousness, with living in the world.

I took a bath, got out of the tub, and I brushed

my leg against the cold, hard, white enamel of the rim. That touch seemed terribly unclean. I carried that sensation away with me, I was overwhelmed with a feeling I could not understand or tolerate, a feeling that was empty, dead, meaningless. I struggled to name it, to make sense out of the experience. I was stuck. I was trapped in a hideous place.

That was my first experience of contamination.

> **Cultures around the world sustain customs that are repetitive and symbolic and serve as obsessive-compulsive symptoms for the group. Religions struggle with problems of contamination and purification.**

The physical world was evil, broken. Things were dirty and poisoned, utterly dangerous and threatening. I found myself performing repeated, useless actions that took over much of my life. I tried to hide, to escape, to avoid contact. If I couldn't I would wash again and again. I would check that the gas was really off, that the door was really locked, that the letter really went into the slot.

My inner state was a place of blood and excrement. I was inevitably contaminated, condemned. I would be overwhelmed by inescapable despair because my feelings had roots in the earth. I was buried in slime.

I always considered myself one of a kind, so I was greatly surprised to be hit by a common, classic, garden-variety condition that was familiar to me from my study of Freud. He wrote about two obsessive-compulsive (OCD) patients who have become famous since, notable also for their odd nicknames. So here we are, the wolf-man, the rat-man, and me.

OCD is a solitary encounter with the raw power of the psyche. It is a great burden, but I see no reason to call it an abnormality or a sickness. Cultures around the world sustain customs that are repetitive and symbolic, and function as obsessive-compulsive symptoms for the group. Religions struggle with problems of contamination and purification. In the Old

The physical world was evil, broken. Things were dirty and poisoned, utterly dangerous and threatening. I found myself performing repeated, useless actions that took over much of my life.

Testament, Job expresses his bewilderment at God's anger. "If I wash myself with snow, and cleanse my hands with lye, yet thou wilt plunge me into a pit, and my own clothes will abhor me." God responds out of the windstorm: "Where were you when I laid the foundation of the Earth? Tell me, if you have understanding. Who determined its measurements... surely you know! Or who stretched the line upon it? On what were its bases sunk, or who laid its cornerstone, when the morning stars sang together, and all the sons of God shouted for joy?" There is no better answer to the problem of OCD.

Years later I formed an intention. I wished that the dark energy I struggled with would embody itself. I prayed to visualize this unknown part of myself, to dream, to see, to meet. I wanted it revealed to my consciousness as an image of a living being, so that I could interact and engage with the force that had tormented me, so I too could meet the God behind the storm.

So the process began. Some months after forming that intention I quit my job in California and went to spend a month alone on a tiny island in a large lake in Maine. I was good at my job and the job was good for me, but the stress of the work, plus the obsessional symptoms plus my continuing substance

Block by block I rebuilt my house, constructed from the ruins of my shattered consciousness.

abuse, all added up. I had joined Alcoholics Anonymous and studied Iyengar-style hatha yoga, and these formed the foundation. Now on the island I had space, both physical and existential, to experience my own consciousness. I played with my pain.

Two early dreams mapped the world I began to explore: a promise and a premonition. One dream marked the height, the unclimbable mountain, the unattainable goal: *I am a seer, a primordial man, standing sturdy and calm, looking down. Below me I see a glowing green valley and a fast-flowing river. I am the water and the water is me.* I awake in tears. The other dream marked the swamp, the muck and sludge through which I must labor on my way to the light: *I am a farmer. The cows and their milk are threatened by something dangerous and impure moving underground.* Feelings of contamination would soon fill my life.

> I am a seer, a primordial man, standing sturdy and calm, looking down. Below me I see a glowing green valley and a fast-flowing river. I am the water and the water is me. I awake in tears.

The island became a magic place. The dark, opaque energy of contamination, the hidden core of my obsessive-compulsive disorder had given me two images in what I hoped would be a series in evolving transformation. I remember sitting writing in my new dream book, weeping with pain and joy. The dead and empty horror of a meaningless, paralyzing neurosis was giving birth to images of healing and hope.

One day I felt a deep sense of contamination in a jacket pocket. I imagined my hand reaching in, and this act of visualization received a response from the inner world. *The hand seems to extend into water, and the water is filled with fish. I grab one and pull it out. It thrashes and trembles violently. I struggle with it and kill it.* I now somehow knew what to do, as if this new inner world were a familiar home. I knew to take the one out of the many. I knew that I might kill the image of the fish without harming the gift of consciousness I had received. This was the beginning of change.

I chose to sign myself in to the best psychiatric hospital I could find, one that specialized in the treatment of anxiety disorders. I wanted behavioral therapy. I liked the simplicity, the pragmatism in what I had read about it. Systematic desensitization, flooding, exposure to stimulus, prevention of response: it seemed to provide methods of learning how to experience anxiety.

I trained in how to approach when I wanted to avoid. I learned not to wash when I felt contaminated. The feelings rose up and overwhelmed me, but now they rose and fell and rose and fell. I became familiar with states of high anxiety. And I began to change my behavior.

No longer must I wash until my arms were raw. No longer must I fling away a handful of contaminated coins.

And the training also gave birth to intense and meaningful imagery. Again and again, this seemingly superficial behavioral technique, exposure to stimulus and prevention of response, gave me access to a deep and flowing world of visualizations. I could now choose more or less at will to move from my daytime consciousness into the world of dreams. Behavioral therapy allowed me to achieve one of the greatest goals of yoga.

Block by block I rebuilt my house, constructed from the ruins of my shattered consciousness.

Most of what I value today came out of the golden heart of contamination. I have inside me a world of dreams that is just as beautiful and strong as the outer world. I have regained much of my lost self, my feelings, my creativity and my spontaneity. I continue to struggle with compulsive behaviors like avoidance and hand washing, but the sense of contamination, however unpleasant, is no longer dark, cold and alien. This is also me. In many ways my affliction has become a blessing: I would not give up this whole process if I knew how, if I could press a button or take a pill.

> Most of what I value today came out of the golden heart of contamination. I have inside me a world of dreams that is just as beautiful and strong as the outer world. I have regained much of my lost self, my feelings, my creativity, and my spontaneity.

Through these years of awakenings and astonishments my understanding slowly evolved. I gained no control over my feelings, but I began to know them as part of me. I was dealing not with physical filth or external danger, but with a spiritual energy that resided in myself. ∎

Body of Poetry, Body of Revolution
Eddie Bartók-Baratta

Eddie Bartók-Baratta is a poet, musician, and sculptor. He has published over 200 poems including in *Bomb*, *Boston Review*, *Ploughshares*, *Harvard Review*, *Massachusetts Review*, and *Denver Quarterly*. He is a member of the Murder Victims' Families for Reconciliation.

What am I here to make in the world? Am I here to make a career? Am I here to make a larger ego? Or am I here to make myself thoroughly known to myself... and to be of use to us?

WILL HALL Much of your poetry comes out of your childhood; tell us about that.

EDDIE BARTÓK-BARATTA Sparrow Hill is the neighborhood where I was raised, the Western slope of Jersey City from where you can see Carny and Newark and Elizabeth. A ten-square-mile city of hundreds of thousands of people tightly pressed together in different neighborhoods of poverty. I was eighth of nine kids in a physically violent, abusive family. There was inappropriate touch, denial of access to food, denial of access to the bathroom, memories of a brother tied or handcuffed to the bed...

As I say that, I am smiling, because my response now is one of larger ownership of my body. I know where I come from and I don't identify as a victim anymore. I am thriving on the other side of this larger experience.

WH How did that change happen?

EB Decades of my life the nights were utterly terrible and eternal, and visions would come. About 1997 I experienced what one might call a "break." I had to self-incarcerate myself in my apartment, I couldn't go out during the day, only at night to shop. I started seeing things. I saw my father coming for me with an axe to core out my ear. How telling is that?

WH An image of a poet losing his ear.

EB It's been a really long road to becoming present to my own body. Many moments came on dark nights at 3 am, and the paper and pen were there when I couldn't find any other support. My poems aren't some kind of code, yet much of the journey is written down in two thousand poems.

WH Can you share one of them?

EB Haunting images visit, sometimes to torment and sometimes to play. How about a poem that brings Ronald Reagan together with the Cowardly Lion?

WH That sounds really promising!

EB *I was not made to sail around the bathtub in a small toy boat.*
Here I am, antithetical to the wishes of my father.

By now you have learned that they killed Ronald Reagan; "they"
being time and patience. They always win.

I am making sushi out of Ronald Reagan's eyelids and feeding it
to the poor. I am using the oily hair from his early movies as thread to
sew the wounds of a second-hand doll.

Who would throw away a stuffed version of the Cowardly Lion?
I found him in the trash, coffee grinds in his ears. Together we peruse

the wet newspaper he was wrapped in.

We are off to Leverett. They are having a midnight sale on a sheep farm. The sheep are in a large circle, seated in chairs in the field. They are sharing their feelings about having been born into a species with thick wool and edible flesh.

In turn, each sheep that speaks hold the Cowardly Lion. They pass him clockwise. That's the direction of the sun's journey.

The sun is the oldest boy in the school. He was left behind one year after another.

He shines on the brutal, the forgiving, and the weird.

WH You can't see this on radio, but Eddie isn't reading, he is performing this poem: it transforms his body.

EB Starting in 1993 I needed to get away from the page in order to move and say things. My body felt too contained, I felt I couldn't get my breath. So I would walk every night and repeat all these poems until they were committed not from memory, but from my body.

The learning process was coupled with insomnia, night terrors, startle symptoms. I took a fire burning inside me and I said "I want to bring this fire out. I want to blaze with it." Doing these poems, I am serving my body and its needs, to channel these things through.

WH You said that body ownership is communal, not just personal.

EB To own this body I have to know my family history, the city and the poverty in which I was raised, the political climate. You know yourself too, Will. When we come together we make this really wild banquet together.

WH Weaving light and dark. Your brother is a real presence in your work; tell us about him.

EB You feel the fear and then you step forward bravely and say, "I have a job for us."

My brother John was murdered in New York City in 1984. And I know where John came from, and maybe something of what led to his death. I stood beside him, from 3 or 4 years old, while my father's belt, or, as we called it, his "strap," fell down on us with the force of the 240 lb man behind it.

WH You wrote a beautiful poem about your brother, "Old New York City Where I Lay My Head."

EB John did not have a voice, he could not do what we are doing right now. But he had basketball, he was very athletic and had a real beauty in his body. After some years of living on the street and being in the mental health system, Manhattan State Psychiatric, Trenton State Psychiatry, he was diagnosed with many things. Anxiety, major depressive disorder, psychosis.

I'm not sure of all of what happened to him, in what state he was found. Some of his madness was definitely addiction, dope, and wine. He was also splitting, dissociating, trying to escape our tremendous history of abuse. And then finally at the age of 27 he was thrown down an elevator shaft in New York.

The paper and pen were there when I couldn't find any other support.

And so whenever I come out I know where I come from, and John comes with me. He was my best friend when he was killed. Some of my toughness is definitely communal; he is in me, he leaves a lot of love in me, he leaves a lot of ferocity in me.

Just as I say that, I can see him sitting next to me and nodding his head with a cigarette the way he would, and saying, "Yeah, man, you tell 'em."

And he would say other things that I won't repeat here... John was a tough guy, and the world, as James Baldwin says, the "too rough fingers of the world," was tougher than he was.

"Old New York City Where I Lay My Head"

I remember visiting my brother at Bellevue. He had come to stay in the mad ward at Bellevue, cutting his arms like a crazy map of where he lived. All high, brilliant, and light.

Brother, don't wanna die in a February with no love. Old New York City where I lay my head.

> For the boy I ate spaghetti with, spitting watermelon seeds and punching each other in the adolescent dark. We were boys learning to be like our father, learning to grow in the shade of that tree.
>
> He had the best jump shot in Jersey City, meat, potatoes, and peas, my brother, one of the brave, Progresso soup, Hi-C and the New York Yankees.
>
> We sat beside each other in the old stadium, baseball gloves in our laps, in the bleachers, waiting for Mickey Mantle to slap a white tongue into our day.
>
> Oh, high, brilliant, that blood — brother don't let me die in a February with no love. On old New York City streets I lay down my head with the boy I ate spaghetti with.

WH "Learning to grow in the shade of that tree." Beautiful...

We were talking before about this language of "disability." Who gets to make the decisions about our bodies. What ability is "dis-"; lesser than or deficient, and what ability is just different. What is diversity and what is impairment?

EB We are "otherly-abled." Will, having been at your house and seeing the neatness of your house, I know something about people who have certain kinds of order. An artist above all is a maker, so to ask oneself a question beyond that, "What am I here to make in the world?" Am I here to make a career? Am I here to advance myself? Am I here to make a larger ego? Or am I here to make myself thoroughly known to myself... and to be of use to us?

I took a fire burning inside me and I said "I want to bring this fire out. I want to blaze with it."

WH Claim that ownership.

EB And this "Us" again, with a capital "U." It's a sacred thing when we come together as this larger body, this larger animal. Or we come together as a destructive larger animal, like when we were kids and tormenting and ostracizing another kid. I think it is incumbent upon us to go back for the true narrative, to do a little word play, not to be recumbent. Not to sit back and say, "Oh well, these things happened, get over it" and then stuff it in my pocket, so that later it can blow up in a social situation or in a partnership or in a meeting, and I can take it out on someone else. Let me know this body, let me know what I am bringing to the table.

WH Listening to your music and watching you perform, that word "ancient" came to me. The flute, your body moving, and the breath. It's just very timeless and something essentially human. What brought you to music?

EB I found the flute at age 13, someone in high school was playing an old nickel flute and I bought it from him for five bucks. It's one of the few things that survived my childhood. I didn't get to have lessons, you know, I wasn't taken from soccer to flute the way kids are taken around. There is much I can't vocalize or write about, yet I can express through music. And my brother heard my flute, saw me play. So it means a lot to me, it is a sacred thing.

I have been reciting poems for almost two decades but only came out performing the flute about three months ago. My body insisted. There is a beloved in there who is like, "Hey, man, what about this?" I used to

My body insisted. There is a beloved in there who is like, "Hey, man, what about this?"

play in Washington Square Park when I was 15 and 16. I had a couple of buddies with me so no one would steal the money or the flute. But then I lost that vocalization, so after all these years I took it back. I started playing again every day.

Last sunday I was performing and got stuck on different melodies. I choked up and my throat started to close. In my body, that was my father telling me "No!" He used to grab my hair, the long hair like I have now, and throw me against the wall, saying "Stop with that black crap. Stop with that boogie-woogie crap." The racism and violence of that man was there at my neck, it was choking me. But I said, "Dammit, I'm going to play the pieces I planned to play tonight. Because this is about us." Let's uplift and celebrate one another.

WH Some of your songs are so fierce, yet others are delicate. You hold both those qualities.

EB We are that, aren't we? There is a myth of a unified self. I know who I am as I am here today, I know that there is a quietude and a gentleness and I know there is a savagery and a kind of ferocity, and I understand about certain limits.

WH The challenge of listening to your body, and the struggle to get the flute out in the world: that's a struggle we all are in.

Let's talk about crossing over and moving energy, putting the history in the moment. Tell us about what you call shamanism, what you call revolution.

EB We can loosely borrow the word "shaman" because the shaman brings forward and addresses the spirits. These spirits reside beyond the dichotomy of good and evil. If I can be at home with the multiplicity of self, then I can be more at home with the multiplicity of the world. The role of shaman, giving voice, belongs to all of us, in how we work to heal one another.

I don't want a language about fighting. We know what society says, we know where the fences and the walls are. We need to come together, gently and lovingly and courageously, meeting one another in our terror, in our beauty, in our wisdom. Revolution reminds me of the word "subversion." Literally, a version beneath this larger version. So a "subversion" is not necessarily setting things on fire. That doesn't do any of us good, it just means more of us get incarcerated or put away against our own will. Instead, subversion means there is a more healing version under the dominant paradigm.

I refuse the language of opposition and fight. I don't even want to fight against the language of fighting. Instead, if there is trauma, if it's another kind of what people call disability, then I want to be present to it. I want to come through it as much as I can, and meet other people who are going through the same. I want to learn from it. ∎

Shifting Realities
Miguel Mendías

Miguel Mendías a performance artist whose work has appeared at the Maryland Institute of Contemporary Art, and is a member of The Icarus Project.

My reality is a construct that shifts, and when I am freed of that construct I can explore things other people would be much too afraid to.

WILL HALL You've had a very different view of reality since you were a child.

MIGUEL MENDÍAS As a kid I was very independent, and always felt I was different. I have a twin brother, and before age five or so I wasn't told I was female, I was part of this androgynous unit. So I rebelled very early on, against gender roles, when I was told I was female.

I was an imaginative kid, and I remember my twin and I used to play war where we blew things up, and I created a special role for myself that was like a witch-doctor. I had magical powers and could heal the soul, do all sorts of healings and bizarre rituals. I don't know where that came from exactly, at a really early age, creating this healer identity for myself.

Around kindergarden I became really sad and withdrawn. I experienced depression and what was later labeled OCD, and started developing trichotillomania after I got lice, when I started pulling my hair and it became its own thing. I remember I had a mysterious illness where I was sick for three or four days, and then just kept on throwing up afterwards, in the bathroom and classroom, like bulimia. I was very isolated, and had friends in the fourth grade who said, "what's up with you, you never smile" and would make a game of it.

WH Was trauma causing any of this?

MM What went on later was really severe, some of the rituals that I did and the self-mutilation. But I wasn't abused at an early age like other children who tend to do these things.

My family is very Catholic and we went to church and Sunday School every week. I started to see that the world had a lot of problems and adults had a lot of problems. I was feeling bad for adults and that they didn't really know what was going on, and I wasn't feeling great about becoming one of them. So from when I was a young kid I had some deeper sense of things, and felt that I had some kind of special role or a calling.

WH When did you start having altered states?

MM I developed a whole secret life early on, hidden rituals and behaviors. I had insomnia, and would stay up late creating an immense world of spiritual helpers.

WH What were they like?

MM There was a family of monster spirits who adopted me even though I was human, and watched over me every night. There was a farmer who lived in the ceiling fan, and shadows who lived on the wall: one was a British soldier with a large nose who became my sentry. My stuffed bear was a companion guide. I told my family, "He's not just my pretend friend, he's a spirit who I encounter through this stuffed animal." And I had two people who lived inside my head, Black Moon and Jeanie, like different aspects of myself. I rarely felt fearful, because I had all these friendly helpers around me. But I didn't talk much with anyone about them.

Later I decided there was something wrong with me and I wasn't going to live very long. I thought sin was innate to my character, that I was flawed. I started punishing myself, borrowing from Catholicism. I would dig into my feet into the edge of the bed, and hitting my head and pressing my wrists. This was when I was about 8 or nine.

There are times I've just thrown myself on the mercy of... riding the current dragon, with no idea what is going to happen, switching different realities.

WH Was the self harm relieving or satisfying in some way?

MM Yes, because I never cried, and when I would do something wrong my mom would say, "I'm telling you that you hurt your brother's feelings, how can you just stand there?" So I would not show anything and get sent to my room, where later I could perform these punishments. Catholics go to confession to receive absolution: I had to do penance, and when I hurt myself, the penance enabled me to feel emotion, to cry a little bit.

I started banging my wrists against the bed or trying to put as much weight as possible. I was afraid the noise might bring attention, so I couldn't do that all the time. I burnt a curling iron onto my wrists, and the tip of my fingers, so when people did see a mark, it looked accidental. The iron's edge hurt a lot and was painful, and served my needs ritualistically, but it healed quickly and it just left very thin, fine lines. Then I started hair-pulling.

WH And this was always when you felt you had done something bad?

MM Often after being confronted I had a feeling of deep shame along with the inability to express myself or defend myself. That lead to the stoicism, the clamming up that got me accused of being unfeeling. At that point I did feel unfeeling, so I would wait until I was alone and could express myself through the ritual.

WH But even though this was very religious, you later rebelled against the church?

MM My dad gave me Edith Hamilton's *Mythology* to read when I was eight, so I asked my dad "What's a myth?" And I started looking at my church as a set of myths, which interested me, but I wanted to study other myths too.

WH When did you start feeling connected to Christ, with a special destiny and healing role?

MM Part of me still feels "Oh this is blasphemous" to say this, but I told my friend in the second grade that I would be the next coming of Christ. Then she told me she had a similar vision. That really irritated me. I thought, "No! How do you know you're Jesus when I know I'm Jesus?! You're not even Christian!"

WH Was she just copying you like kids do?

MM I think so. So as a child I think I was egotistical, but at the same time there was something noble about it, a great suffering on behalf of humanity. I perceived Jesus as a very loving human who helped people. I was sincere in wanting to be like that.

> My crazy mind allowed me to survive extreme situations normal people wouldn't be able to handle.

WH And how did you eventually end up on medications?

MM When I was nine I told my best friend how I was going to kill myself. She was really upset, and I learned never ever to tell anyone. And so for years I lead a dual life: one where I was a normal, even high-achieving, precocious kid, and the other where I self-mutilated, had rituals that no one knew about, and was sad and suicidal. I started overdosing on pills, huge cocktails of whatever I could find in the house, including these gigantic antihistamines that weren't even sold in grocery stores. I became really paranoid, I thought my mother was drugging my food, I was bathing about 8 times a day and shaving a lot and really upset about germs. I had been pulling out my hair so much I was having bald spots. I never wanted to go to school, so I cried every morning. This was all happening freshman year, when I was also varsity cheerleader, voted most beautiful in my class, and was in top 5% of grades.

I was sleeping a lot, all day, and I went to visit my father, who is a social worker, and he said "you seem depressed." Before then, no one had paid attention, so it was a big deal. "Oh my god, somebody sees this." So I said, "What does that mean, you are my father, what should I do?" He said he thought I should go to a doctor and be put on antidepressants. At that point having a label wasn't a hindrance; it was like being saved.

WH Were the medication and counseling helpful?

MM For a while, if for no other reason than I wasn't alone anymore in my world. I don't know how much more functional it made me though, and nothing helped with the hair-pulling. They tried an experimentally high dose of Prozac when I was 17, 200mg. That was the first time that I surfaced from depression, but it also felt incredibly toxic.

> I hitchhike and hop freight trains, and sometimes I lose all my possessions and suddenly I'm somewhere and I don't know anyone. But I almost thrive on this.

I drank a mug of St. John's Wort tea while on that high dose of Prozac, and wound up in the emergency room. I had full-body tremors that were so strong they were almost convulsions, my heart was racing really fast, and I couldn't walk normally. But they thought I was just making things up, and I didn't realize the connection to the St. John's Wort until later. There was a four- hour delay in the ER until I was seen, and part of my agitation was because I was so scared. I didn't know what was happening or why, but I had serotonin syndrome, which can be lethal.

When the intake nurse was going to give me a shot of Ativan, he grabbed my hand and told me to stop shaking, even though the whole reason I was there was because I couldn't control the shaking. He said if I didn't hold still, "I'll jab it in there as many times as it takes," and so he jabbed the needle in. I didn't understand

I thought, "No! How do you know you're Jesus when I know I'm Jesus?!"

why I was getting a needle in my hand. I had a huge contusion the size of my palm afterwards.

WH Some medical professionals mistreated me in shocking ways too, cruel ways. It makes you crazy when nobody wants to believe you, and if we are angry, then there's something wrong with us. How did you get off medications?

MM They tried at least 8 different drugs, including antipsychotics and lithium, saying I needed meds the rest of my life. Somebody suggested it was good to feed your plants menstrual blood, so I did. And it completely killed all of them! I later realized it was because of all the Prozac in my system. It poisoned my houseplants. So I began to see I was surrounded by all these toxins. I realized this wasn't working for me, and I started to resist.

WH Today you are off medications, and your identity has changed to being transgender, tell us about that.

MM Not everyone who is transgender identifies this way, but my crazy mind allowed me to survive extreme situations normal people wouldn't be able to handle. When you are mad you are in some ways not worried about what other people think. It's about being an outsider, and to be transgender is to be outside of gender binaries, to be fluid. My reality is a construct that shifts, and when I am freed of that construct I can explore things other people would be much too afraid to.

WH What are some examples?

MM I hitchhike and hop freight trains, and sometimes I lose all my possessions and suddenly I'm somewhere and I don't know anyone. But I almost thrive on this. I refer to it as going on a walkabout or a vision quest, a complete abandonment of your own identity. Homeless people also can experience something like this, with owning nothing and no place to go. Our identities tend to be shallow: "This is my job, therefore it is my identity." We are typically scared to be really out of our comfort zone. There are times I've just thrown myself on the mercy of... riding the current dragon, with no idea what is going to happen, switching different realities.

I recently decided to quit my job, and my boss asked "Are you unhappy here?" And I just said, "No, no, I just feel intuitively I need to go hop trains, to put myself in the void again." In those few years I had grown a lot from having community, carving out a comfortable niche for myself. My parents were happy because my moods were supposedly stable and I was contributing to society, holding down a job and making decent money. But it was time to stretch myself, and I needed to throw it all away again.

> I recently quit my job, and my boss asked "Are you unhappy here?" And I just said, "No, no, I just feel intuitively I need to go hop trains, to put myself in the void again."

For a long time I considered myself an ally of trans people, but in truth I felt sorry for my trans friends: It's going to be hard, how can they do it, I'm so glad I don't have this affliction. Then I found myself in the same boat. I had this realization, Oh my god, I'm transgender. It wasn't necessarily welcome, it was maybe exciting but also horrifying. From the very beginning it was a calling, but I felt I could escape it. So it took courage to go out into the unknown. Why now? I didn't even know what it meant. Do I have to alter my body? Am I going to have to live as a man? And it was coming to me as This is what you have to do, this is part of your destiny, to evolve spiritually, to reach your potential.

WH Is this connected to how as a kid you felt you had a calling to be Christ and a healer?

MM I knew what the word "shaman" was and I knew from cartoons what a "witch doctor" was. So early on I identified with those sorts of figures,

I thought I had special powers. There is a spiritual component to being transgender. In some cultures, trans people were the shamans and medicine people, the gifted healers and artists. That's what finally made it acceptable to me, that I could resolve it as part of my lifelong spiritual calling. At an early age I knew I was ready for this calling, so I decided now was the time to put my whole life at stake. ■

Meaning In Voices
Eleanor Longden

Eleanor Longden is a researcher at the University of Liverpool and a trustee of Intervoice. She lectures and publishes internationally and is the author of *Learning from the Voices in my Head* (2013).

Voices speak in metaphorical ways about genuine problems in a person's life. It therefore doesn't make sense to shoot the messenger and deny the message.

WILL HALL You've worked as a clinician and researcher on the experience of voice-hearing. Tell us about how you began this journey.

ELEANOR LONGDEN My voyage into voice-hearing started when I was very young. I was forged in a crucible of painful abuse that created a shattered, fragmented child, who would ultimately grow into a crushed and devastated adult. I buried my past; all these terrible memories of fear and shame, horror and terror, I pushed them into a box and sealed it over. But I had essentially buried it alive. This unresolved pain was screaming to get out, and ultimately, of course, it did.

I was 18 when I began hearing a voice narrating all my actions in the third person. At that time I was very distressed, and couldn't advocate for myself or express strong emotion in a healthy way. I was fragmented and crippled on one level, shattered, yet I also tried desperately to push those feelings away and play 'normal.' In the midst of this tumultuous, chaotic internal world, the voice seemed to be reminding me that I was coping and carrying on. I wasn't particularly frightened by it; in fact it provided quite a positive role. So if the voice observed, "She is going to the library," "She is reading a book," it felt rather companionable, reassuring me I was still meeting my responsibilities and doing what I needed to do.

WH And at some point the voice became negative?

EL That happened in a university seminar, where another student would really challenge and belittle me. I never defended myself, because I felt it was vital to appease everyone. I think many children who've been terrorized can become submissive adults who try to keep the peace, keep everything calm and safe. Yet that meant I often came out of those situations hugely frustrated. A part of me, an aspect that was never expressed, felt consumed with rage.

After one such experience of subjugation, the voice said "She is leaving the room," but for the first time its tone had changed, it sounded angry. I was intrigued, and quickly realized that it was expressing my disowned sense of anger. This was an early indication that the voice was closely linked to my emotional life, embodying unexpressed feelings.

Shortly afterwards, however, I made a decision that would have catastrophic consequences: I told a friend about the voice. She was horrified, and insisted I see a doctor, who in turn referred me to a psychiatrist. Seeing a doctor was the beginning of my descent, not only into the mental health system, but also into real madness.

WH You were still in school and functioning as they say, but they were concerned because they assumed voice-hearing equals schizophre-

nia. So you were hospitalized?

EL It's ironic, that somewhere established to offer sanctuary and safety to distressed individuals is often what ultimately breaks them. I swiftly became aware that if I was going to recover my disowned sense of self, then the hospital wasn't the place to do it. They immediately defined me in terms of a biomedical model of disease and disability. It's profoundly disempowering to be told there is essentially nothing you can to do to help yourself except take medication and hope for the best.

> What had previously been an experience, the voice, was now constructed as a symptom. I was encouraged to take an aggressive stance towards the voices, to reject and ignore them.

At one point I was told, "You would be better off with cancer, because cancer is easier to cure than schizophrenia." A message of hopelessness and helplessness; that my voices were a meaningless, aberrant bit of biological bad luck to be endured, rather than a complex, significant experience to be explored. To be told that your mind, the essence of your humanity, is malfunctioning is profoundly terrifying. It encourages you to devolve all power and responsibility to the psychiatric system.

WH And your voices worsened because of being hospitalized?

EL I use the expression a "psychic civil war," which relates to what I was saying previously; being incited to see your mind as the problem. What had previously been an experience, the voice, was now constructed as a symptom. I was encouraged to take an aggressive stance towards the voices, to reject and ignore them.

So now when I heard the voices, I became incredibly fearful and angry. And ultimately this just served to make the voices stronger, more aggressive, and more numerous, they were fighting harder to be heard.

And all the time I was being told schizophrenia is a degenerative neurological disease, and the voices were a sign of deterioration and disintegration; as if I was rotting from the inside.

WH What was your experience with medication?

EL I think if voices are about emotion, then psychosis is the emotional crisis. Psychiatric drugs are designed to inhibit emotion. Yet strong emotion can actually be part of the healing process; learning to fully tolerate, experience, and express it. Voices are a sane reaction to insane circumstances. If you've been terrorized and demoralized in your life, in whatever form that takes, abuse, poverty, exclusion, marginalization... then something needs to happen for you to heal. You need to find a sense of meaning, compassion, understanding, and self-acceptance. And that's hard to do when you are sedated on stupefying drugs.

WH While I was hospitalized I was hearing a very aggressive, ridiculing voice. There was never any curiosity from the staff about it, it was just seen as a symptom of disease, to be "stabilized" with meds like an irregular heartbeat or something. When they did ask about family history, it was to claim my mental illness was genetic. It was only long afterwards that I started to make the connection with my childhood trauma.

EL Those experiences are heartbreaking and I will never cease to be outraged by them. A person's story, so rich and meaningful and painful, being disregarded and disrespected. In this way, I think mental health services can implicitly side with abusers.

At one point I was told, "You would be better off with cancer, because cancer is easier to cure than schizophrenia."

The author Judith Herman talks about this; that perpetrators depend on the universal instinct to look the other way. In contrast, survivors ask us to bear witness to their suffering, which is much harder to do. And so it becomes easier to be complicit with the abuser. Often, that's exactly what psychiatry does.

Jacqui Dillon, the English Hearing Voices Network Chair, talks about a voice-hearer who disclosed his experiences of rape, and his psychiatrist responded "I don't need to hear that, we're here to discuss your schizophrenia." Complicity with silence and denial is so toxic.

WH How did you go from believing the disease model to where you are today?

EL It was a long process. I was instilled with such hopelessness and humiliation about myself that the voices consequently grew much more aggressive. The deterioration was rapid and horrifying, and it exposed me to further victimization. I became a target for vicious, systematic bullying that culminated in physical and sexual assault.

WH Other students targeted you because you had mental health difficulties?

EL Yes. The basic message was "We can do what we like because nobody will believe you over us." That's the universal message of abusers. Unfortunately, as we've discussed, that threat is not entirely without foundation. Even when patients' reports of violation and victimization aren't denied outright, they're often minimized, trivialized and invalidated, and the end result is the same: you are not heard.

Unsurprisingly my mental state deteriorated even further and I withdrew into a nightmarish world of voices, visions, and delusions. It was an awful, prolonged living death.

> Strong emotion can actually be part of the healing process; learning to fully tolerate, experience, and express it. Voices are a sane reaction to insane circumstances.

WH When did you start to come back?

EL My first lucky break was returning to a place of safety, my family home. I have an incredibly close relationship with my mum, who consistently believed in me. She had faith I could recover and communicated that hope to me, a sense of unconditional love and belief: "I'll wait for you, I know you'll come back to me."

I was also lucky to be referred to Pat Bracken, a wonderful psychiatrist who firmly believed that recovery was not only possible, but inevitable. In the first interview he said, "Can you tell me about yourself" and my response was "I'm a paranoid schizophrenic." And he gently challenged that immediately: "Don't tell me what other people have told you about yourself, tell me about you." It was wonderful; for the first time, a professional was seeing beyond my degraded, despairing exterior.

He also gave me a copy of *Accepting Voices* by Marius Romme and Sandra Escher. That was revelatory, a recognition that voice-hearing isn't an abstract, arbitrary indication of mental illness, but rather a significant and understandable experience that can be deciphered and made sense of. That you don't have to just survive, you can thrive.

This process took a long time. But when people started to believe in me I realized that if I wanted things to change, then I had to be an active part of the process. I used to think Pat Bracken and his team saved me, but later I realized they did something much more meaningful, they empowered me to save myself.

I was very fortunate. The damage I endured was catastrophic, but wasn't irreversible, which was largely a matter of luck. That's a terrible thing, because terrorized, demoralized people need more than arbitrary good luck to protect them. I joined the Hearing Voices Movement and had the privilege to meet a range of extraordinary, progressive individuals, who inspired and taught me. This was really energizing and after that, once that healing process initiated, things just kept on improving.

A principal part of that process was making sense of my voices and realizing they had a protective function: they were drawing my attention to unresolved emotional conflicts. I described myself earlier as a shattered child that grew into a fractured, devastated adult. All of those fragments were represented by different voices, each of which needed compassion and care. And the most negative, destructive voices were actually the ones that required the greatest kindness, because they related to parts of me that had endured the most suffering.

WH Tell us about your work helping professionals support voice-hearers.

EL Much of that focuses on "the construct," a tool originated by Romme and Escher. It's based on the premise that voice characteristics are personally meaningful to the voice-hearer and related to their life story. So the example you gave earlier Will, about hearing a negative voice but nobody asking, "What does it sound like, what does it say," that's at the heart of the construct; exploring voice content and formulating it in a way that the voice-hearer understands is acceptable and useful.

We ask about five themes: the voices' identity and characteristics; what triggers them; what was happening when they first appeared, whether they changed afterwards; and finally, the person's life history, their story. We use the information to explore two main questions: "Who or what do the voices represent?" and "What problems do the voices represent?" That information is then used to derive a recovery plan.

In the first phase, that's about safety, finding ways to cope with the voices' intrusions, and reduce fears and anxieties. The second phase is making sense of the voices, using them as clues to internal emotional conflicts that can be understood and healed. And the third phase is reconnection, helping a person reclaim their life, to recover joy, revisit dreams, hopes, and aspirations. A positive future is a fundamental right for every voice-hearer, irrespective of a harrowing past or painful present.

Voice-hearing, essentially, is a meaningful personal event: a story. By reclaiming that story, you can reclaim control of both your voices and your life.

> I was being told schizophrenia is a degenerative neurological disease, and the voices were a sign of deterioration and degeneration; as if I was rotting from the inside.

WH It's a normal human variation, a part of who we are. Part of the human experience.

EL That's beautifully expressed, exactly right: a sign of human difference and diversity.

WH Are you hopeful for more caring approaches to hearing voices?

EL Yes, because The Hearing Voices Movement is so powerful, articulate and political. It adopts a Civil Rights outlook shared by many minority experiences; agitation for social change, emancipation, actions for respect, and working in

In the midst of this tumultuous, chaotic internal world, the voice seemed to be reminding me that I was coping and carrying on.

ways that don't blame or pathologize the individual. It's about changing society's perceptions and psychiatry's perceptions as well. It's no longer justifiable to see distress as part of a disease syndrome, rather than something meaningful and real, an opportunity for learning and growth, even if the lessons are painful and difficult.

As Marius Romme says, voices speak in metaphorical ways about genuine problems in a person's life. It therefore doesn't make sense to shoot the messenger and deny the message. If drugging, sedation and silencing are psychiatry's traditional "cure" responses, then understanding, accepting and integrating the voices' emotional meaning is the recovery response. ∎

From Paranoia to Wholeness
Matthew Morrissey

Matthew Morrissey MA, MFT, is a therapist based in the San Francisco Bay Area who works with children, teens, and adults.

At age 21 I traveled abroad and realized a lot of important things... including that adults don't really know what they are doing! There is no "in control" there in the adult world. And I found that terrifying.

When I got back home I had severe jet lag and wasn't able to sleep, I just couldn't stop my mind from racing. And then I made a big mistake: I smoked some pot, which sent me through the roof. I had a hard time being in my body and had painfully intense feelings of joy and elation. I got into an argument with one of my friends, and he was verbally abusive and shamed me in front of a lot of people. And that was the straw that broke the camel's back.

I felt a existential void open up and terror flood in. I started to have what's called delusions, thinking the world was controlled by very smart, evil people who were actively manipulating things. And it was my future to find the good force, the angels, people who had intelligence and compassion, because I was on their team. But the evil people were psychic and coming to get me. So paranoia set in.

I said to my family, "Okay, I should go to the hospital to get some sleep." But when the psychiatrist started asking questions about things I had been saying, I knew the evil forces had captured me. I just wanted to sleep, but I spent ten days on the in-patient unit. None of the staff talked to me, and I was on a very high dose of Risperdal. It made me drool horribly, and I looked like a zombie. My friends visited and were just like "Wow, where did Matthew go?"

Then the outpatient program was also basically a joke. The staff treated us like little children, it was very demeaning. But one staff person did turn things around for me. He said: "You need to go back to school." So I eventually did go back to Boston University. And slowly but surely, I recovered. The most terrifying thing the mental health system did was to make me feel I couldn't trust myself.

Growing up my mom was pretty verbally abusive to me, and my dad was emotionally distant. I was also bullied in high school terribly, in seventh grade I ate alone in the cafeteria, and you can imagine the shame of that. So I had a lot of trauma. That moment my friend was verbally abusive with me caused all those old wounds to rush back.

People become paranoid for very good reasons. When you've been let down and hurt repeatedly by people who matter to you very much, you develop a basic mistrust of other human beings. That then shows up as paranoia.

This is why it hits people in their twenties, they are trying to individuate from their families. A lot of family systems have their own idiosyncratic, peculiar way of behavior. So when the person goes out into the world all they have is what they've been trained into from the family. They don't know how to get into a social group and make themselves liked. And they become isolated.

Often psychosis is what the psyche does to achieve some kind of balance and safety, so you can live with this mass of chaotic feelings and not be overwhelmed. My emotions were so extreme that my mind had to invent something to signify this catastrophe. And that was where the cosmic battle between good and evil came from. My mind created an image of wholeness out of my fragmented mental state. ∎

Art and Madness
Louis Sass

Louis Sass is a professor of clinical psychology at Rutgers University and author of *Madness and Modernism: Insanity in the Light of Modern Art, Literature, and Thought* (1994), and *The Paradoxes of Delusion: Wittgenstein, Schreber, and The Schizophrenic Mind* (1995).

I wouldn't want to identify them too closely, but there is a structural similarity between modern art and schizophrenic perception.

WILL HALL You're interested in the subjective experience of madness, a "phenomenological" approach shared by Scottish psychiatrist R.D. Laing, and rare today.

LOUIS SASS Friends I knew very well in high school developed psychosis and schizophrenia, and I was dissatisfied with what I read in clinical psychology and psychoanalysis; it just didn't fit what I observed. I was very influenced by Laing, especially *The Divided Self*, and I could identify with what he described as the schizophrenic condition. I saw in myself similar alienation and problematic self-consciousness, so I felt I could make a contribution to the field.

WH Doesn't that lead to question calling something "schizophrenia" at all?

LS I understand people don't want to be saddled with a label that is perjorative. But the word from Greek means "split mind" or "split heart" and I think it captures fairly well what some of it is like. Eugen Bleuler used the term to replace Emile Kraepelin's earlier "dementia praecox," to emphasize schizophrenia as a *different* way of thinking and experiencing, not deficient or lesser, like dementia.

WH It's still not a clear clinical entity with distinct definition, but a catch-all that Kraepelin put on an asylum population that was vast and undifferentiated.

LS Yes, what people call schizophrenia has an incredible diversity of symptoms, and symptoms can sometimes even be antithetical to each other. A patient can feel they are a god controlling the whole universe, but at other times that they are a mechanism or thing, with no willpower or control at all, the opposite of a god. So normal people have difficulty empathizing, and schizophrenia seems incomprehensible.

WH For Psychiatrist Karl Jaspers the defining feature of schizophrenia was being "un-understandable." To me it's more meaningful to say two people have trouble relating, and each sees the other as "un-understandable."

In *The Autobiography of A Schizophrenic Girl*, the author Renée writes:

"For me, madness was definitely not a condition of illness; I did not believe that I was ill. It was rather a country, opposed to Reality, where reigned an implacable light, blinding, leaving no place for shadow; an immense space without boundary, limitless, flat; a mineral, lunar country, cold as the wastes of the North Pole. In this stretching emptiness, all is unchangeable, immobile, congealed, crystallized. Objects are stage trappings, placed here and there, geometric cubes without meaning. People turn weirdly about, they make gestures, movements without sense; they are phantoms whirling on an infinite plain, crushed by the pitiless electric light. And I... I am lost in it, isolated, cold, stripped,

purposeless under the light. A wall of brass separates me from every-body and everything. This was it; this was madness... Madness was finding oneself permanently in an all-embracing unreality. I called it The Land of Light because of the brilliant illumination... dazzling, astral, cold... and the state of extreme tension in which everything was, including myself."

LS People who haven't had this sort of experience are likely to interpret it in three ways: either as deficit, an absence of some rational capacity of mind; as a "Dionysian condition," a lapsing out of rationality into an overly passionate, instinct-driven state of mind; or as a regression into a young child state of mind.

But these interpretations are very different, actually, from what Renée describes. She describes not being overwhelmed by desire but having a tremendous sense of distance and separation from the world. It's not going into the dark caverns of the unconscious but into the land of light, as she describes it, in which things are almost too brightly-lit, too precise, too clearly-seen.

> **It's not going into the dark caverns of the unconscious but into the land of light, as she describes it, in which things are almost too brightly-lit, too precise, too clearly-seen.**

WH So psychiatry and psychology have viewed psychosis as deficit, that your brain is not working properly or you lack cognitive functioning; or as regression, that you sink into a wild or childlike state, something more primitive. But you are going beyond the deficit, and regression views.

LS Central to the experience of schizophrenia are extreme self-consciousness and alienation. One has a tremendous sense of separation: from one's own body, from other people, from the external world, from one's thinking and words: from all kinds of things that more normal individuals are unlikely to feel separate from and think about at all.

WH I myself have a lifelong fascination with scrutinizing interpersonal behavior, and also with the philosophies of language. This interest is fueled by my altered states, when my own participation in language and social interaction codes evaporates.

LS A good example is the "hearing voices" characteristic of schizophrenia. These seem to involve a kind of focal awareness of one's own thought processes. Normally one doesn't hear the words of "inner speech," but just inhabits those words in order to think about something. But in the case of schizophrenic experience there can be acute and direct awareness of the words themselves. Commonly people hear a voice commenting on their behavior, thinking, or feelings.

I was very influenced by Laing, especially *The Divided Self*, and I could identify with what he described as the schizophrenic condition.

WH Everyone seems to have an "inner critic," and you can interact with it just as you can as the hearing voices phenomenon. The Voice Dialogue technique taught in the Hearing Voices Movement wasn't originally developed for voice-hearers, but for everyone, because everyone's psyche is multiple and relational.

LS A similar example is how people with so-called schizophrenia can become very aware of things that we normally just do naturally. You might become aware of the strangeness of what it is to shake hands with another person. Of course it doesn't seem strange to the normal person who grows up in a culture where you have a custom of shaking hands. But if you're in this very self-conscious state, you tend to scrutinize things and then those things become strange. Sticking this lump of flesh out into the space between two bodies and then moving it up and down simultaneously in contact with that other lump of flesh coming from the other person.

And as a result of such an unusual mindset there can be important insights normal people just don't notice. A friend who was diagnosed with schizophrenia would sit in a bar and watch how people moved and interacted, almost like a student of animal behavior. He had a focal awareness of chimpanzee-like rules present in human interaction we don't normally notice, such as the way men held their bodies to impress other people, or to intimidate or be friendly. He thought as an ethologist would see. He was observing things that were really happening, but as a result it was very difficult for him to interact with people.

WH So through the huge diversity of schizophrenic experience there runs a thread of exaggerated self-consciousness. Awareness of yourself and your surroundings is heightened to a break with customary ways people understand things. For me the idea of heightening connects with the spiritual aspect some people discover in these states.

LS I don't want to go quite so far and say heightened self consciousness is always present, but I think it is extremely common and a central feature.

WH Delusions of mind control, for example, can be heightened awareness of real social group dynamics such as deceit and talking behind people's back that are actually in fact going on in "reality." These dynamics can be invisible in ordinary interactions, and professionals and family members often act like these dynamics are not real.

One has a tremendous sense of separation: separation from one's own body, from other people, from the external world, one's thinking and words.

LS In psychosis you can have an of awareness of the artificiality of many societal customs. So you are not "duped." But as a result you wander lost in the world. Conventional social interaction needs you to not have this self-conscious awareness. Psychosis or schizophrenia can involve both an awareness of truth and also be very problematic because of it.

WH And then maybe the person who knows too much becomes a scapegoat.

Language is also an example: in extreme states speech can seem to wander, so-called "loose associations" or "word salad," and then people are told they can't keep their thinking on track.

LS Normally we don't focus on a word we use, just the meaning we want to convey. But in psychosis one may become hyper-aware of the word itself, and be distracted into another line of thought. If the word is "pen," you find yourself now talking about a farmyard rather than about writing implements on your desk. Hyper-awareness can also make a person's

You can have an of awareness of the artificiality of many societal customs. So you are not "duped." But as a result you wander lost in the world.

thinking abstract, and speech can seem meaningless. I gave a Rorschach inkblot test to one person, and instead of imagining images he got into talking about the difference between black and white, and the concept of contrast. What he said was similar to what philosophers might say, but from a different more mainstream point of view it could be dismissed as nothing but "poverty of content of speech."

WH The Minnesota Multiphasic Personality Inventory test was quite a puzzle for me in the hospital.

I still struggle with the idea schizophrenia as a difference given or internally generated "inside" someone. Hyper self-consciousness may also be an adaptation to context, vigilance in the wake of trauma for example. These states can result from a relationship, such as fear of something: an excessive, deep, strange terror that shocks you into an extreme world view. Maybe "madness" then becomes a way out of relational power struggles too terrifying to be named directly.

Tell us about excess of consciousness and modern art, which is often also "un-understandable."

LS Twentieth century art can be very incomprehensible, because it also became preoccupied with hyper-reflexive issues. Marcel Duchamp took a urinal and put it in an art exhibition, a self-awareness, a consciousness of what art is. He was reflexively calling into question the whole convention of art.

In abstract expressionism, instead of using paint conventionally to depict an object such as a landscape or a nude, the paint and surface of the canvas themselves became the work's focus. Alain Robbe-Grillet of the Nouveau Roman literary school was always circling back on the narrator talking about himself. So if you look at twentieth century art, you find interesting parallels with things that occur in schizophrenia, if we see schizophrenia not as regression or cognitive deficit, but as a different, more complex form of awareness.

Normally we don't focus on a word, just the meaning we want to convey. But in psychosis one may become hyper-aware of the word itself.

WH Another example would be the Surrealists, who were fascinated with psychoanalysis, and had a mission to bring dreams to greater social prominence, as in the indigenous cultures they borrowed so much from. Which reminds me of Jung's comment that psychosis is like living in a waking dream.

LS Surrealist Yves Tanguy painted strange, moon-like landscapes of unrecognizable objects: very much like the geometric cubes without meaning that Renée talks about in *Autobiography of a Schizophrenic Girl.* Perhaps that's what the world would look like if you lost all practical relationship with it, so a chair serves no human function, just a strange angular form.

WH Jean-Paul Sartre's novel *Nausea* describes a similar state of extreme alienation.

LS When *Nausea's* central character Roquentin looks at a chestnut tree, he loses awareness we would expect. Instead the tree and its roots take on a strange, hallucinatory quality. That kind of excessive staring plays a significant role in schizophrenic experience.

WH Staring and hyper-awareness seem related to trauma: the fight-flight alert response. Animals stare and become hyper aware when in danger. Philosopher Maxine Sheets-Johnstone suggests psychosis may be a vastly exaggerated physiological startle reflex, a recoil in terror from a threat that reshapes the entire nervous system.

But your direction here is not to diagnose artists, or to pinpoint "prodromal" first signs of illness? You're suggesting a deeper mystery?

LS Someone like surrealist Antonin Artaud clearly was schizophrenic (if that word has any meaning); he spent his last ten years in asylums. Alfred Jarry, a major innovator who wrote the first absurdist play *Ubu Roi*, was very schizophrenic-like. But other modern artists, such as Robbe-Grillet, were conventional. So I wouldn't want to identify them too closely, but there is a structural similarity between modern art and schizophrenic perception.

WH Perhaps one person who is hyper-reflexive gets more of a grip on life and expresses the awareness as a talent in art and work, whereas another ends up funneled into the role of the mad person. Any quality might itself be variation, not abnormality. And no such genes have been discovered, so maybe it's a creative adaptation rather than inherited.

LS That is extremely plausible as well, and a lot of different explanations may be simultaneously true. Or the causes of hyper-reflexivity in schizophrenia and in twentieth-century art may be completely different.

In the twentieth century there are quite a few people of profound cultural impor-

If you look at twentieth century art, you find parallels with things that occur in schizophrenia.

tance who were nearly psychotic or who actually suffered from schizophrenia. But if you look earlier it is harder to find examples of people who had much influence. In 1800, the time of Romanticism, popular art was in a way manic or hypomanic-like: emotionality was much more important than alienation and self-consciousness. The creativity of Lord Byron is very different from the creativity of Samuel Beckett. So the link between madness and creativity also needs to be seen in historical context: it depends what a culture defines as creativity.

WH The question becomes, why does an era value certain kinds of art?

LS There is a hyper-objectivism today, people think they are nothing but their brain, just neurons firing. The artist Andy Warhol once said, "I want to be a machine." He referred to his art studio as "the factory." His vision of the world has no inner life, just things like photographic images. And at the same time it is a world of total fantasy, where "there is no real Jackie Onassis, only images of Jackie Onassis." So you go back and forth between mechanical concretism and extreme subjectivism. That has parallels with schizophrenic experience.

WH How can these ideas we're discussing be helpful to people?

LS For some people the whole idea they are suffering from a mental disorder doesn't make much sense. But notions about hyper-reflexivity gives them a better handle on what is really troubling them, and a way to go in different directions.

WH Some are just more aware than others, in a way that can cause problems for them. Does your work help us see diversity in people, rather viewing them as lacking something?

LS That is certainly one of the goals I have. We have to be more sensitive and start to recognize people's potential insights while at the same time not romanticizing them or neglecting their suffering. ■

I gave a Rorschach inkblot test to one person, and instead of images he got into talking about the difference between black and white, and the concept of contrast. What he said was similar to what philosophers might say.

Salvation By Music
John Rice

John Rice is a DJ and manager of Blue Beat Productions. He lives in Phenix City, Alabama.

The stone the builder refused will become the head cornerstone. That's Christ's main legacy, but it has been completely lost in religion as it is practiced.

JOHN RICE I was born in Montgomery, Alabama and my father was a Methodist minister from a very liberal family. Another minister downtown, at Dexter Avenue Baptist Church, was Dr. Martin Luther King Jr. My father was right there when Rosa Parks refused to get up, and he was one of many white ministers who put his family and himself in danger. The threats were so cruel and so lethal toward anyone supporting integration. Even though I was a shy kid, when I came of age I had a strong sense of conviction and wanted to speak my mind, out of pride for what my father stood for.

WILL HALL What kinds of things were you speaking out about?

JR Racism is still very prevalent in the South today, but it's not as open now: in the '60s it was very ugly. I just said that black children should come to our school. For that I was subjected to a great deal of ridicule.

WH That was courageous. Did you always feel like an outsider growing up?

JR I was extremely rewarded for getting As and everything, but I didn't fit in. I began to be labeled as somebody that didn't "apply himself" in the right way. I didn't really want a scripted life, but I always felt as if I had no choice but to go off to college. I approached it almost as if it were induction into the army or something,

WH And so when you got to college it was difficult for you?

JR Extremely difficult. It manifested itself in a phenomenal desire to go home! I wasn't being educated in a way that would help me. I was living in a dorm and it was a lot like a fraternity.

It became apparent I wasn't going to finish the year. I needed incompletes to not lose the tuition, but the stipulation was that to get the incompletes the college needed some kind of reason. So I went to a psychiatrist who sent me to a facility for a few days of observation. I was extremely naïve about what I was getting into.

The first day the nurse told me one of the most peculiar things anyone ever said to me. She said, "John, if you don't want to stay with us, that means... you need to stay with us."

WH That's the widely used, Orwellian hospital logic of "involuntary voluntary."

JR I was horrified. I then realized the hospital was basically a psych ward.

The next morning nobody would tell me when I would be released. I was put on Haldol almost immediately. The psychiatrist did a lot of tests and told me he "needed to see how I adjusted to the medication." He said when he discoverd what was troubling me they would think about letting me go home.

I was beginning to not be myself. At all. The doctor said this real vague thing about "Well, sometimes when tension is released, we do peculiar things." It didn't make any sense. And I was filling out this form and I closed my eyes for a minute to ponder what was going on, and I realized my eyes were difficult to open. I began to tighten up all over. My neck started turning to the left, and I couldn't turn it back. I called the nurse, and it was like I broke some kind of code. All these people ran in. They flipped on this unbelievably bright light, turned me over, and gave me a shot in my rear. I didn't know anything until the next afternoon.

I was there two and a half weeks, and when I was released I was a complete shadow of the person who went in. Something had happened that I would never recover from. I was so fearful.

WH Those were Parkinsonian side-effects, that rigidity, very common on antipsychotics. And you had never been violent?

JR Oh, no. The only thing I had ever done in my whole life that was contrary was that I didn't want to stay in school. That was it.

WH What happened after you were released?

JR I felt like my life was over. I had always been a huge fan of music, ever since February 9th 1964 when the Beatles were on Ed Sullivan. When I got home my older brother had just purchased the new Paul McCartney album, "*Red Rose Speedway*." It's out of print now. It had the beautiful song "*My Love*" that he wrote for his wife. And my brother played it for me that night... and I felt nothing. I couldn't feel it. Music, the thing I loved most in life, I couldn't in any way enjoy.

Deep in my heart I knew something had been done to me that needed to be undone. But I couldn't make a case for myself because every step I took was just seen as confirming whatever the doctor said. My father asked if maybe the medicine was wrong, and the doctor said, "No. John is the problem, not the medicine."

They said "as soon as you can get him employed, that's what he needs to do. This medication has taken care of the things that were in his way, now he needs to take the initiative." I tell you, all I wanted to do was go to bed. That was the only time I was even remotely comfortable, to lay in the bed and think "This is my room, and if I'm real still, nothing can hurt me at the moment."

The first job I got was on a public works crew chopping weeds with a sickle on the side of the road. I didn't go back the next day. The next job was sweeping the floor at a textile mill. Seven days a week you go in at 7:00 in the morning and they decide when you get off. They fired me after a week: "He's just too slow."

The nurse said, "John, if you don't want to stay with us, that means... you need to stay with us."

Every time I went back to the hospital for follow-up appointments, my parents would say "He just wants to sleep," and "this job didn't work out, that job didn't work out." So the doctor became increasingly hostile. Without my parents in the room he said to me, "You know what you're going to leave me with? One option, John: to put you back in this hospital and give you electroshock treatments. And believe me John you don't want that."

Then I got lucky. My mother was very upset by all of this, but she believed the doctor. She said to my dad, "If he's going to have shock treat-

When I was released I was a complete shadow of the person who went in. Something had happened that I would never recover from.

ments, we can just drive him to a hospital that's closer by." So I saw a different psychiatrist, who took me off the Haldol and didn't prescribe electroshock. Being off of the Haldol was like night and day: I began to show real signs of being human again.

WH How long had you been on the Haldol?

JR I was on Haldol for a full year, which is long enough that you never get over it.

Getting off that drug was like being physically reborn. Stelazine is nobody's friend, and I was in for a long haul, but without the Haldol I began to show initiative, to have more energy, and to be able to become the person I was before.

I started to enjoy music again, in a very limited way. I was listening to Carlos Santana, albums he was making after his initial impact at Woodstock. Carlos and the band got tired of just being rock stars and began to explore jazz, deeper Latin roots, and Coltrane. One record I remember that Christmas was with Alice Coltrane. Apparently the powerful rhythm was sort of getting into me. I was really happy to be back to that part of myself.

> My father was right there when Rosa Parks refused to get up, and he was one of many white ministers who put his family and himself in danger.

WH Did you really start pursuing music at that point?

JR I was the biggest fan that ever was, and that was used as the example of what was distracting me from being a "responsible person." I was always told, "You worry too much about the Beatles and not enough about your studies."

I went back to college and was flunking out; I would go to the local hippie record store instead. That's what Springsteen sang: *"we learned more from the three minute record than we ever did in school."* And I couldn't read books very well because I'd forget the plot, so I began reading Henry Miller and literature that was like a roller coaster, a jazz type of writing, you didn't have to remember the tune, just the groove and rhythm. And jazz music became a real strong fascination; it was totally different from anything anybody around me liked or listened to. Jazz music gave me distance, which I really wanted. I began to build a world inside myself.

WH What was some of the music that was prominent for you?

JR I was really into a lot of things from German producer Manfred Eicher, who had a great independent label in Munich called ECM. He was recording a young pianist who had just left Miles' group, Keith Jarrett. Jarrett introduced me to Paul Motian and Charlie Haden and it grew from there.

Jazz for me was something I could cover myself with. Then as the mid-1970s moved on towards the '80s, suddenly there was punk rock. And, really it is very similar to jazz. I immediately immersed myself in the radical sounds coming out of Great Britain.

> I felt nothing. I couldn't feel it. Music, the thing I loved most in life, I couldn't in any way enjoy.

WH How is punk similar to jazz?

JR I'm sure Manfred Eicher, if he were sitting here, might disagree, I don't know! But rock is not a complicated form of music and can be done with very little else besides feeling. And while jazz is quite complicated, it is rather sterile unless the emotion is very immediate, such as with improvisation. So to me, feelings are paramount and what people think are irrelevant: that is what is consistent between punk and jazz.

Then in December of 1980 the Clash released their third album, *Sandinista!*. I had been hearing reggae influence all over punk rock, but when I heard *Sandinista!*, it wasn't just reggae, it was the extended dubs. And boy, it hit something in me. It was a rhythm different from anything I had ever heard, and it just had such remarkable power.

At first I thought the Clash had invented dub, but before long I discovered the truth. There was a very small community of engineers and musicians making music as powerful as scripture, yet completely without words. Dub was able to move a person spiritually just by the vibrations themselves. There's a mystical quality to it that I can't explain. Jamaican dub, it began to teach me things. I became more self-aware than I would have ever dreamed.

Publicly I was still in the darkness with medication. I did get some retail jobs, but I had a tremor from the Stelazine that I was very embarrassed about, very ashamed of. It affected my confidence and work. But privately I was becoming deeper and deeper involved in this sound that came from Kingston Jamaica.

One song that deeply affected me was "Soul Rebel," from Bob Marley. It connected me back to where I was born. Dr. King is a rebel in your soul, see? There is a great power in his rebellion that's very consistent with the Gospel, but hardly ever seen in Christianity as it is practiced. It's the ability to follow your own path to save your soul. You have the power to be yourself no matter how much courage it takes. And that really struck a chord with me. And "Redemption Song," that beautiful line he sings (and I hope I can say it without my voice breaking): *"emancipate yourselves from mental slavery. Nothing but ourselves can free our minds."* I hung onto that song. and I still do.

WH That is beautiful. Do you consider yourself part of the Christian and Rastafarian tradition?

JR I have broken with my family, and been told my father wouldn't approve of some things I say. I'll tell you what I believe: I believe that my father spoke for a Christ that is the part of anybody who stands up for people who don't have anything. The idea in Scripture is that the stone the builder refused will become the head cornerstone. That's a very powerful image and it really was Christ's main legacy, but it has been completely lost in religion as it is practiced.

I don't believe that some are "saved" and some are "lost." Bob Marley read the Bible every day and was greatly influenced by the Gospel, but he didn't think of any human being as "lost." He knew that was a whitewash, no pun intended there, of something more powerful.

Jazz music gave me distance, which I really wanted. I began to build a world inside myself.

So I was on Stelazine for thirty years, but the fire that was kindled by Jamaican music never died. And I became obsessive about music. I began to explore almost every phase of jazz and Broadway and really old, roots country. I would go from one obsession to the other, always retaining that foundation of the way I heard things through Jamaican music.

Then the psychiatrist I saw at a public clinic died. For the first time in my life I felt like I had just enough courage to say to the new doctor, "Review my whole chart and tell me if I am on the right medicine." And that is when everything changed. He told me to stop taking the Stelazine, just like that.

I went through months and months of the most horrifying cold-turkey withdrawal you can ever imagine. But when I came out on the other end, I was me again. It left me with a really bad short term memory, but

I don't believe that some are "saved" and some are "lost." That was a whitewash of something more powerful.

all the knowledge of all of the types of music I was so obsessive about for years was still there. And suddenly I didn't have to be obsessive about any one type of music, now all of it made beautiful sense to me. Certainly with reggae as the cornerstone.

That's when my mother helped me start a sound system business. I really do keep up with everything, and my music is remarkably diverse because of that. I'm a unique DJ in that I really dig Cole Porter as much as I do 50 Cent. ∎

Singing in the Dark
Susan McKeown

Susan McKeown is a Grammy award-winning vocalist and composer celebrated world-wide for her contributions to traditional Irish music, as well as her knowledge as a historian and folklorist. Her album *Singing In The Dark (2010)* is a benefit for mental health recovery.

What if there had been open conversation when we were teenagers? What if we had discussions about the family secrets, secrets that later came back in such a violent way when we were older?

WILL HALL What led you to create your album *Singing in the Dark*?

SUSAN MCKEOWN Several years ago my ex-partner had severe depression and behavioral changes that were really shocking to me. When I looked for help, it led me to question what my own family had been through. I was angry at the mainstream mental health discourse and the glossy ads from the pharmaceutical industry; it was irritating that there wasn't any way to talk at a deeper level, to deal with each other as human beings. Making *Singing in the Dark* was my response: it's the album I wished I had when we were going through that traumatic time.

WH What went on in your own family?

SM In the group of five teenagers I grew up with, there was me, a brother and sister whose father died by suicide, and then two friends, one of whom murdered the other. This all happened when we were in our twenties and thirties. It was so upsetting to us all. I felt, "What if there had been open conversation when we were teenagers? What if we had discussed the thoughts in our heads, what if we had felt safe doing that? What if we had discussions about the family secrets, secrets that later came back in such a violent way when we were older?" So I developed an interest in talking about things that aren't talked about, and the connections between culture and mental health.

WH Like most communities, these tragedies are just overwhelming. There are the formalities of grieving, but so much stays buried or at best just gets talked about behind closed doors with counselors.

SM I have been recording albums of traditional Irish music for years, and learned about a ritual in Ireland called keening. Keening comes from the Gaelic word *caoineadh*, to cry, to grieve. It was a very funny and formalized ritual where people could let things out for three days.

You might have heard of the Irish wake, and there's various stereotypes of that. But for centuries before, keening was a time to celebrate the person's life as well as to grieve. You could cry and mourn, and it was an opportunity to express things about the social context and recent community history. It was led primarily by women, and women spoke out about injustices they had witnessed, such as domestic violence. So when somebody died, keening was a safe place where anyone could express things and nothing could be said against them. People grieved the dead, banging the boards of the coffin, tearing their hair, gathering together. The lament of the keening was a kind of otherworldly sound coming from these women, who as young girls had watched the older women keening and learned the art from them.

In the fourteenth and fifteenth centuries, the Catholic Church sent orders down to parish priests to wipe out the keening process. I'm having discussions with many other Irish singers about this, we weren't taught it in school and we are researching it and want to claim it because it's our tradition.

WH A tragedy happens, and the community comes together in a ritual space to express emotions and for certain truths to come out. Was this a political threat? Was that why the Catholic Church suppressed these rituals? It makes me think of the Church's suppression of women when their healing practices were called witchcraft.

The bishops instructed local priests to stop the women and take back control of the funeral practice, to bring it under the directive of Rome.

SM The bishops instructed local priests to stop the women and take back control of the funeral practice, to bring it under the directive of Rome. Angela Bourke writes about this.

WH It's interesting to me how culturally today we say the same thing: this is not for us to talk about, we need experts and counselors and doctors. So when your partner had this very deep depression and behavior changes, it started a whole journey for you, discovering secrets in your own family?

SM In my family there is trauma going back generations. I can see the effects today of keening being wiped out by the church, within families and between men and women. My mother died when we were all between fifteen and twenty-three. We didn't have any tools to deal with her death, it was just shocking to us, there was no family sit-down to talk about it. Within six months most of my siblings moved out, and I lived with my dad for the next six years. I always wanted to talk about things, but there wasn't a space for that, even though everybody was in pain. A lot of my drive today as an artist is connected to that family experience. It's one of the inspirations for my album "Singing in The Dark."

WH Your album takes famous poems about madness and sets them to music. Tell us about that.

SM One of my favorite poems is by Theodore Roethke, who was fifteen when his father died and his uncle died by suicide. They had been commercial gardeners and done quite well in their town in Saginaw. Theodore had grown up in giant greenhouses and the influence of nature in his poetry is right there. It's such a beautiful poem, connecting his suffering with nature in an incredibly hopeful way.

> ### Excerpt from "In A Dark Time"
> ### Theodore Roethke
>
> *What's madness but nobility of soul*
> *At odds with circumstance? The day's on fire!*
> *I know the purity of pure despair,*
> *My shadow pinned against a sweating wall.*
> *That place among the rocks—is it a cave,*
> *Or winding path? The edge is what I have...*
>
> *A steady storm of correspondences!*
> *A night flowing with birds, a ragged moon,*
> *And in broad day the midnight come again!*
> *A man goes far to find out what he is—*
> *Death of the self in a long, tearless night,*
> *All natural shapes blazing unnatural light...*

WH One of my favorite lines is devastating: "What's madness but nobility of soul at odds with circumstance." That's such a map for discovering who you are and what those states mean.

SM Another poem I love is "Her Kind" by Anne Sexton. When Sexton began going to therapy after a breakdown, her therapist recommended she start writing poetry. She did, and now she's one of the greatest American poets, winning numerous awards including the Pulitzer Prize. The opposite advice was given to the Irish poet, Maeve McGuckian when she had a breakdown: her therapist recommended she stop writing poetry!

And I learned about McGuckian from another great Irish poet, Nuala Ní Dhomhnaill, who wrote "But how could we do that, it's poetry that keeps us alive."

"Her Kind" is a phenomenal poem about Anne's struggle with society, trying to be the perfect wife and mother and caregiver in the 1950s,

> ## You could cry and mourn, and it was an opportunity to express things about the social context and recent community history. It was led primarily by women, and women spoke out about injustices they had witnessed, like domestic violence.

and also give care to herself, every woman's struggle and every mother's struggle. Anne had other levels of struggle that she was going through as well, and there's messages in this poem that speak to us all.

"Her Kind"
Anne Sexton

I have gone out, a possessed witch,
haunting the black air, braver at night;
dreaming evil, I have done my hitch
over the plain houses, light by light:
lonely thing, twelve-fingered, out of mind.
A woman like that is not a woman, quite.
I have been her kind.

I have found the warm caves in the woods,
filled them with skillets, carvings, shelves,
closets, silks, innumerable goods;
fixed the suppers for the worms and the elves:
whining, rearranging the disaligned.
A woman like that is misunderstood.
I have been her kind.

I have ridden in your cart, driver,
waved my nude arms at villages going by,
learning the last bright routes, survivor
where your flames still bite my thigh
and my ribs crack where your wheels wind.
A woman like that is not ashamed to die.
I have been her kind.

WH Such a different quality from the Roethke: defiance.

SM There's beautiful footage on YouTube of Anne reciting that poem right into the camera, in a very seductive, very provocative way. There's something there we all long for, to be so bold as to *really* express ourselves.

WH So we should thank Anne Sexton, and also apparently her therapist at least a little for having encouraged her to write poems. I wonder Susan, do you ever feel there are times when you need to stay away from your creativity, to help your own mental wellness?

When Anne Sexton began going to therapy after a breakdown, her therapist recommended she write poetry. She did, and now she's one of the greatest American poets.

SM I haven't experienced that myself. But I've always felt there's a time to put it out in the world and there's a time to just express it to yourself. I can feel when something is coming, it feels like it's coming from somewhere outside of myself. It's my call to pick up on it and put it down on paper, or pick up the guitar and start finding out what it is, because I know it's going to be something key to my own journey of self discovery. Creativity has always been fruitful for me, I'm so happy to say.

WH For me the creative process is very connected to the inner critic process. I can become blocked or shamed and judge myself for not doing it right or not doing it well enough, or not being able to do it at all. Sometimes, I do just step back from it but it's not the creativity, it's the self-sabotage that comes along.

SM There's a documentary about the architect Frank Gehry talking about the moment when you begin a work, that you have to let the creativity flow and how difficult it is because you get in the way. All these voices

Making *Singing in the Dark* was my response: it's the album I wished I had when we were going through that traumatic time.

come to tell you that you're not good enough and you've got to tidy up your office, and he says he's always tidying up his office and seeing all these other things he needs to do.

So, as Roethke would say, "Which I is I?" It's about trying to find the voice that lets you get out of your own way.

WH What do you make of the fact that so many artists describe creativity just as you have, something is coming through you, something from beyond who you are?

SM It's not something I can explain! But it connects to some of the most profound experiences I've ever had in my life: being there when my father departed this earth, and the moment when I gave birth to my daughter. The energy that was present was something that I could not explain. I feel so privileged to have something blow through my hands or through my voice, I just feel privileged.

Roethke said that when he wrote one of his most famous poems, it came to him in a evening and he wrote it in half an hour. As soon as it was finished he knew it was one of his greatest works. And so he got down on his knees with gratitude.

WH One of the poems on your album is "Crazy Woman" by Gwendolyn Brooks.

SM When I came across this poem, I just thought it was so beautiful and so simple. She was a poet from Chicago and her parents must have spotted her talent early, because as a teenager they introduced her to the poet, Langston Hughes, and Hughes encouraged her to get published. She ended up becoming the first African-American to win the Pulitzer Prize.

"The Crazy Woman"
Gwendolyn Brooks

I shall not sing a May song.
A May song should be gay.
I'll wait until November
and sing a song of gray.

I'll wait until November,
that is the time for me.
I'll go out in the frosty dark
and sing most terribly.

And all the little people
will stare at me and say,
"That is the crazy woman
who would not sing in May."

I shall not sing a May song.
A May song should be gay.
I'll wait until November
and sing a song of gray.

WH It's an interesting way of understanding madness, suicide, and depression: as a kind of desperate resistance, as rebellion. We can't romanticize these experiences and the suffering associated with them. But conflict, with an oppressive society or an oppressive relationship or oppressive family, or even conflict between parts of ourselves , can drive us crazy.

SM This is something you see in poetry. And it makes me think of my own songwriting, how I address my own struggles with the way things are around me.

It's about trying to find the voice that lets you get out of your own way.

Our reactions to trauma are perfectly normal considering the environment or the circumstances, but then they're perceived by other people and they react. Things are not just self contained, but they occur in relations with others.

WH What's next for you?

SM One project is an album of fairy songs from the Irish tradition, many of them in Gaelic and hundred of years old. They're from people who lived with the belief in the fairy world, that the faery realm was ever present and very close at hand.

WH Some of us do still live with that belief!

SM What I find so interesting about these old songs is how they resonate in a contemporary way. So I love researching lyrics that are only available now in books and bringing them to today's audience. ∎

Breakdown and Breakthrough
Mel Gunasena

Mel Gunasena is a video activist, writer, poet, and artist. She is the director of *Evolving Minds*, a documentary on psychosis, spirituality and self-help; and *The Mayan Word*, on the spiritual view of the indigenous Maya.

WILL HALL What led you to making your documentary *Evolving Minds*?

MEL GUNASENA I was forcibly hospitalized after experiencing an altered state of mind that, for me, was a powerful spiritual experience. I have always been interested in shamanism and meditation, and believe I was accessing dimensions of reality that were potentially beneficial for humanity. To outsiders, I seemed crazy.

I felt incredibly infused with energy and I was stronger than ever before in my life. I could see reality clearly, could perceive other people's thoughts, and was very sensitive to energy. Though frightening, it was also exhilarating and powerful.

The primary insight from my altered state was how governed we are by fear. From childhood on, government, the media and society all try to control us to not really be who we really are and not live up to our full potential. In today's society, people are cut off from their roots, their source of power. My altered state was all about connecting with the cosmos, with everything that exists on the Earth and into infinity.

WH So you freed yourself from this fear and started to actually see what is going on?

MG Absolutely. But because I hadn't done it slowly and in a controlled way with spiritual practice, I was launched into a dimension where I didn't know how to be. I think it is important for people to have one foot in both worlds: to be in the ordinary yet be able to access these dimensions. A lot of people labeled psychotic and winding up in hospitals have launched themselves into other dimensions without knowing how to return or operate within the boundaries of society. So you don't, for example, go running down the street naked or whatever it is that might get you locked up. If people want to run down the street naked, why not? But we live in a society where doing such things is illegal, so...

WH We just had the Naked Bicycle Ride here in Portland, so social convention around what is crazy or normal is arbitrary! What were you doing that led to being launched into these other dimensions?

MG I experienced a lot of trauma in my life. And while I was in India, in the Himalayas, I started using LSD as a psychological healing tool.

WH Many spiritual teachers in Buddhism, like Jack Kornfield or Ram Dass, got their start on the spiritual path through psychedelics, and then adopted disciplined practice. So there is a strong connection, but psychedelics of course have a lot of risks. What did you experience?

MG I was spending a lot of time in the wilderness in the mountains, and began experiencing increasingly powerful dimensions. I didn't have the proper support or guidance, though, and this led me to lose my way. I started to live more in other dimensions than in the everyday. Ordinary day-to-day things, like taking care of myself, started to be less important. I was focused on spiritual insights: I got into a state of mind where I didn't want to sleep, I wanted to be awake, alive all the time. This burns out the body.

WH You said you experienced trauma; how did that relate to your spiritual insight?

MG People who experience trauma often create other dimensions so they don't have to experience their trauma. Their mind goes elsewhere.

WH Becoming a medicine person or shaman can in many cultures mean

I felt incredibly infused with energy and I was stronger than ever before in my life. I could see reality clearly, could perceive other people's thoughts, and was very affected by energy.

enduring an initiatory illness or trauma. Maybe dissociation becomes a problem when you don't have guidance on how to navigate, but it's actually a skill, not a breakdown.

MG It's not something I would recommend! But trauma doesn't have to cripple you. You can use it to develop yourself.

WH What led to you being locked up?

MG My family was very worried about me, and my sister flew to Thailand to bring me back to London. I was in complete shock because I had spent the previous six months in the wilderness, where I felt I had come to my true state of being. My family couldn't accept it, and when my own mother saw me at the airport she didn't even recognize me. This really affected me.

When I got back to London I was scared and felt I needed a place where I could feel safe. I have a very strong connection with horses, so the obvious thing to do at the time was to go and be with the nearest horses. There were stables around the corner from our house... but it happened to be where the police horses were kept! Very early one morning I jumped over the wall of the police station, climbed into the stable, and lay down under one of the horses. For the first time in days, I felt completely safe. But when the police saw me they took me straight to the psychiatric hospital.

> My family couldn't accept it, and when my own mother saw me at the airport she didn't even recognize me.

WH You were trying to take care of yourself and find some healing?

MG Yes. In hospital, nobody spoke to me. They put me in a room and observed me through a Plexiglas window for a few hours. Suddenly, without warning, four men rushed into the room, pulled down my pants, and injected me in the ass with antipsychotics.

They locked me in a room for four days, and every time I woke up they re-injected me. I was absolutely terrified. I really thought that I had been kidnapped by the forces of evil and they were going to kill me. It felt like I had started to experience and perceive very powerful and beautiful things, but that the psychiatric system was trying to stop that. They were trying to destroy that ability in me.

WH You make me think of my own confinement in an isolation cell; I blacked out in terror and rage when I was locked in, I didn't even remember much until I read the hospital's account in my medical files.

MG I was forced to take medications, and a psychiatrist told me that I had a mental illness and I should take psychiatric drugs for the rest of my life. Luckily, because I had studied about altered states of consciousness and been an activist, I didn't believe him.

WH How did you get out of the system?

MG When I came out of hospital I had to do a complete detox. For months, I was very scared. I just had to just trust that everything was going to be ok. I slowly weaned myself off medication. I was very particular about my diet and became a recluse until my strength and confidence returned. I ultimately healed myself mainly through diet, vitamin and mineral supplements, resolving my trauma, and through friends and family support. Not psychiatric intervention. ■

Crash Course in Urban Shamanism
Will Hall

Spiritual practice is not for everyone, but sometimes survivors of psychosis have a calling to discover the truth in the world's mystical traditions. This essay, written in 2004, summarizes some of the lessons I've learned exploring altered states.

Shamans are the magician spirit healers in tribal, indigenous societies around the world. Anthropologists use the word "shamanism," borrowed from the Tungus speaking people of Siberia, to mean the commonalities between different traditions: shamans find their calling through a life-threatening initiatory illness or mental crisis like psychosis; go into visioning and trance to connect to other realities; shapeshift out of their regular self to identify with animals, spirits, and even disease; and return to the ordinary world to share skills of healing and creativity. Living at the edge of society and defying conventional norms, conduct, and even gender, shamans are respected as powerful community links to the divine.

Can we learn from these traditions without romanticizing them? Can we remember that people are people everywhere, that war, oppression, and exploitation are also found among tribal societies? While also valuing the tremendous wisdom of people living close to the earth, including insights into the spiritual gifts sometimes wrapped up in what gets called "psychosis?" Traditional societies create rites of passage; how can people in modern societies explore and develop these gifts as part of recovery?

Traditional shamanism means being part of

a living indigenous society, apprenticing in it and learning its ways. To take this approach, you need to be accepted by teachers who are part of that culture. If you're an outsider, don't be racist: never use a culture's spirituality without guidance and accountability, and always support cultural survival and land struggles against colonialism and industrial expansion. Traditional peoples need real respect and practical activism, not more plastic, new age medicine men.

"Urban shamanism" is a broader approach, respecting indigenous societies while rediscovering the roots of tribal mind for modern people. Urban shamans reinvent spirit healing and find ancient patterns in new forms. All of us have ancestral links to shamanic cultures if we go back far enough, because all societies have origins in tribes and all societies practiced magic. There are no rules and no end to learning and creativity, as we reawaken our indigenous minds and recreate spirit healing in new ways.

Does the altered state that got labeled psychosis mean you are having an initiatory illness into becoming a wounded healer? Are there gifts to untangle from the trauma in madness? Many societies have elders to identify when crisis is an initiation, and to mentor people into using their gifts wisely. Urban shamans may need to recreate that mentorship, or find it within ourselves. Without the guidance of traditional shamanic cultures, the answers will be up to each of us.

Here are some signposts to exploring urban shamanism:

Join with wilderness. Everything you need to know is found in the wildness of nature. Get out of the corporate monoculture of our cities. Wander forests, deserts, beaches, and mountains every chance you get. Go off trails, climb trees, sit silently on the earth, sleep under the stars, find music in rushing water, watch animals, thrash in the ocean, follow footprints, listen to birds, stare at clouds, study plants. Seek out pockets of wildness in the hidden edges of the city. Learn the natural history and ecology of your home.

Tracking and awareness. Listen to and question everything in your outer and inner landscape. Ground yourself firmly in the sight, sound, smell, and touch of your present surroundings as if you were tracking animals in the wild. Slow down, then slow down even more, until the virtual world fades and the real world comes into view. Cultivate your skills with meditation and sensory awareness practices. Remember to observe the observer: our inner emotions and sensations are an important territory to explore, and offer vital clues not just to your mind, but also to the world around you. Stillness and sensitivity will guide your attention to what you need to follow. Always come back to the here and now, it's the most magical place of all.

Experimental attitude. Go on your direct experience of what works. Don't take anything you were told or read just on faith, use trial and error and healthy skepticism. If you wonder if you are just making things up in your imagination, find out: treat it as if it were real and study the results, like a scientist doing an experiment. You may discover that reality isn't passive, but is collaborative, creative, and participatory.

Find pathways to visionary states. Food, media, driving cars, work, computers, and drugs all hypnotize us into ordinary reality. Take back control of your consciousness and start accessing visionary states on your own terms. Check out new tools: follow your intuition to find ideas, methods, and practices you are drawn to. Dancing, drumming, drawing, writing, puppetry, music, sex, silence, fasting, meditation, ritual... all are possible ways to pass from this reality to the next and back. Open your intuitive side, welcome the unknown, focus on body sensations and emotions, and learn about altered states and imagination. Walk new routes through your city, open up to unexpected music, poetry, and art, follow hunches and look for signs. Be curious about unexpected interests and odd sources of power, especially what comes into your life seemingly on its own, or that fascinated you in childhood. Try out new identities but be ready to drop them when they've outlived their usefulness. Your body is the only tool you truly need.

Listen to your dreams. Don't just interpret intellectually, actualize your dreams by keeping a journal, drawing images, dialoging with characters, acting out different parts, and looking for clues in waking life. What is the dreamer telling you? Notice uncanny coincidences, track dream-like synchronicities, and explore underground pathways between unrelated events. The more you pay attention to dreams the more dreams you'll have, and you'll discover that waking life is itself a dream.

Hunt lost energy. Addictions, spacing out, numbing your body, dull friends, toxic food, consumerist media, bad sex... there is a long struggle ahead of you to reclaim all the energy you lose, and put it instead towards awareness and healing. Treat the things you are ashamed of as invitations to find hidden sources of strength. As you clear your own stagnation, follow what inspires you and respond to the alive energy of moments, ideas, plants, places, and people. Break the habit of who you are. Surprise yourself.

Explore your calling. Study your crisis and collapsed self. Listen to the voices, look at the visions, and feel the crazy energies of your madness, with a fresh eye towards what wisdom or learning might be behind it all. Imagine that there is something essential for you to discover in the painful parts you might wish would go away. Notice what remains unfinished and unresolved, and sense how your energy is drained when you don't listen to the missing parts of yourself. Do this when you are strong, grounded, and have solid support from your community.

Learn from your ancestors. Find out as much as you can about your family and roots. Be on the lookout for eccentric, artistic, mad, activist, indigenous, and nonconformist relatives who may also be on a visionary path. Pay attention to the struggles for survival that your ancestors went through, and honor any unmet hopes and dreams still felt by the living.

Beware ego tripping. Your true needs are in a mysterious flux; learn techniques to put the goal-directed ordinary self in its proper place. Can you practice seeing through the stories you tell about what is missing in your life? Don't pray or wish for specific things like a new apartment or marriage, only general things like a home or love. Let the details be a constant surprise as you focus on the magic and beauty of the larger pattern.

And above all: Watch out for getting overwhelmed. Come back to strong grounding practices, clear awareness, and a healthy life first before exploring the unknown. Pace yourself. Be clear about your purpose as a healer, and don't let any power or uncanny phenomena you encounter distract you from your integrity and ethics. Forge firm bonds of trust and honesty with beloved friends. Get your feet on the earth before you take off for the heavens. ∎

Maps to the Other Side
Sascha DuBrul

Sascha Altman Du-Brul is one of the co-creators of *The Icarus Project* and author of *Maps to the Other Side: Adventures of a Bipolar Cartographer* (2013)

Lo and behold, I'm taking these drugs and they seemed to be helping me. I felt really strange about it.

WILL HALL Tell us about the origins of The Icarus Project in punk rock and the New York City counterculture squatter scene.

SASCHA DUBRUL When I was 13 my dad died, and I ended up leaving the world where I grew up, the culturally mainstream upper west side of Manhattan, and venturing down to the "underworld" of the lower east side of New York. In the late 80's it was a thriving community of anarchists and squatters and freaks and folks living in abandoned buildings and Thompson Square Park. It was a really different New York City than the New York City that exists now. I got into punk rock and was at the Tompkins Square Riots and watching my friends getting beaten bloody in street battles with police. I felt free for the first time in my life, and part of a community. I never really fit in and now I found a whole bunch of other people I could relate to.

The 1980s were a wild time, lots of homeless people out on the streets, lots of underground economy and culture. Reagan had let out all these folks locked up in mental hospitals, and promised them community support. But that didn't manifest, and folks were really struggling. So at 14 I found myself in a park with a bunch of crazy homeless people and runaway teenagers, and, lo and behold, I felt like I fit in somewhere. It's a funny thing to say, but its true, that's the origin of my relationship to the mad pride movement.

Many of us didn't have families that supported us, or community structures that were intact, so we were lucky to find something. There were all these ways that you could play and adopt an identity. Part of the whole American culture is giving up where you come from. So I adopted punk and anarchism, with a whole tribe of people who had my back.

Human beings are social creatures. We want to be a part of the community. People don't talk about God much anymore but people really want that experience of oneness. Yet everyone's just sitting alone in front of computer screens talking to each other on social networking sites. I think there's something fundamental about cathartic experiences. I was raised in a really secular environment, we didn't go to church or synagogue. At a punk rock show a band is playing and people are packed into a dark space dancing all over each other, it's super crazy, your heart is pounding and you feel you're part of something totally incredible. It's like church, I suppose.

When I was 20 I dropped out of school and started traveling, riding freight trains and having all these adventures. It was being true to myself. I'd been tied my whole life and I'm now I was going to be free, to live wild.

WH And then something turned at some point, and there was a hospitalization?

SD I had a lot of pressure from my family to succeed academically so I pushed myself in college in a way that wasn't healthy for me. And in New York City I was used to smoking what we'd call Mexican dirt weed, and suddenly I got out to the Pacific Northwest for school where the marijuana and coffee are really strong. So one day I had an allergic reaction to penicillin and was in a lot of pain, and also had a reaction to Prednisone I was taking. I thought I was going to die, I had all kinds of energy. I didn't need to sleep and I was running so fast. I started finding all these messages in the billboards and the radio.

I was reading Plato's allegory of the cave: people staring at shadows and one guy breaks free, realizes everything is just shadows of the real. I had this really transformative, spiritual break, an awakening.

If I'd been raised religiously I would have been talking about God, but I was raised by a man who read Marx, so I talked about revolution. I had a messianic feeling like I

At a punk rock show your heart is pounding and you feel you're part of something totally incredible. It's like church, I suppose.

was a bridge between worlds, visions about the world ending and us living on something like television. Years later when Myspace and Facebook emerged I got chills because it was similar to my visions coming true.

In hindsight it is clear what was going on, but at the time I didn't have anyone around who had any sense of what I was going through. My friends didn't know what the hell to do with me so they put me on a plane back to my mom. In New York the whole thing just cranked up another 10 notches. I wandered the streets and talking to spirits knowing I was going to die. I walked down to the train on 23rd street, hopped onto the tracks and started walking all the way to Christopher Street, that's a long way. They pulled me off the tracks and sent me to Bellevue. I was in the hospital for two and half months, on Depakote and Haldol and two weeks in the quiet room.

WH Let's turn to what helped you heal. You became involved in the beginnings of the permaculture movement and the radical farming scene?

SD Permaculture started as a movement in Australia in the late '70s, and is a way of looking at how humans design things, the land that they live on and the food they grow, to model it after how things happen in nature. I was a part of taking that set of principles and helping to popularize it within the DIY anarchist community. I had a gardening column in a punk rock magazine called Slug and Lettuce for eight years.

WH So you were promoting gardening among punk rock kids?

SD Yes. I grew up on the 12th story of an apartment building in Manhattan, so gardening was an incredibly empowering experience. Growing plants to seed and then saving the seeds and then planting them again the next year... I had never seen cycles of nature, I was so consumed by the urban environment. In the early '90s the multinational chemical company Monsanto engineered seeds to reproduce sterile, so-called 'terminator seeds.' It was a big wake up call about the importance of saving our own seeds, and taking the power back from corporate agriculture business giants and putting it into the hands of the community. So we created a community seed library.

WH That theme of protecting diversity continues with The Icarus Project.

SD At the end of the '90s people came to Seattle to protest the World Trade Organization's takeover of the world. Between November of 1999 and September of 2001 when 9/11 happened a whole lot of us were busy working on radical projects, and it looked like a lot of change was going to happen really fast. Then the big boot came down and stepped on us... we had to go back underground.

If I'd been raised religiously I would have been talking about God, but I was raised by a man who read Marx, so I talked about revolution.

In 2001, I was hospitalized again, this time in Los Angeles and spent a month in county jail. It was eerily similar to the experience I had when I was 18: not sleeping for a long time, thinking the world was going to end, thinking I was being broadcast live on television on all the channels. I came out of it pretty humbled, and taking medication. I never thought that I'd be doing that. Here I was promoting sustainable agriculture and working against Monsanto and the chemical companies, and I am thinking What am I doing? I'm taking these drugs, and the pharmaceutical companies are so evil on so many levels. They just want me to be addicted to these drugs! But lo and behold, I'm taking these and they seemed to be helping me. I felt really strange about it.

WH It broke your black and white view of the world, good and evil?

SD Yes, especially within my community. Anarchists are known for being very free and very open... and not always very tolerant of differing ideas.

So I outed myself in the punk rock gardening column I wrote, and then wrote a cover article for the San Francisco Bay Guardian. The response was huge, I learned that when you bare your soul to a bunch of strangers, inevitably there's a whole lot of strangers who want to bare their soul back. One of the people who wrote me was Jacks McNamara, and that was where the idea for The Icarus Project came from. Now more than 10,000 people are registered on it from around the world, and there are local groups all over North America.

WH This was when community forums on the Internet were relatively new.

SD We are really inspired by the LGBT movement reaching young people. The movement finds freaks and kids who feel really alienated and alone and gives them a space to feel like superstars, teaches them their history and gives them a community to be a part of. Mad Pride is parallel to Gay Pride.

WH Were you able to sustain the momentum of the early days of Icarus?

SD In 2008 I was in the midsts of stepping back from The Icarus Project, and I had another crazy psychotic breakdown, it was really dramatic. To take care of myself I went and lived at a yoga ashram for 9 months The regimented schedule where I was up at 5am every morning, meditating, chanting and doing yoga then working all day was super useful as I put my life back together.

I'd never lived in a spiritual community, but I figured out pretty quickly that the same kind of folks who would gravitate toward ashram life you would also find at an Icarus meeting. Folks who have a hard time in the world outside, and who are searching and looking for community and meaning. Although we don't use the language of spirit, it became really clear that there is something very spiritual about what we do at The Icarus Project.

I started to realize that neither madness nor pride are things to cultivate to have a happy life. Mad Pride is a political dead end: a powerful point of unity, but doesn't give us a map of where to go next. For me "Mad Pride" goes all the way back to the punk rock identity that I had as a teenager: "us'" against "the world," we're the freaks and we're the outlaws.

But that's only the beginning of the story. We need to lay foundations for a movement that can embrace large segments of society, both ourselves for who we are and our differences, and also really look at our potential. People in my generation who are a part of the "Mad Movement" don't even know about the Human Potential Movement in the '60s and '70s. It

I want to see the marriage of social justice and visionary spiritual movements, and a reinvention of what it means to be "healthy" and "sick."

was this incredible explosion of creativity and visionary ideas: Eastern spiritual practices intersecting Western psychology, Gestalt Therapy, the Encounter Movement, Humanistic and Transpersonal Psychology, the Soteria model.

I want to see the marriage of social justice and visionary spiritual movements, and a reinvention of what it means to be "healthy" and "sick." I want us to talk about how oppression makes us crazy: how race class and gender are more important than "brain chemistry." I want us to cultivate skills to take better care of one another. I want us all to make maps to break out of the biopsychiatry labyrinth, and build a new world from all of our beauty and brilliance. ∎

Communicating With Psychosis
Dina Tyler

Dina Tyler is direc-
tor of the Bay Area
Mandala Project, co-
founder of Bay Area
Hearing Voices, and
coordinator of peer
support services at an
early psychosis inter-
vention program in Al-
ameda County, CA.

I practice a *being-with* approach that I would have wanted when I myself was struggling.

Between the ages of 18 and 22, I was diagnosed with attention deficit disorder, severe depression, bipolar disorder, and psychosis. And I discovered the meaning of life: I experienced intense feelings of oneness with the universe; I was filled with empathy for the plight of humanity; I felt connected to the most powerful force of divine love, and I figured out a plan that would take me to becoming the first female president of the United States.

All of these amazing experiences were immediately met with resistance by family and friends. I was put in a psychiatric hospital. I was told I had delusions of grandeur, hallucinations, and a "manic episode." I was treated like a "bad patient" because I refused to take medication and I complained about side effects. When I was sexually assaulted by another hospital patient I was told by staff it was a symptom of my mania, that it happened because I was "hypersexual." I was strip searched for my own "protection." I left the hospital on high doses of lithium, Zyprexa, Risperdal, Tegretol, and Klonopin, so much medication that I felt numb and unable to communicate.

I learned to no longer trust the people who were supposed to help me. At 24, I came off all of my medications and began fighting against my diagnoses. I wanted desperately to regain the truth I learned in my altered state, and turn it into a philosophy of how to live my life.

I discovered years later that what I called the meaning of life was already recognized as a very famous theory in psychology: Maslow's hierarchy of needs. My vision of becoming the "supreme human beings that we are meant to be" was what Maslow had called "self-actualization." What if someone had taken the time to talk with me about this in the hospital? All I needed was someone to listen to me, to validate me, to help guide my thinking.

This entire ordeal, and the stigmatization I faced from diagnosis, shaped my direction in life and the person I became. Today I work with young adults recently labeled with schizophrenia. I facilitate support groups and provide individual peer support, especially to those considered "difficult to engage" or "reluctant to seek care." I practice a *being with* approach that I would have wanted when I was struggling: forming a relationship, putting the person at ease, and showing them I am not there to judge.

For example, I visited one woman in the hospital who said she was receiving God's guidance to harm herself. Whenever others had tried to convince her to accept a mental health diagnosis and stop wanting to hurt herself, she would only shut down and not talk. Instead I wanted to let her talk about the messages she was receiving.

In the beginning we would just walk around the hospital ward and then sit and pray together. She asked me to change my make-up and dress in "girly" clothing before I met with her, because she wanted me to be "less intense." Then we talked about hair and nails and even did each other's make-up.

After slowly building a relationship, we have begun to discuss her inner conflicts and past traumas. She recently said to me, "Life is hard but you never give up!" I have hope that she can find the meaning behind her experience: that was what not only helped me to heal, but also to grow. ∎

Voices of Everyone
Rufus May

Rufus May has worked as a clinical psychologist for 19 years. His interest in psychological and community development approaches to different states of mind is rooted in his own experiences of psychosis and recovery in his late teens.

I have facilitated Hearing Voices groups in Bradford UK for 13 years, where people get to know their different voices and what the voices' needs might be. By meeting the voices half way and honoring the deeper longing they represent, the voices gradually become a lot easier to live with. Like angry people, angry voices want their emotions acknowledged, through dialogue or symbolically with artistic expression. An angry commanding voice might need the person to be more assertive. Or an angry voice might be distressed, and need calming activities and environments. People are less overwhelmed when they learn to look after the emotional needs of their voices.

I became interested in the Hearing Voices Movement approach because of its acceptance and curiosity towards voices. I had a psychotic breakdown in my late teens, and making my experience into a medical problem didn't help. What did help was acceptance from friends, acceptance I was lucky to have. I learned creative ways to express my emotions, and I found an active role doing care work and later went on to train as a psychologist, determined to understand and respect unusual mental experiences.

Many voice-hearers in our group have found by getting to know the voices they are getting to know different parts of themselves and their ancestry, their family history and conflicts, suffering and unfinished struggles. This kind of inquiry might benefit us all. We all have different parts that take the lead in different situations: competitive parts, parental parts, and people-pleasing parts. I have a chameleon part that is good at fitting in and emulating the characteristics of people around me. I have a compassionate part that wants to help people who others may have given up on. I also have a comfort eater when I am stressed, a defensive part when I feel vulnerable, and a laid back part that likes to watch films and take naps and daydream. *No part of us is good or bad.* My fighter part, for example, channeled carefully, can help me in sports or activism or defending myself from physical attack, though it could be a problem if I don't give it space in my life, and at times it has been aggressive to people I care about. And my caring part helps me in many areas of my life, but it has been experienced by some people as controlling when I let it take over me too much.

It is natural that different contexts bring out different parts of us, but often we have a very compartmentalized approach to this inner community of selves. In Western society the responsible, productive and protective selves get rewarded. Unless we make a concerted effort, creativity, spirituality and playfulness get less space to express themselves. In many settings showing our vulnerable sides is not acceptable. Often people use alcohol or other drugs to numb some parts and thereby access other sides of themselves. The more we become aware of our different parts, their wants and needs, the more we can reduce conflict between them and have more choices in how we respond.

I meet a lot of people who have blocked off and separated from parts of themselves, probably since childhood as a survival technique to get through confusing and terrifying circumstances. This dissociated self may be experienced as a voice or as a part that takes over our consciousness. Rather than seeking to get rid of voices or dissociated selves, another option is to start a peace process. Learning to look after the needs of different parts of myself, rather than resent them, has helped me navigate the wider world. ∎

The Most Powerful Medicine
Steven Morgan

Steven Morgan was trained as a Georgia Certified Peer Specialist in 2004. He helped create a peer-run respite, was executive director of the peer-run agency Another Way in Vermont, project developer for Soteria-Vermont, and works for Intentional Peer Support as operations manager.

A treatment plan shouldn't suggest tightening the screws in the cultural machinery that crushed your soul in the first place.

STEVEN MORGAN From an early age I carried around a lot of rage and felt disconnected, though you might not have known it from the outside. Sometimes I wanted to die, but then I would come out of it and have these wonderful highs. That went on for many years without seeing it as a psychological problem. It was just who I was.

When I was about 22 I got into a relationship with a woman who was diagnosed with bipolar disorder. I read Kay Jamison's *Touched With Fire* and it reminded me of myself. I had gone through tough periods, including drinking alcohol, and wasn't sure if I could handle going down that far again, so I brought myself to a psychiatrist, and was quickly diagnosed.

WILL HALL People think about going from a depressed to a manic state as a mysterious cycle that just exists, that it must be "biological." But you are suggesting that it has an emotional basis?

SM Our bodies carry around experiences and traumas and releases them through all kinds of expression. Because I wasn't in touch with feelings of rage and humiliation, they would overtake me as if from nowhere. I would try to push them down, but they never went away. Instead, those feelings found paths to break through in new, insidious ways. I was always caught in webs of obsessions and compulsions that complicated matters.

Now that I'm not on medications and not pushing feelings down, I'm able to handle them differently. I say, "This is ok. This is part of the human experience." I'm not seeking happiness in my life, I'm seeking to be real with whatever my feelings are.

WH What happened when you saw the psychiatrist?

SM My whole worldview changed. I started to see myself as having a chemical imbalance in my brain, and I started to label a lot of my experiences as manic or depressed. I rewrote my history to fit into clinical phases of mania and depression. I stopped viewing hard times as existential crises and started diagnosing them as medical problems.

At first it was relieving, because it at least pretended to explain what was going on. But as I started re-labeling everything in my life, I also started to take on tremendous despair. I did that for about six or nine months before my spirit shouted, "No way! You are casting off this label." So I quit medication cold-turkey.

Then I made the mistake of jumping right into an intense job where I was out of my element. I had a really rough time and broke down. When that happened, I re-evaluated my life and decided, "Bipolar is something that you really have. This is a problem that is going to be with you for the rest of your life."

That started a series of psychiatric hospitalizations. I even started manifesting behaviors just because they were part of the diagnosis, as if

I were learning to be ill.

WH So you swung back to believing the diagnosis.

SM I just fell apart. I didn't have access to a sense of self or my body or emotions. I had erected mental walls to block off fragments of myself, and now these fragments were hunting me, literally hunting me in my dreams. I went through a period of time where I was very bad off. I subscribed to the "mental illness" worldview and was in and out of hospitals.

I was in despair for a long time, but at the same time I decided I was going to make a film about bipolar disorder. I had just gotten out of a relationship and the film was a way of dodging those feelings. I started pushing myself really hard and allowed myself to get high. I ended up crashing and going in the hospital again.

> Meditation can become just another medication. If emotions come up, I know how to meditate to get them to go away. But if you do that, those emotions are going to come back at you.

It's amazing that we think hospitals are places of healing, because it's just the opposite. You're not met with the human connection we need. In fact, a lot of the mental health profession is designed to stay disconnected from you, and to see you as an object. In a crisis, what I need more than anything is a human being who cares about me, who will sit and be there with me for hours on end. That is totally unavailable in a hospital.

But this time, when I got out, I said, "I'm going down the wrong path. I'm going to do whatever I can to stay out of the hospital forever." Because the experience was just awful. I had applied for social security disability benefits, and I realized if I didn't change my life dramatically I was going to end up a mental patient for life. And even though I was still paralyzed with intense emotions, the fear of that drove me to push through. I said, "This is going to get better. This is going to get better. This is going to get better."

WH That inner strength was crucial; do you think people can learn to cultivate it?

SM I think people can learn to be more resilient. People have different temperaments. Ever since I was a little kid I was a curious and deter-

Feelings of rage and humiliation overtook me as if from nowhere. I would try to push them down, but they never went away. Instead, those feelings found paths to break through in new, insidious ways.

mined individual in a lot of ways. So I think part of it is my spirit, but for me that's a two edged sword, these qualities also have a shadow that can be destructive.

And we shouldn't expect everyone to be determined individuals who want to conform to our standards of success. That's not for everybody. It's the responsibility of the society, culture, and family to provide an environment that brings out people's strengths, whatever they may be.

WH The mainstream model is individualistic, but many people need community, interdependence, and relying on each other.

SM Absolutely. A treatment plan shouldn't suggest tightening the screws in the cultural machinery that crushed your soul in the first place. Not everyone's treatment plan should be "get back to work." We have to look at diversity, which is a wonderful opportunity for larger cultural and social change.

If we see people who are breaking down as indicators of the larger whole that is in trouble, we can start to ask, "How can we allow everyone to use their voice?" But I don't see that. I see our society becoming more rigid, more insistent that everyone meet capitalistic ideals. If someone hates their job, we don't say "Quit your job," "Change the work environment," or "Be an activist about it." We say, "Go back to work and take your Prozac so you won't know the difference."

WH Yes, whatever happened to helping each other and taking care of each other? As a collective we are responsible for not just leaving it to the individual.

What helped you get off medication and find a way forward?

SM I started to read a lot of Eastern spiritual texts, the *Bhagavad Gita*, the *Tao Te Ching*, and Zen texts. I was attracted to the idea of letting go of expectations. We're taught to have ambitions and goals to achieve happiness and success. The paradox is that when you let go of expectations, you get more in touch with your nature. Some people think Buddhism is nihilistic, that you give up on life and repudiate worldly things. You don't. When you learn how to just be, you end up getting what you really need but didn't know you needed. And that can manifest in so many ways. It doesn't mean you abandon your family, leave your job, and go live in the desert. Though I like the desert too!

> If we see people who are breaking down as indicators of the larger whole that is in trouble, we can start to ask, "How can we allow everyone to use their voice?"

When I got out of the hospital I also started therapy for the first time, nine months with a Jungian psychologist who was spiritually-oriented. We dove into my highly active dream life and the bigger questions they raised: what does it mean to be a man in this world? What does it mean to be a human being with a collective past? Human beings are not isolated, we've been evolving for hundreds of thousands of years, and that is in our blood and soul.

I started to reconnect with a life source I had lost connection with. Through validation and support I explored that connection, and that source responded.

I analyzed my dreams during the daytime and at night they would send me new messages in response. The back-and-forth of imagery, mythic symbols, clues, dead-ends, and big questions propelled me towards a more integrated state. I discovered an incredible healing potential that is within us. In a way, my dreams acted on what medications had intended to resolve, but much more profoundly: they healed the roots, not just trimmed the branches.

For instance, big animals used to hunt me in my dreams. There I am in the middle of the ocean with sharks coming after me, night after night. As I explored things in waking life, I started talking to the sharks in dreaming life. Pretty soon I was partying with the sharks on the beach. Then they disappear for months, and later when they return, I now hunt them.

WH That is an amazing metaphor for changing the relationship to a part of yourself, befriending yourself. Sharks are themselves hunters, so maybe you integrate it all into one whole.

SM Symbols and myth express something that we can't describe in language. It's definitely not "evidence based practice!"

> ## We shouldn't expect everyone to want to conform to our standards of success. It's the responsibility of the society, culture, and family to provide an environment that brings out people's strengths.

WH The most important things in life are heart-based practices, not evidence-based practices. I learned that from a psychology textbook called *The Little Prince*... So what were some of the other things that helped you?

SM I also started working again as a peer support worker, as part of the recovery movement that values lived experience and trains people who've been psychiatrically diagnosed to work in the mental health system for change. That gave more meaning to my life, as I learned how to relate to people in different ways. I also sobered up, which was significant.

WH How did you get sober?

SM I saw the destructiveness of alcohol, and when I started to work I had more of a focus and less need to drink. Meditation also put me back in touch with my body, to appreciate my body. I don't necessarily want to put toxic stuff into my body.

Later that year I had a meditation experience that altered the course of my life forever.

WH What happened?

SM I sat in front of a white wall bathed in moonlight, and had a vision of a wise man in an ancient world. As I continued to meditate, a lot of energy came up inside me. At first I thought, "Don't go with this energy, just observe it." Then I remembered reading earlier that night of a Zen master who said, "Go with what comes in meditation." So I let the energy overtake me.

> Now I say, "This is ok. This is part of human experience." I'm not seeking happiness in my life, I'm seeking to be real with whatever my feelings are.

The energy put me through all sorts of rituals. I became an elephant and a snake, and even started to bite my cat! I watched myself disappear in a mirror, all these crazy things happened. Hours later I realized something internally had really shifted. But I wasn't frightened at all; it very much felt right.

I started meditating every day. I was hallucinating for several months, and would go to work and see auras, patterns, and colors everywhere. I was just in a different state of consciousness, I don't know how else to explain it.

It started to die down, and I realized I would probably become attached to it, which I did. I would meditate and be like, "Damn, where did all those great colors go!"

I've had these visionary experiences since I was young: when I was seven I saw the Virgin Mary. If you try to repress these visions they will keep coming at you. A lot of my work has been to get back in touch with them and the place from which they came, and as I've done that they've actually lessened.

WH Like the dream with the sharks. What are the dangers of meditation and spiritual experiences? Sometimes people go in that direction and it gets them into trouble.

SM I never felt like I was going to lose touch with consensus reality. But in the West especially, meditation can become a vessel for inflating a sense of self instead of becoming more honest. So for example, I used to

I've learned that meditation is not about a blissful state or even a clear state, but about coming closer to what already is: exploring, acknowledging, and being with it.

meditate in the woods and harmonize with the wind, and I found a lot of power in that, but one step too far and it's "Wow, I am special," or worse, "I'm superior to others." I have to be very careful about that.

Another danger for me is that meditation can become just another medication. If emotions come up, I know how to meditate to get them to go away. But if you do that, those emotions are going to come back at you. I've learned that meditation is not about a blissful state or even a clear state, but about coming closer to what already is: exploring, acknowledging, and being with it, as opposed to just moving around it.

WH Meditation is often portrayed as "this good thing that you should do," like taking vitamins or going to the gym. But it's more complicated than that, a whole realm in and of itself that has downsides and pitfalls and well as huge benefits.

SM Maybe this is just the people I am drawn to, I don't know, but with people who have made significant recoveries in their life, just about everyone will describe some kind of spiritual connection. Not necessarily meditation, but prayer, a higher self through community, or their own way of finding God. It's powerful medicine. ∎

Awakening in the Dream
Paul Levy

Paul Levy is author of *Dispelling We-tiko: Breaking the Curse of Evil (2013)*, and *The Madness of George W. Bush: A Reflection of our Collective Psychosis (2006)*. He is the coordinator of the Portland Padma-Sambhava Buddhist Center and works with people in private practice.

Thus shall you think of all this fleeting world:
A star at dawn, a bubble in a stream;
A flash of lightning in a summer cloud,
A flickering lamp, a phantom, and a dream.

— the Buddha, *Diamond Sutra*

A life-transforming spiritual awakening, something that until then I had only dreamed about, introduced me to psychiatry.

In 1982 I emerged into a more expansive and whole part of myself: I was beginning to recognize the dreamlike nature of the universe. I was filled with enthusiasm; so much so that the anti-bliss patrol was alerted and I got put into psychiatric hospitals. The more I tried to express my realization that we could awaken and help deepen each others' lucidity, the more the psychiatrists saw me as crazy. They (mis)diagnosed me and medicated me out of my mind, and my spiritual awakening got extinguished. I felt traumatized, literally, made sick, by the treatment I received.

Thankfully, after I got out of the last hospital I began meeting Buddhist teachers. Instead of pathologizing me for experiencing the dreamlike nature of reality, they were teaching just that. The same fundamental insight which got me diagnosed is in fact the very pith essence of all of the great wisdom traditions from around the world. Needless to say, I was happy to find myself in such good company, though I wasn't overly thrilled at being left to deal with the resulting psychological clean-up operation, aftermath of a most unnatural, and unnecessary, psychiatric disaster.

Spiritual awakenings typically become catalyzed by severe emotional crisis, often growing out of unresolved abuse issues from childhood. This was certainly true for me. Healthy and pathological factors are co-joined: the idea is to nourish the healthy aspect so it becomes stronger, and then the pathological factors naturally fall away as they become integrated into the wholeness of the newly emerging psyche.

Over the years, I've deepened and stabilized my realization of the dreamlike nature of reality. I bring people together in what I call "Awakening in the Dream Groups." We take seriously, and step into, the idea that we are actually inhabiting a collaboratively created dream. The group is a ritually-created alchemical container, tailor-made for this contemplation.

Meeting in a meditation circle, a facilitated conversation collectively inquires into the nature of our present experience. We see how we are collaboratively dreaming up both the world and ourselves moment to moment. We discover we are each others' "dream characters": embodied reflective aspects of each other. If something triggers us with a strong emotional reaction, instead of seeing the person as the cause and the problem, we practice looking at what inside of *us* is the source of being triggered. This opens up a new world of possibilities for healing: being in relationship creates magic and medicine for the soul unlike anything else.

When people are brought together with the intention of waking up, it insures that a "guest" will be invited too, i.e., the unconscious, with its shadow. Whereas most spiritual groups are primarily identified with love, peace and harmony, and don't welcome any shadow energies, we inquire instead into the deeper process that is animating conflict and friction. We learn that most people are secretly thirsting for a safe place to get into their stuff and play it out, to unlock and liberate the deeper energies that shape their lives.

This is true evolutionary magic available to us as a species: there is a way of being together where we can activate our collective genius, conspire to co-inspire each other, and dream ourselves awake. ∎

Inbetweenland
Jacks McNamara

Jacks McNamara is a genderqueer writer, artist, and healer; co-founder of The Icarus Project; and subject of the documentary film *Crooked Beauty*. Jacks' book of poetry is *Inbetweenland* (2013).

I embrace the archetype of the "wounded healer." My writing, art, and healing work are motivated by trying to be there for people in ways no one was there to help me.

WILL HALL How did your creative journey with mental health and The Icarus Project begin?

JACKS MCNAMARA I grew up with a family that meant well but did me a lot of harm. I had "mental health issues" from a young age. I was a volatile, intense, depressive, elated, creative, brilliant, and devastated child / teenager / adult. My family was really alcoholic, raging, unsafe, neglectful: very chaotic. And I'm also adopted, which I've come to realize also makes a huge difference, being given away at birth to strangers.

I've never been a person with filters to block

out either the beautiful or the terrible aspects of the world. I have always had an acute sensitivity to injustice. From a young age, I remember when I would hear my mom saying racist things or see bad things happen on television. I needed to talk about it and figure out how we could end it. Plus I had a really creative mind that wanted to problem-solve.

WH At what point did that lead to an extreme state?

JM A lot of it had to do with drugs and alcohol. In the six months before I went into the hospital I had dropped out of college and was traveling around the world, thinking that I was a queer Jack Kerouac taking on Europe and Egypt, doing a lot of different drugs and drinking a lot. It was a wild ride.

During my trip to Europe and Egypt I was also sexually assaulted, which I completely blocked from my memory for six years. I got back from that trip opened up in all kinds of ways, pretty overwhelmed. I had just climbed Mt.Sinai, done all these incredible things, more than my system could hold together. That combined together with trauma in my childhood, and I finally erupted.

It started out amazingly. I thought I had found the key to human salvation, that I could literally save the world by telling everybody how everything is interconnected, that the carbon in their bodies comes from exploded supernovas, and this would end racism, classism, and poverty.

WH Goals you haven't necessarily given up on, though, right?

JM No, I would love to see that happen... I just don't think I'm going to do it single-handedly!

But then the wheels came off: everything started to fall apart and degenerate, a horrible black mass of chaos and nasty inner voices and not being able to function in consensus reality at all. I ended up in the psych ward.

WH So are trauma and creativity connected for you?

JM By walking through the fire yourself you learn how to help other people walk through it too. I was pretty indoctrinated into the message that I was broken, that I was a lifelong mental patient. Such a depressing, hope-

> **Can we say "Hmm, we have these beautiful, tricky, dangerous wings to use. Can we come together as a community and learn how to use them?"**

less idea. So today I embrace the archetype of the "wounded healer." My writing, art, and healing work are motivated by trying to be there for people in ways no one was there to help me. Trying to fill the voids I saw, to write the book I needed that wasn't there when I was fifteen.

WH How did you move beyond those messages you got in the hospital?

JM A lot of it had to do with meeting Sascha DuBrul and starting Icarus, finding someone else out there who had similar life experiences. Folks that get diagnosed with bipolar have an oversized appetite for life, an adventurous and big spirit, bigger than what consensus reality permits us. And so we run into obstacles...

I used to be really into the book *Be Here Now* by Ram Dass. He has this great page where he writes, "part of how you end up in psychosis is that you try to run through the doorway of heaven, but you still have your ego on." So there's this hunger to just run right through the door of Heaven, but I haven't learned all the tools to be grounded and know myself well enough before I transcend myself.

WH Tell us the story of Icarus.

JM In ancient Greek mythology, Icarus was a boy imprisoned in a maze with his father Daedalus. Daedalus was an inventor and he made wings out of wax and feathers so Icarus could fly out and get free. But he warned Icarus not to fly too close to the sun, because his wings would melt and he would crash into the ocean and drown. But Icarus was really intoxicated with his new power, and he flew too close to the sun and they melted and he crashed.

And so the metaphor is if you have wings, how do you learn to take care of them? Instead of squashing ourselves into the maze of having a disorder, can we say "Hmm, we have these beautiful, tricky, dangerous wings to use. Can we come together as a community and learn how to use them?"

Navigating the space and continuing to be alive on Earth means being willing to have one foot grounded in reality. Things like taxes and traffic and family relationships. And also navigate spirit and electricity, ideas and passion. To really to see both as two feet walking, two sides of the same coin. If we could have it, we would live in the sky all of the time. But you can't just get rid of one side. You have to learn how to be in both or you're not going to stick around.

WH I like the idea of learning from both sides, and even our parents or psychiatrists might have valuable words of caution when we are dealing with really powerful forces.

You talk a lot in your poetry about being queer and experiencing the world differently than people around you. That's also played a big role in my own trauma: being targeted for my sexuality, a sense of not fitting in and also "I'm not in the straight world and I'm not in the gay world, then where am I?"

JM When you first knew me I was still bouncing back and forth between trying to be straight, very unsuccessfully, and being in queer relationships and freaking out. I wasn't accepting my own gender identity.

WH So what is the relationship between being queer and madness?

JM It depends. Being queer doesn't give anyone a mental health issue, but homophobia and trans- or gender-phobia, harassment, abuse, and oppression all do. I was yelled at, things thrown at me, lots and lots of harass-

I've never been a person with filters to block out either the beautiful or the terrible aspects of the world.

ment. Always being very vigilant, knowing that I probably wasn't safe; trying to have my back covered, being aware who might come at me, is it safe to walk down the street, who do I have to pretend to be. I couldn't rest in the world if I looked gender-variant.

I tried to start a gay-straight alliance at my high school in rural Maryland; I was told I couldn't do it because people would pull their kids out of the school. When I came of age there was no Ellen Degeneres, there was no famous gay person to look at, or even a non-famous gay person. It was all just completely closeted and terrifying.

WH Just finding each other, making community happen, is so vital.

And there is something very powerful about queerness, moving beyond genders. There is something magical about going beyond the thing you have been given.

JM It opens you up to a lot of different sides of human experience, I mean talk about something that forces you to live between worlds!

WH Is this why you chose to title your book *Inbetweenland*?

JM Well *Inbetweenland* kind of chose me. As much as I try to pick a side to be on and say "This is my side," there isn't a side, there isn't a box or a category that fits. And so how do we learn to just live in Inbetween-

When I finally found medication that worked it was like the negative, black voice, hysteria, suicidal despair... it just stopped. I could think again clearly enough to leave my relationship and see the steps to put my life back in order.

land? It's an ongoing struggle for me, daily. But Inbetweenland is where I am, and where a lot of power is. This culture has a lot of boxes I don't want to fit into.

WH Can your impulse to make art and poetry take you too far and lead to madness?

JM They are very closely related. In the middle of writing *Inbetweeen-*

land I lost my mind again. I ended up locked in the psych ward again this summer, which I could not believe, after thirteen years.

WH What happened?

JM Writing brought up a lot of intense material and required me to be alone with my tortured, tempestuous, beautiful muse. That doesn't lead to mental stability. I also developed horribly painful repetitive strain injury and had to quit work completely. Chronic pain can really do your head in. It hurt to hold books up, I couldn't send text messages, I couldn't drive my car, I couldn't do my dishes, I couldn't use the computer. The whole structure of my life fell apart. And I also had some really intense relationship turbulence.

Folks that get diagnosed with bipolar have an oversized appetite for life, an adventurous and big spirit, bigger than what consensus reality permits us.

WH What helped you get out of that space?

JM One of the things, honestly, is medication. I tried a bunch of different meds, but over the years I have become much more sensitive to side effects, and I can't take the drugs that used to be helpful. When I finally found medication that worked it was like the negative, black voice of hysteria and suicidal despair... it just stopped. I could think again clearly enough to leave my relationship and see the steps to put my life back in order. I went into intense physical therapy and just focused on my health, on rebuilding my body.

WH The question of medications is related to the image of *Inbetweenland*: **if we're trapped in either/or, either meds are bad or meds are good, we can miss the reality of what might help.**

JM I was trapped last summer in "I have no options, there are no more options. I have tried everything and there are no more options." If there was a beautiful mad, free sanctuary I could have gone to, to put me up, feed me organic food, take me hiking, give me a great Jungian-somatics therapist to work out my existential dilemmas, a sugar momma in the sky to foot my bills so I didn't have to worry about holding down a job, paying my rent, keeping my life together, then I don't think going on the meds would have been a necessity. But in this world?... No one is going to pick me up and carry me. I need to keep functioning in consensus reality. And for me that is where the meds come in as a tool.

WH I ask myself that question a lot: if the circumstances were ideal, would we still sometimes need medications or confinement? If you look historically, madness always has some core of deep mystery that doesn't seem to want to go away. We can romanticize indigenous and traditional cultures, and say, well, people had a place, they were recognized. But sometimes they weren't. Sometimes they just killed them. Or they just drove them out, or sometimes people just wandered and ended in tragedy. And even in the most alternative, progressive programs they consistently document encounters with mad people they just have no idea how to deal with other than medications or confinement.

JM That's deep. I think some of this is intergenerational and comes from way back. I carry trauma that is not my own. I'm adopted and was born to a woman who the entire time I was in her womb she knew she had to give me away. She was unemployed and stressed out, her super-Christian

When I came of age there was no Ellen Degeneres, there was no famous gay person to look at, or even a non-famous gay person. It was just completely closeted and terrifying.

parents were pressuring her to get rid of the child that she didn't intend to have, and then here I come into the world. I deal with a lot of depression, a lot of feeling like I don't belong on this planet.

My birth dad found me when I was 21. He's diagnosed bipolar, his brother was diagnosed schizophrenic, and I have multiple other family members who have also been diagnosed bipolar. And they are all creative people, beautiful, fascinating, turbulent, smart people. They didn't raise me or impart a bunch of behaviors through the environment. So I don't know what to make of that. I've developed a complex idea of inheritance, what it means for madness to be "inherited."

If certain kinds of stress happen, I am likely to respond to that stress through, for instance, getting manic and getting depressed. Other people might develop breast cancer, so did their mom and so did their sister. Or they might turn to an addiction. Even if a piece is inherited, I don't think that makes it a disorder or a dysfunction. I believe I inherited a sensitive disposition. I am sensitive to chemicals and food, I am sensitive to other people's emotions, I can feel what everybody else in the room is feeling. That is part of my huge gift. And it makes my life really difficult.

WH I like the idea of sensitivity because it isn't necessarily weakness or greater vulnerability, it's just different. Sensitivity can be positive and an incredible asset.

You also write a lot about sex in your poems.

JM A big part of mental un-health is having huge vibrant parts of myself that I felt I needed to hide. I'm a very carnal and sexual being and I'm coming to a place where I can just be real and explore and write about it. Sex is a very sacred force when people can be embodied, respectful, and present. Sex can also be a force for violence and destruction, particularly in the hands of men misusing their power, but sex can be a force of great healing and connection to the divine.

WH Certainly many people who might be abuse survivors may need to stay away from something strong or explicit, but it doesn't mean entire communities have to recreate the taboo against sex all over again. Ironically, it's when we don't talk about sex that it gets more dangerous, and abuse is more likely to happen.

JM I feel lucky to spend much of my life in the San Francisco Bay Area, where there is a lot of permission to talk about sex, drugs, life... whatever it is. Out loud.

"The Right Words"

It is the day after Christmas and I'm on my way home from a threesome. The glory in my surrendered hips is quickly being replaced by a familiar smoking shame. The winter's first snow has just begun to fall and I am driving through a raw gray world half dream half shine brick buildings softened slightly and everything obscured like my body I have floated partway out of my eyes that are suddenly a little too bright a little too focused my heart tight in its cage as I drive down Atlantic Avenue I search for the words the terrified deer in my chest needs to hear to move on and after making it too complicated it turns out to be so simple. I love you survivor body. Anxious and numb I still love you. You're doing such a good job. After enough repetitions my breath settles into my thighs and she lowers her gaze, bounds back into the woods.

"Inbetweenland"

I wish someone had told me that I would get out of the burning house. Or that I had already escaped a long time ago and it lived on only in my muscles and my mind. I wish someone had handed me the word "survivor," placed it in my palms like a blossom or a drill. Told me to build altars and hang hinges carefully. I wish they had told me I could stand up any time, open the door, leave.

My best friend and I used to talk about choosing Earth and sky. We traveled between borders leading workshops for survivors who had known rocks that whispered, billboards that shout conspiracies and cosmic truths, electric hearts impaled on apocalypse sunsets over ruined cities and paper mountains speaking myths that evaporate like water off hot pavement when you finally come down. Into the world of toothpaste and toilet paper, fathers and sons, appointments, diagnoses, mania, psychosis, but we knew we were caught trying to fly out of mazes built by kings and corporations. Where your wings melt when you finally make it over the sea. When we mentioned keeping one foot in both worlds, everyone in the room would exhale, eyes like fireflies switching on at dusk. Permission. This, too, was real. Inbetweenland. Both.

You don't have to choose between sanity and the ruthless night.

It's 2012 and I am lying on the floor of a small room while a therapist in a black muscle tee emblazoned with "HOPE" in white letters draws infinity symbols above my eyes. I follow her fingers and I freeze as usual until the images come. The shadow shapes of men, my father leaning over, thick stories, heat, suddenly the impulse to roll onto my side, stand up, open the door, leave. For the first time I do. Outside the world is big as snow, bright as a waxing moon, full of people. My hands are full of tools, my eyes are full of horizon, I am enormous. A child landing in an adult's miraculous skin.

"Third Gender"

One. I remember when I turned my last skirt into a tablecloth because I only wanted to be one gender now and it was not girl. I remember when everything changed, I turned the tablecloth back into a skirt.

Two. The red purse was the last present my mother ever gave me. I hid it under the bed and then I got sober and she went into a coma. It was easier to look like a girl when I went back to Virginia. The neighbors liked me with long hair. The purse was actually pretty and had good pockets. I carried it to the hospital every day.

Three. When I was seventeen I wrote a short story about castrating cucumbers after cars of drunk men threw packs of playing cards at me. Queen of hearts, ace of spades, they swerved directly at me, 2am, screamed at my tits. When I cut all my hair off two days later, I felt hideous and proud. Properly gay, and partly invisible. No one is screaming now but my mom.

Four. They called me Sinead O'Connor, they called me G.I. Jane, they called me crazy and called me "sir" when I shaved my head in a foreign country. Small children asked if I was a boy or a girl. The men shouted out shop windows to ask where my hair was. Finally I gave up and told them I sold it to buy my plane ticket home. They stopped asking me why I wasn't married. They stopped asking me anything at all.

Five. We had gone to my mother's favorite restaurant and drank enough wine to be pleasant. We were supposed to be celebrating something. When we got home, she burst into tears all over the kitchen counter, all she was thinking at dinner that night was that she hoped everyone thought I had

had chemotherapy and that's why I had no hair.

Six. He told me I had always had a lot of third-gender energy before I knew what that meant. He thought it was a compliment, I thought I was an alien. I don't remember another word he said. I remember going home and putting on a black dress and trying to be beautiful.

Seven. Now my lover tells me I am handsome and she tells me I am pretty. Sometimes I open my ribs for her. I bought a black tuxedo vest on eBay. It has one rhinestone button. I will wear it. She will wear a short skirt and flower in her hair. She calls me her "ex-boyfriend" and she calls me a "zebra," she squeals when she discovers my underwear is all covered in hearts. ■

Teenage Mental Patient
Leah Harris

Leah Harris is a mother, storyteller, survivor, and activist. Her writing has been published at *The Huffington Post*, *Truthout*, *Mad In America*, *Off Our Backs: a Women's Newsjournal*, *Adbusters*, and *CounterPunch*. Leah was also the past technical director for *Madness Radio*.

i wanna tell you
what it's like to be a teenage mental patient
to have your every movement
scrutinized
your every uttered word
analyzed
then to be accused of paranoia
when you point this out

this is what I learned inside:
in order to get out you have to hide
how you feel. You have to lie
until you don't even feel real.
it's torture and after enough pain
you learn to play the game.
you walk the walk, and talk the talk
and smile and take your meds
and every morning make your bed.
speak of goal-set-ting
grad-u-ating
and job get-ting

you can always tell the new admits
wild-eyed and still high on coke, crack,
zyprexa and prozac, jacked up on speed
still bleeding from their wounds
after a self-mutilation gone too far
gauzy white bandages encircling
fragile
wounded
wrists

i saw Lil' Brazy, 14 year old LA Blood
so engulfed with anger and indignation
at her incarceration
it took two grown women and men to subdue her
they held her down and shot her up
she was tranquilized like an animal
like the unreachable wounded animal
they considered her to be
oak grove institute was a mad warehouse
for troublesome kids of all sorts
jason was 10, told adults to fuck off
for which they labeled him with tourette's
jack was a cross-dressing nirvana fan
andy's mother hit him, he hit her back
and was labeled "oppositional"
kizzie and li'l brazy were hood rats
marie's crime was developmental disability
sue idolized michael jackson "obsessively
sarah-lynn had satan worshipers for parents

sue and sarah-lynn loved one another
for which they were put on
20 foot-restriction
cause you ain't allowed
to love no one in there
yeah, they look down on that in there

and me
I was a majorly depressed
severely-emotionally-disturbed
borderline-personality-disordered
obsessively compulsive
medium-to-high suicide risk
with bipolar tendencies
who wore too much eye-liner and fishnet stockings

wrote poetry that didn't make sense to them
skipped school sometimes
and dreamed of being editor-in-chief
of my high school paper
before they locked me up

the reigning philosophy is that youth is pathology
cause so-called crazy kids
aren't allowed to be kids
you are forced to be patients
you are drugged
under-educated
over-therapized
psychiatrized
and victimized

this is what we learned on the inside:
it's not life on the streets
turning tricks for the next high
or being a poor immigrant kid
doing what you have to to get by
it's not daddy's touching
it's not mommy's drinking
it's your own disordered thinking

and we don't mention the word "trauma"
because here's the explanation for your life's drama:
your brain is broken
and we'll fix it
with institutional food,
lack of sunlight and fresh air
and we'll fix it with drugs
we'll fix it all with drugs
the newest drugs
the legal drugs
just don't get caught with the ones
that make you feel good

they're not allowed in here

i remember us crazy girls
wild with boredom and rage
scraping anarchy symbols
into our skin
with an eraser
the only weapon we possessed
trying to erase the skin that held us in
watching scab turn into scar
growing bitter and old inside
watching the days go by

we were released, all of us, one by one
sentences determined by
1) our insurance policies and
2) our acting abilities

sent back to the people institutions society that oppressed us
to the adults who abused us in the first place
out of their own fear ignorance and pain
and so we'd soon end up on the back wards again
hanging on to one another to survive
trying to keep alive some shreds of hope
in our hearts, grasping onto fading dreams
as our spirits slowly came apart at the seams

that's what it's like
to be a teenage mental patient ■

A Savage Insult
Clare Shaw

Clare Shaw is a survivor-activist, a founding member of the National Self-Harm Minimisation Group, and author of the children's book *Otis Doesn't Scratch (2015)*, illustrated by Tamsin Walker. The Arvon Foundation described her as "one of Britain's most dynamic and powerful young poets."

"The diagnosis of borderline personality disorder appears to be an enduring pejorative judgment, rather than a clinical diagnosis." That's what UK's National Clinical Director for Health and Criminal Justice, Louis Appleby, said 22 years ago.

But today, service users and survivors still report ongoing discrimination and degrading treatment from being diagnosed borderline.

The borderline diagnosis lacks scientific validity or reliability. It is gender biased and pathologizes people's coping strategies. It is a label put primarily on women, at least 70% of whom were sexually abused as children. Borderline parallels notorious past sexist diagnoses such as hysteria, which creates overwhelming stigma. Borderline is also arguably one of the labels most feared by staff and patients, who associate it with phrases such as manipulative, attention-seeking, untreatable, and untrustworthy. Borderline is used as a punitive diagnosis, a garbage bin for those judged "bad" patients because they are troublemakers or fail to "respond" to treatment. The list of assumptions going along with borderline is so derogatory it has been described as "little more than a sophisticated insult."

And a diagnosis of borderline destroys lives. I should know, borderline is my primary diagnosis. When we listen to the voices of those who have been diagnosed, there is no debate: the diagnosis is hurting people. Badly.

"Having the diagnosis of borderline has never been a positive experience, it's always hung over my head like a dark cloud." (Jo)

"In many ways it is a relief to be diagnosed... At last you have it irrefutably confirmed that you are wrong and always have been wrong. And it makes

such sense ... you have nothing else to blame but yourself" (Clare Shaw)

"It became clear to me that the diagnosis had caused women more distress than whatever took them to services in the first place. [...] No other diagnosis smears the woman's character, trustworthiness and validity of her distress as much as borderline does" (Louise Pembroke)

My personality disorder diagnosis confirmed and deepened the most negative messages given to me throughout my life. My diagnosis told me it was own my fault services had not been able to help me. My diagnosis meant my childhood trauma and violence were just marginal details. My diagnosis meant I was never going to get better: there would always be something wrong with the person that I am.

I live with the legacy of that message every single day.

Language within mental health is more than just semantics. Phrases like "personality disorder" deform thought and practice. They position the diagnosed as "other" in our distress, and tell us that our very being is "disordered.'" A borderline diagnosis dismisses any role for social context to explain our experiences, and pushes our voices, opinions, and histories to the margins of society.

The diagnosis of borderline causes extensive damage to the people it is supposed to help. It leads to bad practice in services rather than meaningful support. It is therefore imperative that professionals, practitioners, activists, and academics stop promoting this regressive and traumatizing label and all others like it.

We may decide that alternative diagnoses, such as "Complex Post-Traumatic Stress Disorder," offer more helpful, less devastating alternatives. Or it may be that any diagnosis at all is flawed. Either way, we must listen to the voices of those subjected to these labels. We must accept a simple reality: the words we use to describe ourselves and each other really do matter. Language can help. Or it can hurt. And even kill.

If not for this diagnosis I wouldn't have tried to kill myself the second time. Because that's what happened. Being diagnosed borderline escalated my suicidality into a realm previously unknown to me. It caused me to feel subhuman. It's lethal. ∎

Recovery from Being a Professional
Daniel Mackler

Daniel Mackler is filmmaker of *Open Dialogue* and *Take These Broken Wings*, which have both been translated into 20 languages. He was a psychotherapist in New York City for 10 years.

My training as a therapist went against something in my nature. I didn't realize it at the time, but therapist school tried to make me arrogant, to feel I was better than people I was working with, that I was somehow different. My training told me I knew, or should know, the answers. And that the people I worked with didn't.

Well, what about all those times as a therapist when I had no clue what to say?

This was especially true when people had serious problems that had no simple solutions. How was I supposed to be an expert when I had no idea what to do? No wonder my colleagues were sending people to the hospital and pushing them on meds. To retain our supposed expertise, therapists needed to get rid of these "difficult" people, and fast. They were a threat to us.

I finally figured out that my job was to go against my training, and instead trust myself and the people I was sitting with. My job wasn't to save anyone. Rather, I needed to be honest about who I was, and to listen. Just listening, I learned, was more than many people ever got when they asked for help from professionals. And when I listened to people, I actually learned a lot more from their experiences than I'd ever learned from my professors. Honesty opened the doors to real conversation. ∎

Post -Social Worker Trauma Disorder
Cheryl Alexander

Cheryl Alexander is a trauma-informed and holistic psychotherapist who uses energy work in her practice. A past Freedom Center volunteer, she was also co-host of several *Madness Radio* shows.

Four years after graduating as a social worker I realized I had been traumatized: not only traumatized vicariously by witnessing abuse at my school internship, but also traumatized by how the college responded when I reported this abuse.

At the outset of my graduate studies at the prestigious Smith College School for Social Work I believed entry into such an auspicious establishment could only promise good things for the future. But I quickly discovered that the faculty's mainstream model didn't make much sense to me. My requests to explore 'psychosis' using more spiritual, holistic and constructivist perspectives were largely dismissed. I was left unable to understand how a person's mental health could be truly addressed by focusing on a perceived pathology of the brain alone.

My internship on a locked psychiatric unit confused and horrified me: traumatized adolescents were routinely physically, mechanically, and chemically restrained. Staff, who appeared like bouncers, frequently straddled and bruised children as a disciplinary measure, dragging them across the floor when they would not comply with orders, and forcibly injecting them with Haldol, an antipsychotic drug.

These locked units were a culture of sanctioned

violence. I will never forget meeting a young girl who was deeply embedded in the foster care system and taking about 6 different types of medication. During the short time I knew her in the hospital, her weight skyrocketed. One day I was co-facilitating a therapy group and she tried to join the group. But she had been placed on "restriction," and even though I welcomed her, two male staff dragged her out of the room on her back, each one yanking her by an arm. They threw her into solitary confinement in padded room.

When I wrote an affidavit and reported this and other hospital incidents to the appropriate authorities, I was disciplined by my school. My teachers mandated I see a therapist and advised me to take medical leave.

This experience left me extremely fearful and critical of the social work field I was about to enter. My conviction about the misguided and dangerous nature of the mainstream model grew stronger when I was invited to work as an ally of Freedom Center, a local group of psychiatric survivors. Freedom Center validated my efforts to speak up when I witnessed abuse. I learned that openly identifying myself as a trauma survivor was one of the most powerful ways of collaborating with people needing help.

Although I did eventually graduate from social work school, I was uneasy and ashamed in my new role of social worker. I found myself exposed to the same oppressive practices again and again, and I became frustrated with the personal and professional limitations of my social work education. After illness forced me to take some conscious time to reflect, I knew Smith College's attempt to train me in the art of pathologization and an "us and them" model had failed.

In my work now I do not pathologize or have an agenda. There is a complex environmental context to everyone's "presentation"; people adapt and respond in various ways to the trauma and social oppression they've been through. Often people come to me after leaving therapists who pressured them to take psychiatric medications, or wouldn't support discontinuation. Today I meet people exactly where they are at, to find more effective ways, using the perspective of mind, body, and spirit. Our goal is to move forward in the world with greater wholeness and integrity. ∎

Discovering R.D. Laing
Adi Hasanbašic

Adi Hasanbašic is a gestalt psychologist in Sarajevo, Bosnia and Herzegovina. Founder of Metanoia, he has published articles on critical psychiatry and translated the *Harm Reduction Guide to Coming Off Psychiatric Drugs*, *Friends Make the Best Medicine*, and Theodor Itten's *Rage: Managing an Explosive Emotion* (2013). In 2012 he was awarded Laureate of the Farah Tahirbegovic Foundation for mental health activism.

"What we call 'normal' is a product of repression, denial, splitting, projection, introjection and other forms of destructive action on experience. It is radically estranged from the structure of being..."

"We are bemused and crazed creatures, strangers to our true selves, to one another, and to the spiritual and material world—mad, even, from an ideal standpoint we can glimpse but not adopt..."

"Madness need not be all breakdown. It may also be break-through. It is potential liberation and renewal as well as enslavement and existential death..."

— R.D. Laing

I've always sought to explore the depths and unknown territories of experience. That personal search led me to study psychology, because it is supposed to be the science of the soul and human mysteries. How wrong I was! My enthusiasm was stopped when I found that the focus of University study was not, as I had hoped and imagined, human beings, but instead statistics, labels, and research, where humans are just numbers placed into some kind of category.

Reality became too hard and superficial. By my third year of studies I fell into a deep psychological vacuum, and withdrew from the outside world. Facing a school that industrialized the human experience, I doubted my motives and lost my strength. For nearly ten months I stopped going to the University or taking exams, searching for my way out of this void.

One day as I was wandering the city I came across a man who was selling books on the street. I bought a used paperback that sparked a new life in my bones; the book was R. D. Laing's *The Divided Self.*

Laing seemed a savior: he was why I returned to the field of psychology. For the first time I discovered what I was searching for: human beings as a diversity of inner richness. Laing's words and knowledge helped me find my own path in life.

After finding someone who spoke my soul language, I wanted to find others. I live in a wounded country, Bosnia and Herzegovina, and daily I see the psychological ruins of the past: men alienated from themselves, soldiers who survived war now slowly dying ignored by the society they defended, people swallowing pills to make it through another day. I tried to make sense of this insane world that claims everything is alright. In the morally corrupt context I live in, who do I want to be?

I decided to found an Association and name it Metanoia, a Greek New Testament term that Laing used that means a transformative change of heart. Metanoia is dedicated to valuing human differences and affirming persons with psychiatric experience. Metanoia is a collaboration of experts by education and experts by experience. We have a radio show, create art, publish books, organize support groups, offer trainings, and collaborate with regional groups in Croatia, Slovenia, and Serbia.

In Bosnia we all suffer and we are told to keep quiet. But we are not sick: we are hurt, and we want society to know. We want everyone to feel they have a place and value in life. And at our events our pain has a voice. ■

"She came in three months ago
She is still in
She still feels like screaming
She has never screamed"
— R.D. Laing

Electroshock
Linda Andre

Linda Andre is an electroshock survivor, director of the Committee for Truth in Psychiatry, and author of *Doctors of Deception: What They Don't Want You to Know about Shock Treatments* (2009)

I had electroshock in the 1980s, and my experience was typical: I lost five years of my life, everything was erased as if it had never happened. I was only 25 at the time, and that was extremely traumatic: memory is your life. I also suffered permanent cognitive disability, which limited my potential.

Shock treatment was invented in 1938, an ere of anything goes when it came to mental patients: lobotomies, sterilization, and euthanasia. The idea originated with treatments where patients were overdosed with insulin to go into a coma, because doctors observed that patients who survived were calmer. There was also a crackpot idea that epileptics didn't have mental illness, so let's induce seizures as a treatment for mental illness.

Doctors applied electricity to pigs, and when they saw the pigs get up and run away they decided it was safe to apply electricity to humans. They rounded someone up, shocked him against his will, and said he was calmer and more lucid.

Of course a person's behavior is going to be changed when they are shocked, because shock treatment produces an acute organic brain syndrome. But that doesn't mean they are improving from their so-called mental illness, the same changes would happen to anyone you give shock to. It is known by neurologists that any head trauma can cause delirium, euphoria, and personality changes, and administering electricity to the brain to induce a seizure is essentially induced head trauma. And then it's repeated, 15, 30, or more times as shock "maintenance."

The 1970s were critical for the electroshock device manufacturers and the doctors with financial ties to the industry. We were just coming out of the lobotomy era, and informed consent laws started to get passed. The industry got scared and started to lobby. They adopted a public relations strategy: claim that shock is new and improved and call it 'electroconvulsive therapy' not 'electroshock.'

You hear this claim repeated over and over in the media. But the electricity is the same, and anesthesia, oxygenation, and muscle relaxants? All of these were already in use in the 1960s.

Anesthesia and muscle relaxants don't make shock safer, they raise the seizure threshold of the brain so more electricity is needed to induce a seizure. And oxygenation was originally invented to make seizures longer, not safer. Seizures are dangerous: the brain is hardwired to protect itself against seizures.

The patients' movement advocated for simple studies to determine how much damage is caused. But the industry and APA blocked safety research. To this day the FDA has never required manufacturers to do safety studies, though the FDA still has shock devices listed in Category 3, meaning the benefits have not shown to outweigh the risks.

Should we as a society be offering untested treatments?

Patients are assured there are no long term adverse effects, but the UK Institute of Psychiatry conducted an exhaustive systematic review in 2006, published in *Advances in Psychiatric Treatment*. They concluded that even with a very conservative estimate at least one third of patients had significant permanent amnesia. It's a very different picture than research manipulated by the shock doctors and manufacturers.

If you tell a big lie often enough people will believe it. We want to believe that technology is advancing, science is progressing and things must be better. All we are asking for is this: honesty and true informed consent. Instead, we have industry deception on the scale of the tobacco industry. That's why a growing movement and I have dedicated ourselves to exposing the lies around electroshock therapy. ∎

Medication Liberation
Laura Delano

Laura Delano is an editor at *Mad In America*, founded a withdrawal support group, and consults with individuals and communities. She is on the board of the International Society for Ethical Psychology and Psychiatry and the board of the National Association for Rights Protection and Advocacy.

When I had a feeling or thought, I would ask myself, "Is this my feeling or is this my medication? Do I even have any genuine feelings?"

WILL HALL You took psychiatric medications for over ten years?

LAURA DELANO Yes, I was first medicated at age fourteen, and it was a profound existential insult. Having that "bipolar disorder" label put on me made me feel so alone, completely separated from humanity.

WH What was going on that got you the diagnosis?

LD Intense anger and rage. I was hitting puberty, beginning to question everything about my life, and I was confused. I didn't have a good relationship to my emotions, always trying to push down uncomfortable feelings, and it just got to a boiling point. I felt like I was possessed, I felt like Jekyll and Hyde. I was sent to a doctor and I described my anger to him as "uncontrollable," and I think that is why they said, "This is more than typical teenage angst." The psychiatrist said the anger was a sign of mania, and that I had bipolar disorder.

I was always told, "This is chronic. You will have this for the rest of your life."

At first I said "Screw you" I am not taking medications. My defiance was an asset. Looking back now it was definitely one of my biggest assets: self preservation.

But then I felt so lost in my life, I was suicidal and completely separated from other people. I had this realization that something must be seriously wrong with me, because I had tried everything and I wasn't getting better. I thought to myself, "They must have been right all along. I must be bipolar." So I went back to a psychiatrist, who put me on medications after our first session.

WH What would you have wanted to say to yourself instead?

LD I would say "What you are going through might just be an episode, a period in your life that you will move through and come out the other side of. You are human just like every other human being around you. You are not abnormal, you are not broken, you are not dysfunctional, you are not diseased. You are feeling emotions, which are human things, and you are feeling them in intense ways. Take some time to find people you trust to help you figure out why you are feeling this way. The answer does not lie in a bottle of pills; pills will take you even further from yourself. Despite what they're telling you, you are not broken forever. You are not broken even in this moment."

WH Many people reach a point of desperation, and the diagnosis and medications feel like the only place left to turn.

LD After seeing the new psychiatrist, I actually felt these incredibly powerful, positive feelings, and a sense of hope. It was amazing, I hadn't felt hope in such along time. I truly believed everything was going to be ok, because they were going to fix me. But for the next nine and a half years my life grew continually darker and more hopeless.

As the years went on, more medications were added. I kept telling myself, day after day, year after year, that eventually the drugs would fix

I was on nineteen different medications over more than ten years. In 2010, when I began to taper off, I was on lithium, Lamictal, Effexor, Ativan, Abilify, and Seroquel.

me. It never happened. I was on five medications at the same time, in very high dosages, and the suicidality got worse and worse. I lived all through my twenties assuming that I would never make it past thirty. When I look back now I realize that I had no faith in myself, because I'd come to believe I was broken, and had absolutely no power to change my life.

WH What medications were you taking?

LD I was on nineteen different medications over more than ten years. In 2010, when I began to taper off, I was on lithium, Lamictal, Effexor, Ativan, Abilify, and Seroquel. I had the impression that the more medications I was on, the more "sophisticated" my meds regime was. It sounds perverse, but I was kind of proud, that I was so "sick" I needed all these modern drugs. I had a little pill bag I brought with me everywhere I went, like my security blanket.

WH You get attention from experts who wield special neuropsychiatric jargon. For many people it's a ritual that assures you you are being taken seriously, that your suffering is real.

LD It's human to need an answer, that something is only valid and legitimate if you have a definition for it and a label to explain what you are going through. But it's freeing to be in a place today where I don't need an answer why I feel certain things, other than because I am a human being.

At the time when I was on medications my diagnosis was the only meaning in my life, and I worked very hard at being a "good patient." I was on top of my "symptoms," reporting back to my doctor. It made me feel important to be a part of the medical dialogue.

WH Somehow those "dialogues" tend to go well only as long as the doctor leads. How did medications fuel a ten-year downward spiral?

LD On medications I was profoundly emotionally, physically, and existentially disconnected from myself. I felt I was performing a role in life; nothing felt genuine. The medications also took a physical toll. My thyroid stopped functioning from the lithium, so now I have hypothyroidism, an endocrine disease. I had sexual dysfunction, cognitive issues, memory issues... I didn't even realize it wasn't normal to have chronic gastrointestinal problems. But the most important effect was existential. I was a slave to these medications; they were in control and I had no agency in my life. When I had a feeling or thought, I would ask myself, "is it my medications or is this my feeling? Do I even have any genuine feelings?"

Take some time to find people you trust to help you figure out why you are feeling this way. The answer does not lie in a bottle of pills; pills will take you even further from yourself.

WH Were the medications helping with your symptoms?

LD Definitely not. They were perpetuating the symptoms. At one point I was on both an anti-narcolepsy medication and a sleeping medication *at the same time*. It just didn't make any sense. I was on 80 mg of Prozac; and 400 mg of Provigil because I couldn't stay awake during the day, which is just a massive amount. So basically I was taking intense dosages of speed, and I was "manic" all the time during the day, racing thoughts, inability to sit still, feeling really "grandiose." And of course at night I had such bad insomnia from the stimulants that I would be on 10 mg of a sleeping pill which would bring me down so much and I'd feel very depressed. But instead of looking at the pills I was taking, they called me a bipolar "rapid cycler" because I was going through these highs and lows. At the time

I believed it was all medically sound, and that it was my so-called "treatment-resistant mental illness" causing these problems.

WH Did they inform you about any risks?

LD The told me about minor things like headache and constipation, and that side effects would settle down in a few weeks as my body adjusted. They didn't tell me about any potentially permanent side effects. Two months after I started lithium, my primary care doctor called and said she had never seen abnormal thyroid levels like mine. The lithium had

I had this realization that something must be seriously wrong with me, because I had tried everything and I wasn't getting better. I thought to myself, "They must have been right all along. I must be bipolar."

given me thyroid disease. But then when I told the psychiatrist, she said, "You should feel grateful that you have Hashimoto's disease, because out of all the auto-immune diseases, it is the most manageable, it is easy to get it right with medication. So you should feel grateful." And I remember then actually feeling guilty for being so angry that my thyroid had stopped working. I thought, "Oh my God, who am I to be so angry? I should be grateful." I was in a place where I had lost my voice: the unequal power dynamic was so real I was unable to question the doctor. The power psychiatry had over me was total.

WH Did the meds affect your suicidal feelings?

LD I believed my suicidal feelings were just a symptom of my bipolar disorder. I had a very serious suicide attempt in November of 2008 but actually, in the weeks leading up to that, I had recently been on high doses of Lexapro, Klonopin, and Lamictal, which had given me akathisia. Akathisia is a drug-induced agitation and inability to be still; I had this very intense energy vibrating through me. Leading up to the attempt I was incredibly "manic," that's how I understood it at the time. I saw no other option than to take my life. Today I'm just so grateful am still here. I look back and see that it wasn't me that wanted to die. It was medicated me.

WH How did you change your belief you had bipolar and needed these medications?

LD In February of 2010 I found myself on a locked psychiatric ward. I wanted to kill myself, but at the same time also I didn't. I just knew that if something didn't drastically change, I'd die.

I decided to quit alcohol, which was a daily part of my life after college. Ironically, alcohol became the only thing keeping me alive, because it helped me not care how hopeless and lonely my life had become. After I quit drinking I got enough mental clarity to start wondering, "Who am I off of all these drugs?" Eventually I asked my psychopharmacologist if I could try coming off. My "treatment team" did not agree for quite some time, but I persisted. Eventually, I began to taper off.

WH What difference did sobriety make?

LD Quitting alcohol ignited a sense of agency and a glimmer of hope. And then, two months after I started reducing the medications, I found Robert Whitaker's *Anatomy of an Epidemic*. I couldn't put it down: it was my "Aha!" moment. I realized that the meds, in fact, might have been making me "sicker" all along.

WH Was the withdrawal difficult?

LD I tapered off five drugs over five months, which is very, very fast. In the beginning, I had a lot of light sensitivity and exhaustion. I felt like I never had a moment of peace. The insomnia was horrible, and because I'd been on sleep medication for ten years, I was scared I'd never be able to sleep on my own again. Very strange smells came out of my skin, toxins of some sort, and terrible acne broke out all over my face, neck, chest, and back, in

I'd come to believe I was broken, and had absolutely no power to change my life.

a way that I had never experienced before. I felt profound despair and intense, debilitating anxiety. The anxiety was beyond anything I had ever experienced. It was physical agitation so bad I wanted to rip my skin off.

I also had a really horrendous experience coming off benzodiazepines. I had absolutely no balance, no equilibrium. I had vertigo all the time, my head ached, the migraines were so intense that I just wanted to tear my head open. I had cold sweats. It was so horrible. It was really hell on earth.

The psychiatrist said the anger was a sign of mania and that I had bipolar disorder.

WH What helped you through this?

LD I leaned on my 12-step community at the time: people dealing with their own emotional and physical pain, and learning how to live with their feelings. I couldn't have done it without that community. I was also lucky to not have to worry about things like rent, a job, or caring for children. I lived with my family for almost a year as I was withdrawing.

WH How long did it take to actually start to feel better?

LD For the first three months it was hard to get out of the house, and things kept getting worse. At six to eight months in I began to feel less bad. At about a year and a half I actually started to have moments of feeling good, when I felt like I was physically healing and slowly starting to settle into my emotions. Today I am off meds completely and I have my life and my health back.

WH What advice do you have for others who might want to get off medications themselves?

LD It helped me to view the emotional, physical, and mental pain of withdrawal as a signs my body and mind were heal-

Today I'm just so grateful I'm still here. I look back and see it wasn't me who wanted to die, it was *medicated* me.

I also had a really horrendous experience coming off benzodiazepines. I had absolutely no balance, no equilibrium. I had vertigo all the time, my head ached, the migraines were so intense that I just wanted to tear my head open.

ing. That helped me find meaning in the experience, to feel like I could keep going.

There is no one right way to come off drugs, but it is important not to rush into anything. Take some time to really think about how you want to do it and who you want to support you. Who is going to be there for you? ∎

Psychiatric Drugs and the Rise of Mental Illness
Robert Whitaker

Robert Whitaker is the author of *Mad in America: Bad Science, Bad Medicine and the Enduring Mistreatment of the Mentally Ill*, named by Discover magazine as a best science book of 2002; and *Anatomy of an Epidemic: Magic Bullets, Psychiatric Drugs, and the Astonishing Rise of Mental Illness in America*, winner of a 2010 Investigative Reporters and Editors award. He received a George Polk medical writing award and was a finalist for the 1998 Pulitzer Prize. His new book is *Psychiatry Under the Influence: Institutional Corruption, Social Injury, and Prescriptions for Reform* (2015).

Right at the beginning of the antipsychotic era the research literature reveals a paradox: short term efficacy, but perhaps increased long term chronicity.

(Excerpted from a 2012 talk at Powell's Bookstore sponsored by Portland Hearing Voices.)

The puzzle at the heart of my book *Anatomy of An Epidemic* is this:

We have a conventional history of psychiatry that says, "Thorazine arrived as an asylum medicine in 1955, and that kicked off the psychopharmacological revolution, a great advance in care of mental disorders." In 1998 for example US Surgeon General David Thatcher wrote,

"Prior to 1955, psychiatry lacked treatments that would prevent people from becoming chronically ill. Once we got drugs, they prevented people from becoming chronically ill, and now we have a wide array of drugs safe and effective for a wide array of well defined psychiatric disorders."

Yet at the same time the number of people under government care for mental illness disabilities has gone from about 1 in every 468 Americans in 1955 to about 1 in 184 in 1987: 1.25 million people. And today there's more than 4 million people on Social Security disability payments due to mental disorders, a tripling in the last 20 years. In 1987 as a society we spent about 800 million dollars on psychiatric drugs, and in 2013 more than 40 billion dollars. US spending on mental health services doubled between 2001 and 2007, and is expected to increase another 50% in the next 8 years.

So the question is this: If indeed medication was a great leap forward that prevents people from becoming chronically ill, why is the mental illness disability rate rising so rapidly?

And with bipolar disorder you have to ask, where did all the bipolar patients come from? 40 years ago, bipolar was a rare disease of roughly 1 in 3,000 to 1 in 10,000 adults. Now it's about 1 in 50. From 1 in 5000 to 1 in 50 in 40 years. What's going on?

For a while I believed schizophrenia was a biological problem from too much dopamine activity, and that the antipsychotic drugs, by blocking dopamine activity, fixed that abnormality. Medications were like insulin for diabetes, and you would never take insulin away from a diabetic. I was a complete believer.

But then I came upon two studies that didn't make sense, which made me start to question conventional beliefs. Harvard Medical researchers found in 1994 that outcomes for schizophrenic patients had declined in the last 20 years, and were now no better than in 1900. And the World Health Organization (WHO) studied schizophrenia outcomes in poor countries, especially India, Colombia, and Nigeria, and found they were much better than outcomes in the US and six other rich countries. The WHO concluded that living in a developed country is a "strong predictor that you will never fully recover from schizophrenia." Only 16% of patients in poor countries regularly took medication, versus 61% in the rich countries. So I began doubting medications necessarily lead to better outcomes, and that was the reason I decided to write *Mad in America*.

I started looking more deeply at the evidence. It turns out that brain researchers never found that people diagnosed with schizophrenia suffer from too much dopamine activity. Steven Hyman, Director of the National Institute of Mental Health (NIMH) in the late 90's, a neuroscientist, and Provost of Harvard University, wrote, "There is no evidence of a dopaminergic lesion as a cause for schizophrenia."

In 1987 we spent as a society about 800 million dollars on psychiatric drugs, and in 2013 more than 40 billion dollars.

And in 1984, the NIMH actually said, "It doesn't look that any perturbation of the serotonergic system is a primary cause of depression." Kenneth Kendler, Co-Editor in Chief of *Psychological Medicine* summed up this whole history in 2005, and said, "We have hunted for big simple neurochemical explanations for psychiatric disorders, and we have not found them."

So if the drugs aren't treating chemical imbalances, what are they doing?

The brain is extraordinarily flexible in trying to maintain its normal functioning. Thus when Prozac makes more serotonin available, the brain immediately starts putting out less serotonin, to compensate for the presence of the drug. Receptors for serotonin decrease and become abnormally low in density. The drug tries to accelerate serotonergic activity, and the brain compensates by putting on a brake.

With an antipsychotic, it's the same thing in reverse. An antipsychotic such as Haldol or Thorazine blocks receptors for dopamine. In response, the brain's presynaptic neurons put out more dopamine and increase dopamine receptor density. Newer antipsychotics work the same way.

So what's happening? Hyman in "A Paradigm for Understanding Psychotropic Drug Action" wrote that these drugs "work by perturbing neurotransmitter systems in the brain," which then "undergoes compensatory adaptations...trying to maintain its normal homeostasis." As a result of medication, the brain begins operating both "qualitatively and quantitatively different than normal."

Now, that does not necessarily mean that the medications are bad. It just means that you're not normalizing function. The drugs are not serving as an antidote to a known disease. And if a drug abnormalizes function, there's a risk of side effects and long term problems.

Great advances in medicine often result from deciphering the disease process: a magic bullet kills a bacterial infection. But we haven't discovered the biological causes of schizophrenia, depression, or bipolar disorder, and we don't have antidotes for those disorders.

So we have to put the puzzle of the drugs' effect on long-term outcomes together like this:

First, what were the outcomes for mental disorders in the era *before* medications? And when drugs were introduced, did clinicians observe something new about the course of the disorder? Were people getting better, or relapsing more? What did long-term randomized studies find? Was there any resulting chronicity? And with modern imaging technology, do the drugs cause morphological, physical changes in the brain?

Prior to 1955, before the medication era, probably 25% to 30% became chronically ill: the minority, not the majority.

From 1945 to 1955, in the pre-medication era, surprisingly 70% to 75% of first episode schizophrenic patients would be discharged within 12 to 18 months. Without medication. Only about 30% would be chronically in the hospital. 5 years after the first episode, roughly the same results: 70% to 75% are living out in the community and not on disability, and the employment rate is above 50%. Prior to 1955, before the medication era, probably 25% to 30% became chronically ill: the minority, not the majority.

And one footnote: did the drugs lead to deinstitutionalization, as is commonly claimed? The number of chronic schizophrenia patients in

1955, after Thorazine came in, was roughly 260,000. 8 years later, it was basically the same. Instead, deinstitutionalization began in 1965 when we passed Medicare and Medicaid, which meant the Federal government shared the costs allowing states to empty hospitals. A political change led to deinstitutionalization, not the arrival of antipsychotic medication.

There is of course evidence for the short-term use of antipsychotics. Studies in the 1960s showed people in a psychotic episode did better with drugs in six weeks than they did taking placebo. But that's short term efficacy. Then you have to ask, "How long should we keep people on the drugs?" At the end of 6 weeks, yes the drug-treated patients are doing better. But in the first longer term study, at the end of one year, the drug treated patients were *more* likely to have been re-hospitalized.

The evidence for long-term use of antipsychotics comes from drug-withdrawal studies. These were studies in which patients who had responded well to antipsychotics were either abruptly withdrawn from the drug, or maintained on the drug. As might be predicted, those abruptly withdrawn from the medication relapsed at a much

A political change led deinstitutionalization, not medications.

greater rate than those maintained on the medication. And that relapse was seen by the researchers as evidence of the disease returning, and thus they concluded that the drug prevented the return of psychosis.

But you can see the problem here: maybe the relapse is a result of drug withdrawal, not a return of the disease.

Is the any other type of evidence in the research literature for long term efficacy of using antipsychotics compared to non-medicated patients? Higher unemployment rates? No. Any functional improvement? No. There is *nothing* in the research literature.

So, if we go back to the 1960s study which found a higher rehospitalization rate in the medicated patients at the end of one year, we see, right at the beginning of the antipsychotic era, that the research literature revealed a possible paradox: short term efficacy, but perhaps increased long-term chronicity. Indeed, doctors started seeing, in their medicated patients, a revolving door syndrome. They saw people get better with pills,

40 years ago, bipolar was a rare disease: roughly 1 in 3,000 to 1 in 10,000 adults. Now it's about 1 in 50.

but next thing you know they're coming back to the hospital.

In addition, several researchers noted that people who've been exposed to medication have more severe relapses. Samuel Bockhoven did a retrospective study for the NIMH of patients treated in 1947 without meds, compared to patients he's treated with meds in the 1960s. The 1947 patients fared better, particularly in terms of functional outcomes. He wrote, "Rather unexpectedly, these data suggest that psychotropic drugs may not be indispensable. Their extended use in aftercare may prolong the social dependency of many discharged patients."

In the 1970's, the NIMH ran 3 randomized trials on people put immediately on antipsychotics, comparing them with an experimental group of people not put on meds, who were instead treated with psychosocial care to get them through their psychotic break. If, after 4 or 5 weeks the psychosis wasn't abating, then the patients in the experimental group might be put on the medications. This design might be called a "selective use" model of medications.

In each of the three studies, the experimental group had better overall outcomes. Those who never went on medications had the best outcomes.

For instance, in one study by Maurice Rappaport, 24 of 41 patients in the experimental group got through their psychotic break without being exposed to medications. And that group had by far the best 3 year outcomes, had the lowest relapse in the following 3 years, and the best global functioning. Another study by the head of schizophrenia research at the NIMH, Loren Mosher, had similar findings.

Rappaport, wrote, "Our findings suggest that antipsychotic medications is not the treatment of choice at least for certain patients if one is interested in long term clinical improvement. Many unmedicated hospital patients show greater long term improvement, less pathology at follow up, fewer rehospitalizations, and better overall functioning in the community than patients who were given chlorpromazine, (Thorazine) while in the hospital."

William Carpenter who led the third NIMH study, also concluded that they saw better outcomes in the unmedicated group on the whole. Indeed, many of the non-medicated patients told him they found it gratifying and informative to go through their psychotic episodes without their feelings numbed by drugs. Carpenter speculated that the medicated patients didn't have that same learning experience, and as a result they might be less able to manage subsequent life stresses.

Loren Mosher wrote this conclusion about his study, "Contrary to popular views, minimal use of antipsychotic medications combined with specially designed psychosocial intervention for patients newly identified with schizophrenia spectrum disorder is not harmful but it appears to be advantageous. We think that the balance of risk and benefits associated with the common practice of medicating nearly all early episodes of psychosis should be reexamined."

And is there any evidence base for long term efficacy of antipsychotics in the research literature? Higher unemployment rates? No. Any improvement over long term? No, there is nothing in the research literature.

So in the 1970's, these three NIMH studies showed that selective use of antipsychotic medication produced better outcomes. Carpenter then raised this provocative point: "There is no question that once patients are placed on medication, they are less vulnerable to relapse if maintained on neuroleptics." Once they go on. But what if these patients had never been treated with drugs to begin with? He writes, "We raise the possibility that antipsychotic medication may make some schizophrenic patients more vulnerable to future relapse than would be the case in the natural course of the illness."

At this point two researchers from McGill University came up with an explanation: "supersensitivity psychosis." The drug causes physical changes that lead to dysfunction in the dopamine pathways in the brain. The researchers knew that many patients taking antipsychotic medication were developing tardive dyskinesia, a sign that the basal ganglia, which is run by a dopaminergic pathway, is no longer working properly. So maybe the drugs induced a similar dysfunction in the limbic system, another area of the brain that relies on dopamine, and this leads to a tardive psychosis. When that happens, the two researchers wrote, "the illness appears worse" than ever before. "New schizophrenic symptoms of greater severity will appear."

Now, that does not necessarily mean that the medications are bad. It just means that you're not normalizing function. The drugs are not serving as an antidote to a known disease. And if you're abnormalizing function, there's a risk of side effects and long term problems.

Then in the 1990's MRI technology revealed that antipsychotics cause the basal ganglia to swell over 18 months and the frontal lobes to shrink. These changes are associated with a greater severity of schizophrenia symptoms. Nancy Andreasen, former Editor of the *American Journal of Psychiatry*, said that antipsychotics drugs cause the frontal lobes to slowly "atrophy" over time.

Meanwhile, studies where patients were off meds showed that many recovered over time. Courtney Harding of Boston University followed a group of patients released from Vermont State Hospital, and at the end of 25 years one third were completely recovered: no symptoms, working, etc. And these recovered patients were all off medications.

Now a study by Martin Harrow is really important. He's been following a group of schizophrenia patients for decades, and found that two years after initial diagnosis there wasn't much difference between medicated and unmedicated patients in terms of outcomes. But by the end of 4 and a half years, the recovery rate for those off medication was 40%, versus 5% of those on medication. That difference in recovery rates showed up at the end of 15 years too. People off meds were doing better long term. Thus, in 2008 Harrow told the American Psychiatric Association, "I conclude that people off antipsychotic medication long term have better global outcomes."

So in 2008 Harrow told the American Psychiatric Association, "I conclude that people off antipsychotic medication long term have better global outcomes."

But even though that is the best long term study we have of medication outcomes, it did not appear in any American newspaper. It was basically just kept hidden from the public.

Other diagnoses raise similar questions about medication efficacy. For ADHD, an NIMH study that began in the early 1990's found that at the end of 14 months there was some benefit for the drug treated group versus the non-drug treated group. And that was the big press release, But at the end of 3 years? The study showed being on medication was not a marker of benefit, it was a marker of deterioration.

Now let's look at depression. In the 1960's psychiatrist Jonathan Cole summed up the standard view: "Depression is on the whole one of the psychiatric conditions with the best prognosis for eventual recovery with or without treatment. Most depression are self limited." Nathan Kline wrote in 1964 that "In the treatment of depression one always has an ally in the fact that most depressions terminate from spontaneous remissions."

But today about 85% of first episode depressed patients end up with a pretty chronic course when treated with medications. So depression switched from an episodic illness to a chronic illness in the antidepressant era.

For bipolar: how do we go from diagnosing 1 in 5000 people to 1 in 50? About a third of the people with a bipolar diagnosis have been exposed to illicit drugs before their diagnosis. These drugs may stir a psychotic episode, a manic episode. And antidepressants can also act as a stimulus: among people with depression who take antidepressants, somewhere between 20 and 40% convert to bipolar. Indeed, one study of bipolar patients found that 60% had their first manic episode *after* being treated with an antidepressant for depression. Meanwhile, 10 to 20 percent of kids on ADHD medications convert to bipolar long term. In short, initial use of psychiatric medications can iatrogenically create a bipolar patient.

In the past bipolar, which used to be called manic-depressive illness, ran an episodic course. 75% to 85% of people would go back to employment, and there was no long term cognitive decline. In 1969, George Winokur wrote: "There is no basis to consider that manic depressive psychosis permanently affected those who suffered from it. In this way, it is of course different from schizophrenia. When people recover from an episode, they usually have no difficulty resuming their usual occupations."

What about today? For bipolar, good long term outcomes, with people employed and staying out of the hospital, have declined from 85% to 35% With people on drug cocktails, cognitive decline begins to appear after about 5 years. Summing this up, Ross Baldessarini wrote "Prognosis for bipolar disorder was once considered relatively favorable, but contemporary findings suggest that disability and poorer outcomes are prevalent, despite major therapeutic advances."

Today about 85% of first episode depressed patients end up with a chronic course if treated with medications. So depression has switched from an episodic illness to a chronic illness.

So what's the solution here? The plea here is not against drugs. The plea here is for honesty. At the very least, for psychotic episodes, we need a system of care that allows some people to not be medicated. We need a system where those who want to go off meds get support for doing that. With depression for example, in Britain you can actually go to your doctor and come back not with a prescription for an antidepressant, but a prescription for exercise. Various studies, including one by Duke University, have shown that exercise produces the best long term stay-well rate.

One thing we have to do, in response to these poor outcomes, is challenge the storytelling. For the past 35 years, we have been told a false story about the nature of mental disorders and what the drugs do, and we the public need to know what science is really revealing about this paradigm of care.

Here is how this false storytelling came about. The National Alliance for the Mentally Ill (NAMI) started as a grassroots organization with noble aims. But it also had an

The plea here is not against drugs. The plea here is for honesty.

agenda to absolve mothers of blame for causing schizophrenia, which was a popular psychoanalytic theory at the time. So NAMI, during the 1980s, embraced and promoted the notion that schizophrenia is a brain disease, in order to remove that idea that mothers were to blame for their child's schizophrenia. NAMI helped popularize the notion that psychiatric disorders were due to chemical imbalances in the brain, which could then be fixed by psychiatric drugs. The pharmaceutical industry and the American Psychiatric Association joined in that storytelling.

The APA obviously has financial reasons for wanting to promote drugs, because their prescription authority gives them an advantage in the drug-prescribing marketplace; other mental health professionals do not have prescribing powers. And the pharmaceutical companies of course have obvious reasons to promote the chemical imbalance story too. So in the 1980s you see these three storytelling forces come together: NAMI, the APA, and the pharmaceutical industry (which provided funds to both NAMI and the APA.)

We need to break up that storytelling coalition. When the Harrow study was published saying recovery is 8 times higher for unmedicated patients, did NAMI have it on their website? No. Did the National Institute of Mental Health issue a press release on it? No. Did the American Psychiatric Association issue a press release on it? No.

Why not?

The reason of course is that Harrow's findings went against the story that NAMI, the APA and the pharmaceutical industry have been telling us for decades.

I think this is one of the biggest moral challenges of our society today. We need to have psychiatric care in this country informed by honesty, as opposed to being informed by storytelling that serves financial and ideological interests. ∎

Beyond Meds
Monica Cassani

Creator of the web magazine *Beyond Meds*, Monica Cassani is a social worker and a person whose life was severely ruptured by psychiatric drugs. She writes critically about the system as well as about holistic pathways without medication.

After two decades on psych meds I came off a six drug cocktail in about six years. This proved to be a gargantuan task, and left me gravely disabled.

In retrospect I see that a core, vital part of me was always still there during the drugged years, a part that was learning and remembering, so I could eventually come off and become med free.

Today I no longer believe that I "lost" my life to drugs. It is tragic I could not be more conscious during those years, and that my body became toxic, polluted, and painfully ill. But my experience was not lost: it was stored in my body, to be processed when I got free of drugs, and to inspire me to help others avoid what happened to me.

Psychiatric drugs are agents of trauma. Part of the healing process for me and many others is working through layers and layers of trauma, trauma inflicted in the past as well as by psych drug use and exposure to the dehumanizing psychiatric system. Because trauma becomes embodied, body-oriented therapies are very important. I healed mostly through self-enquiry, meditation, yoga, and ecstatic dance.

Before I began to find wellness, drug withdrawal made me much sicker: I was one of thousands of people who develop serious protracted withdrawal problems that lead to grave disability. Protracted withdrawal is an injury to the autonomic nervous system that exists on a spectrum: some people are hardly impacted at all, while others are made very ill. I was bedridden and non-verbal for a couple of years.

Despite this, I have never had a moment of regret for freeing myself from these drugs. Today I have a clarity of mind that is so beautiful I cry to think about it. Though my creativity and sense of purpose were stolen from me for almost half my life, today I have them back. Even while gravely impaired I was grateful, because of what I was able to regain.

My healing journey meant learning about our deeply holistic natures as human beings. Everything matters. The body you were born with. The body you have today. Your relationships with others and the planet, the food you eat, the air you breathe, how you move your body, and the thoughts nurtured in your mind and soul.

That is what seeing ourselves as holistic beings means: understanding our relationship to everything in our environment and our bodies, what we're born with and how it's all connected. It's not some sort of New Age hogwash. It's just plain and simple reality.

Through that slow, painstaking, and ultimately joyous process, I've healed and brought wellbeing back to my body/mind/spirit. I now do everything with care and a sense of respect for life. Eating nourishing food and spending time in ways that nourish myself and those around me.

We need each other in this process. The most important thing to me these days is building a non-coercive, healing community. *Beyond Meds* was both a lifeline for me when I was bedridden and a service to others, so they might avoid harm like what came to me. I'm profoundly grateful for the community *Beyond Meds* created.

Community doesn't require giving up your autonomy and self-determination: psychiatry and the mental illness establishment often steal both. I envision a world where people are empowered to make choices that they find work for them. Everyone's path is going to be different. Respecting and celebrating that great diversity is key. ■

Myth of the Chemical Cure
Joanna Moncrieff

Joanna Moncrieff, MD, is a senior lecturer at University College London, a practicing psychiatrist with the National Health Service, and the author of *The Myth of the Chemical Cure: A Critique of Psychiatric Drug Treatment* (2009).

Taking psychiatric drugs is like using alcohol for social anxiety. Alcohol can be helpful for social anxiety, but that's not because people have an alcohol deficiency. It doesn't do anything about the cause of the anxiety.

WILL HALL How did you develop your critical perspective?

JOANNA MONCRIEFF When I started working in psychiatric hospitals almost everyone was on at least one medication. It didn't seem to be making that much difference, and was causing a lot of secondary problems. Yet other doctors thought it was wonderful and believed people were getting better because of the drugs. That made me go and find out more.

WH What did you discover?

JM Prior to the 1950s drugs weren't seen as addressing any fundamental underlying problem. And then that changed. Psychiatrists started to believe the drugs were reversing a psychotic disorder and bringing people back to normal. Except that there wasn't any evidence of that.

WH Wasn't Thorazine innovative because it was a tranquilizer?

JM Yes, and the first people who prescribed Thorazine / chlorpromazine recognized this clearly. They wrote how Thorazine slowed you down and created a state of psychic indifference without just sedating you and sending you to sleep. The barbiturates used previously just made people very sleepy.

Psychiatrists thought it was a great breakthrough, but at the time they also did recognize it was creating an *abnormal* neurological state. It wasn't reversing an underlying disease. But then gradually psychiatry started to believe it was an "antipsychotic" and that it was somehow reversing processes that led to psychosis.

WH They are tranquilizers that work on the higher brain functions: people lose motivation and become indifferent. I've been on antipsychotics: Trilafon, Navane, and Mellaril. I remember blacking out, and a kind of vice or cotton or wool around my mind. I was sluggish and groggy, wandering around or standing for a long time, then sitting and watching television.

JM Parkinson's is a neurological disease caused by a deficit of dopamine in the brain. We need dopamine for movement and thought. The antipsychotics block dopamine production, and create a deficit of dopamine. They're inducing an artificial Parkinson's type state: people slow down, get very stiff, lose facial expression, and their thought processes slow. A high enough dose causes obvious Parkinson's-like symptoms. What

I think is happening at lower dosages is simple: they're causing milder symptoms of Parkinson's disease.

WH This is where the "Thorazine shuffle" comes from. And this drug effect happens when anyone takes the drug, with or without psychosis. Even animals: antipsychotics are used in veterinary practice. There is no targeting of some psychosis process. But nonetheless this led to the idea of dopamine imbalance causing schizophrenia?

JM Yes, it was calming people down by blocking dopamine, so scientists concluded over-activity of dopamine was the cause of schizophrenia. The theory assumes that if the drugs do something, they must be curing a disease, not just having a tranquilizing effect on anyone.

What psychiatric drugs essentially do is like using alcohol for social anxiety. Alcohol can be helpful for social anxiety, but that's not because people have an alcohol deficiency. That's because alcohol causes a state of intoxication to anyone, and that intoxication is characterized by social dis-inhibition, which can be useful if people are very socially anxious. It doesn't do anything about the cause of the anxiety.

WH So all psychiatric drugs are psychoactive, they change consciousness. They are intoxicants?

JM Psychoactive drugs including everything we prescribe in psychiatry and also taken recreationally. There's no fundamental distinction between them.

People take recreational drugs because they have nice effects, and make people feel good. Most psychiatric drugs don't make people feel good. But that doesn't mean that they're not having psychoactive effects.

WH People take some recreational drugs for emotional coping: or "self-medicating," and some psychiatric drugs are also

> Psychoactive drugs include everything in psychiatry and also taken recreationally. There is no fundamental distinction between them.

used recreationally, such as the benzodiazepines and Adderall. I don't think this is an anti-drug perspective, it's more about honesty about how and why drugs can be useful. The problem is that in psychiatry an institutional authority is saying, "this is treatment for a disease."

We need to understand psychiatric drugs *as drugs*: chemical substances that create an artificial state. It might be useful to take them, but we have to treat them with respect and use them wisely.

JM We need to understand psychiatric drugs *as drugs*: chemical substances that are alien to the body, that create an artificial state, with all sorts of dangers and hazards. It might be useful to take them, but we have to treat them with respect and use them wisely. They don't reverse or treat some disease process.

WH Is there research on how psychiatric drugs affect you in general? Like there is research on alcohol or recreational drugs?

WH We don't know very much about these drugs because we haven't looked at them as drugs. The research is on how they affect a presumed disease. We've been obsessed with "Do they alter the dopamine receptors?" or "Do antidepressants raise your serotonin levels?" instead of looking at all the other things they're doing. The focus has been on the supposed benefits of treatment for disorders.

WH A lot of people are told, "If you don't take these medications, you will you have another episode, and you could end up dead from suicide."

JM When I first went into psychiatry in the 1990's, manic depression was a very rare condition with severe episodes of mania or depression that last for several months. And now we have the idea of milder versions: you are bipolar if you have mood swings. Many people with ordinary emotional fluctuations are diagnosed with bipolar disorder, and put on potentially very toxic drug treatments for it. Yet all the research on the effects of drugs is done with the small group of people who have a much more severe and obvious problem.

WH Tell us about lithium.

JM It's an alkaline metal and it's very, very toxic. It can easily kill people, and people taking lithium have blood tests to be sure and not take too much. It's quite obvious, from volunteer studies on people without a bipolar diagnosis, that lithium toxicity has sedative effects. It dampens down the nervous system, slows up thinking, slows up reaction times, it makes you feel very groggy, and possibly also reduces creativity and spontaneity. So of course it's going to slow people down if they're manic, but that doesn't mean it's a specific treatment for bipolar at all. It's going to do that to anyone.

WH There's no targeting effect on some presumed bipolar mechanism in the brain, just as antipsychotics don't target psychotic mechanisms? The beneficial effect is mild lithium toxicity?

JM The effects lithium has in normal people easily explain the effects it has on someone with mania or bipolar disorder. I don't think you need to have any additional explanation. No one's come up with a credible theory about what it might be doing that is specific to manic depression or bipolar in any way. There are various speculations, but nothing concrete has ever been found.

Research into whether lithium reduces the risk of relapse and crisis also has lots of problems. The studies are done on people taking lithium for a long time already, who then stop lithium all of a sudden. Stopping lithium is such a shock to the body that it can actually cause a manic episode.

> Of course lithium is going to slow people down if they're manic. It's going to do that to anyone, but that doesn't mean it's a specific treatment for bipolar at all.

WH A psychotic crisis might sometimes be medication withdrawal, not some underlying condition.

JM If there are any problems, everything is blamed on the illness, and then the solution is to increase the medication. That makes it incredibly difficult for people to get off of medication. They don't take into consideration the withdrawal effect.

WH And there hasn't been much research on the medication withdrawal process?

The increasing use of psychiatric medication is a symptom of consumerism. The idea is that it must be possible to buy a solution for everything, that every aspect of life is marketable.

JM No, very little.

WH What about the so-called mood stabilizers?

JM Starting in the 1980's, someone thought that manic depressive episodes were similar to epilepsy, so let's try anti-epileptic drugs. These drugs also very sedative, like antipsychotics and lithium.

The concept of a mood stabilizer is very misleading because none of these drugs has been shown to stabilize, or reduce mood fluctuations in normal people or in anyone. They don't do that, they're just sedative drugs. But these myths are supported and repeated as part of industry marketing to make being on drugs more palatable.

WH Lithium was once very popular in patent medicines, and was in 7Up soda and beer. People say "Well, it's a salt. It's a natural salt."

JM The toxic effects of lithium are severe neurological suppression: people become sedated and confused and get a tremor. It will have an effect on the kidneys and the gastrointestinal system. One of the points

I've been trying to make is that the supposed therapeutic effects of lithium are milder manifestations of those toxic effects. One early psychiatrist called it "The treatment of the manic patient by lithium poisoning."

WH What should parents do if their children have behavioral problems but don't want them on medications?

JM Up until fairly recently, all these problems would be addressed without drug treatment, by social workers and psychologists. They'd identify the cause of the behavioral problems and identify any issues at school.

WH And now the problem is in the child's brain.

JM Professionals are no longer looking at the entire social context and system around the child, and how this might be producing the problematic behavior.

WH Do psychiatric medications have an aspect of social control?

JM Yes, and they should be more democratically and openly debated. I think society does need to control some people's behavior sometimes, but we need to do that honestly and not overstep boundaries. If it's dressed up as medical treatment, there's nothing to stop the system from heavily drugging and controlling people in a very authoritarian way for a long time. That happens to some people in the psychiatric system.

WH Sometimes people take medications as a useful, and risky, tool. But I've also seen what amounts to psychiatric slavery: your life is owned by your case manager, and your thought are shackled by medications. Few people who work in the mental health field admit this is happening.

> The concept of a mood stabilizer is very misleading. None of these drugs has been shown to stabilize, stop, or reduce mood fluctuations in volunteers or indeed anyone. They don't do that, they're just sedative drugs.

JM There's a big push to medicalize problems. And if drugs weren't taking our attention away from social problems, there might be greater resistance to economic trends that make people's lives difficult. Instead we blame individuals.

The increasing use of psychiatric medication is a symptom of increasing consumerism, really. The idea is it must be possible to buy a solution for everything, that every aspect of life is marketable.

WH What do you think about the growth of so-called psychosis early intervention programs, where the idea is to catch the disease in its early stages??

JM The pharmaceutical industry has produced, supported, and paid for lots of journal issues and sponsored conferences on early intervention into psychosis. Psychosis has become a popular term, which is completely understandable, schizophrenia is a very stigmatizing and frightening label. Historically psychiatrists have been a bit more reluctant to use the schizophrenia diagnosis, and were therefore hesitant to start antipsychotics. So the idea of early intervention into "psychosis" as a diagnosis makes it easier to start people on antipsychotics early. Which expands the market for these drugs.■

Studies show that stopping lithium is risky once you have started it, but not that starting it in the first place is a good thing.

Socially Constructing Drugs
Richard DeGrandpre

A former editor of *Adbusters* magazine, Richard DeGrand-pre is the author of *Ritalin Nation: Rapid-Fire Culture and the Transformation of Human Consciousness (1998)*, *The Cult of Pharmacology: How America Became the World's Most Troubled Drug Culture (2006)*, and *Empathy Test - A Henning Jenkins Novel (2011)*.

It turns out it's not actually true. Animals will also prefer candy just as much as they prefer cocaine. It all depends on what their social environment is.

WILL HALL What were some things you discovered in your work as a behavioral pharmacologist?

RICHARD DEGRANDPRE If you actually look at the scientific studies, our most basic commonsense ideas about how drugs work breaks down. The first class I took for my PhD I thought, "This is amazing." So I pursued it more and more, and there are hundreds of studies referenced in my book *Cult of Pharmacology*. I did a lot of research that was funded by the drug agencies with the US government such as the National Center on

Drug Abuse. What I learned about psychoactive drugs (mind-altering drugs) was a real eye-opener, so I pursued it more and more.

WH Your book emphasizes the power of the mind over chemistry and the importance of social context in creating drug effects. Give us some examples.

RD A researcher can take a group of rats, and let them push a lever to self-administer cocaine through an IV catheter. We know that these animals will indeed self-administer cocaine. The media commonly say these studies show animals will simply "self-administer themselves to death."

WH We've often heard those studies, that the rats will prefer cocaine to water or food, because cocaine is that addictive, right?

RD No, it turns out it's not actually true. Animals will also prefer candy just as much as they prefer cocaine. *It all depends on what their social environment is.*

In one study, a group of animals that self-administer cocaine was compared with another group of animals. They're getting exactly the same exposure to cocaine, same time of day, the only difference between the two groups is whether they have the power to administer the drug by choice or not. With just that difference, choice, the actual physical toxicity of cocaine to the brain is dramatically different. The groups choosing to self-administer are much more likely to be able to cope with cocaine than the animals who are having it forced on them, even with the same dosages. When they looked at the brain physiology of these animals, one choosing the drug and the other being administered it, the basic metabolic, anatomical effects of the cocaine were radically different.

So even in a very simple animal experiment, the way cocaine affects the brain can be dramatically different just because of one small difference in the environment, in this example the ability to choose. It's not in the drug.

This breaks down that idea that if we know what the drug is, then we can know what effects it causes on the brain. In fact, we don't know anything about drug effects on the brain if we don't know the history of the organism and the social context. And if the social context and environment have such a huge influence in animals, you can imagine how influential social context and environment will be for the brains of human beings.

WH This relates to what I often see with psych drugs. Different people have very different side effects, even with the same drugs at the same dosage. We're told these are genetic differences, or size or body type, but my sense is people who are more empowered in their medication decisions tend to have fewer drug side effects than people who are less empowered.

This whole idea flies in the face of the popular understanding, which says something like, "A chemical has molecular properties that do something biologically, and this chemical mechanism leads to toxicity. Medication is a chemical and biological phenomenon; the brain is a physical object independent of environment that is shaped by chemical influences like drugs and medications. And that's all there is to it. "

You're saying that actually that's just not true? And not on some philosophical level, but on the level of provable, replicable laboratory studies on animals?

RD That's correct. Even in basic animal testing you can't predict response to a drug, whether short term or long term, just from the chemistry of the drug itself. You can say general things that will happen, like nervous system arousal or sedation, but even that can be very different from animal to animal.

Drugs aren't *inherently* addictive.

WH People can have very different responses to caffeine or alcohol, for example, which goes against the idea these drugs are simply stimulating or sedating.

RD What research studies usually do is look at common basic main variables about drugs. They don't usually consider other key variables such as social and environmental context. If they did, it would expose the weakness of general, simplistic descriptions of drug effects that describe effects caused simply by chemical interactions.

WH So such social factors as isolation, impoverishment, and choice are key to understanding drug effects, even in laboratory animals? The "brain effects" can't be really known independently from the environment?

RD That's right. If an animal is in a social environment, if it's not isolated, then it is less likely to self-administer a drug. And in for example monkey studies, if an animal is higher in a social hierarchy, then it is less likely to self-administer a drug. If the animal is provided with candy or some

Even in a very simple animal model, the way cocaine affects the brain can be dramatically different just because of one small difference in the environment.

other delight, it may choose it over drugs. There are many research studies that show how the so-called "possession power" or allure of a drug is not just simple pharmacology.

If we really want to get at the meaning of drug use and drug problems, we need to go to the social and historical roots. For example, cocaine and heroin were both widely used a century ago, with far fewer problems than they have today.

WH Your book is fascinating about the history of how the same drugs have been illegal, legal, or medicalized at different times.

RD Today heroin, cocaine, and marijuana are dramatically different than they were a century ago, because the things we *think* about them as a society have changed. As social expectations change, actual drug effects change dramatically as well.

There are many studies showing how a drug effects someone who doesn't know what drug it is they are taking. A person thinks they are given alcohol but aren't, or thinks they are injecting heroin but aren't, and the effects of the drug become different. Expectation around the drug seems to play at least as big a role as the pharmacology in explaining drug experience.

That even holds true for long-term withdrawal. There were studies where heroin addicts in residential housing were told, "If you have bad withdrawal symptoms, you don't need to work around the residence." Then they would tell a different group the opposite, "Even if you have bad withdrawal you still have to work." And as a result of the expectation, the physical withdrawal effects for each group were dramatically different, not just reported but actual physical effects, getting sick or not

Even in a basic animal model you can't predict response, whether short term or long term, just from the chemistry of the drug itself. You can say general things that will happen, like nervous system arousal or sedation.

for example. In a context where people expect to have severe withdrawal, then the actual physiology of the withdrawal will be more severe and more debilitating. In the opposite context, where the expectation is for mild withdrawal, then there will *physiologically* be more mild withdrawal.

WH One of your examples is opiates are used in hospital settings, where the withdrawal effects are much, much less than in street use.

RD Drugs are not *inherently* addictive. We're told today that "If you are exposed to morphine ongoing/chronically, your body will become dependent on it, and then you will experience all this withdrawal, and the withdrawal will drive you back into drug use." Those kinds of messages don't prove to be true.

I have a friend who heard about my book and my ideas about drugs and thought I was crazy. Then it happened that she went into the hospital and was put on chronic morphine, daily for three months. She was

The model of addiction as a disease is based on cartoon logic: supposedly if you expose the brain to drugs over a long enough period of time the brain, regardless of social environment, become dependent and addicted. No, that is just a cartoon.

worried the whole time that she'd be an addict when she left. But when she did finally leave the hospital she had no interest whatsoever in using opiates.

A more dramatic example is from the US War in Vietnam. There was a very high use of heroin and other opiates in Vietnam because they were so cheap and widely available, just like alcohol is available over here. The US government became paranoid that a huge addiction epidemic was coming, that all these soldiers would return home and bring their opiate addictions with them, and create new drug markets for heroin.

Researchers discovered that even former Vietnam soldiers who did seek out heroin when they returned home didn't tend to continue using it. There was a very low "re-addiction" rate. This totally contradicts the idea that if you are an addict you will continue to be an addict, you will seek drugs, etc.

Why didn't addicted soldiers continue to take heroin? Because the social environment where they were using heroin in Vietnam was so dramatically different from the social environment they came back to in the US. It's just like the patient leaving the hospital: they just didn't want to use those drugs when they came home. But if you send them back to Vietnam? They will gladly use them again.

WH Social context factors, such as poverty and oppression, are key to understanding addiction, but get covered over with reductionist claims of biological cause-and-effect. But are you saying a person's drug response is purely socially constructed? I certainly have seen completely diverse responses to the same drug.

RD There is no sharp distinction to be made between the brain/biological on the one hand, and the psychological on the other. Everything that is psychological is at the same time biological. Our thoughts and our feelings all have substrates in our brain, in our physiology, and in our biochemistry.

Scientific studies demonstrate again and again the power of expectation, even with prescription drugs like benzodiazepines, the so-called anti-anxiety drugs like Valium and Xanax which are extremely dependence-inducing and much more addictive than heroin. When a person thinks they are being taken off a drug their withdrawal is much worse than when they think they are still on it, whether in fact they are being taken off or not. To really understand the effect of taking a drug and the effect of withdrawal, we have to look at what people are thinking, what people are feeling, and the situation they are in socially.

> People believed stories about marijuana "possession" when marijuana was used by a sub-population. We say the same today about other drugs with other marginalized users, like meth and crack, while another dangerous drug, alcohol, isn't demonized because it is more mainstream.

WH And it's actually shown in studies, just by *telling* someone you are reducing their drug dosage, but not really reducing it, they will actually start to experience withdrawal effects?

RD That's right. That's true for benzodiazepines as well as for heroin. If you tell heroin addicts that they're going off the drug but you keep them on it at the same dose, they will nonetheless experience withdrawal. There are many studies showing people can have severe withdrawal just because they think they are being taken off a drug, even if they aren't, or very little withdrawal effects when they are still on a drug but are actually being taken off.

WH With heroin use, the risk of overdose is higher in an unfamiliar physical location, even with the exact same dosage, because expectation and social construction shape drug potency. Teaching users about this is a widely known harm reduction principle.

RD The same thing has been shown with cigarette smoking, incidentally. If you switch the cigarettes to very, very low nicotine or very, very high nicotine, there is not a very good correspondence between the nicotine level and the withdrawal experience. There are individual differences, always. But in general we see the belief system has very dramatic effects on drug experiences.

WH So addiction isn't a disease, it's a life situation, a history, and a whole human experience?

RD The model of addiction as a disease is based on cartoon logic: supposedly if you expose the brain to drugs over a long enough period of time then, regardless of social environment, the brain becomes dependent and addicted. No, that is just a cartoon. You cannot ever explain addiction by looking just at drug exposure *alone*.

WH So this helps explain why the same drug can be normalized, crim-

Studies show people can have severe withdrawal just because they *think* they are being taken off a drug, even if they aren't, or very little withdrawal effects because they think they are still on a drug, but are being taken off.

inalized, or medicalized at different times in history.

RD At the end of the nineteenth century, people used opiates, marijuana, and cocaine in a lot of elixirs and patent medicines over the counter. There were many people consuming the very same drugs back then that today we think of as demons. Cocaine and opiates were viewed then the way we view alcohol today. Today we see alcohol as a drug that's not perfect, a drug that may be addictive and risky for some, but is acceptable for most people.

And today we accept alcohol in part because of the diverse range of people that use it, just as back then a very diverse population used cocaine or opiates in these patent medicines and so they were accepted and not easy to demonize. But when alcohol was used largely by a targeted sub-population, Irish immigrants, we did demonize it, and we had Prohibition.

We see the same thing today if we look at crack cocaine use and street use of methamphetamine. Those drugs are easily demonized today because of who uses them.

WH In the case of marijuana, wasn't racism toward Mexicans part of making marijuana illegal?

RD There were strong stereotypes about Mexicans and blacks not being able to control themselves. You read this today and you think, "This is crazy, people actually believed marijuana would make you a rapist?" But that very idea was published in *The New York Times* and *Scientific American* the same way they publish stories today about methamphetamine and crack cocaine. People believed extreme stories about marijuana "possession" when marijuana was used by a sub-population. We say the same thing today about other drugs with other marginalized users, like meth and crack, while another dangerous drug, alcohol, isn't demonized because its use is more mainstream.

> **What if a person can't tell a medication side effect from the reason they are taking the medication in the first place?**

WH So demonizing some drugs is a way of scapegoating people with less power. How then should we look at psychiatric drugs, in your view?

RD We need to be better educated about the drugs we are taking, instead of just relying on a physician who says, "This is a magical substance, you can't really understand how it works and I'm the expert on who should take it and how much, and therefore... Here, take this."

Often with psychiatric drugs nobody is equipped to distinguish between the side-effects of the drug and the problems the person is taking the drug for in the first place. An example is the many individuals who take the SSRI antidepressants and then want to kill themselves. But what if a person can't tell a medication side effect from the reason they are taking the medication in the first place? They will have a very difficult time deciding if they should be given more or less of the drug. In many cases people are just given higher doses of the drugs supposedly to eliminate their "symptoms," but the symptoms are actually being produced by the drugs.

WH The same catch-22 is true of other psychiatric drugs as well.

RD Once the person is taking a drug, we sometimes forget what they were like before they went on it. How the person seems might not be their so-called mental illness, but the effects of the drug itself. The horror story of antipsychotic drugs is that we give up the humanity of the person for the side-effects of the drug they take. We lose sight of the many ways to intervene and manage psychological problems without drugs.

Once psychiatric drugs are involved, it makes a person's life story much more complicated to understand: you don't know what is the person and what is the drug. The person can sometimes get, along with their family and everyone around them, lost in the drug experience. ∎

Belief in Pills
David Cohen

David Cohen is a professor at UCLA. His co-authored books include *Challenging the Therapeutic State* (1990), *Your Drug May Be Your Problem* (2007), and *Mad Science: Psychiatric Coercion, Diagnosis, and Drugs* (2013). He created www.criticalthinkrx.org to reduce drugging of foster care children.

It's a myth that a substance's effects are wholly found within the substance. All human studies about drug effects show this, and this explains why results of studies vary so widely.

So what does account for drug effects? Studies show the personality of the helping professional goes a long way to explain whether a person finds a drug usefu or not , probably more than the drug itself. Regardless of whether the professional is a biological psychiatrist or a humanist, clients rate themselves as improved depending on common factors: the relationship, how the professional appears to them, how enthusiastic and sincere and hopeful the professional is, and how suitable the healing context appears. And the definition of "effective" is itself not an exact science.

Overall, if the helping professional truly believes in the treatment's worth, you will tend to feel better, or interpret your feelings as "improvement," whether you have been prescribed Zyprexa or marathon running.

Depending on context, beliefs, attitudes, and expectations, anything, *anything*, can work, including a placebo sugar pill or sham surgery. And remember that what "works" is itself a belief about "working." The idea of "needing" a drug is itself borrowed from medicine, where real bodily lesions are targeted, but makes little sense in "mental health" treatment, where the ultimate goal is changing your feelings and behavior.

But it's not just all in your mind or up the power of positive thinking. There has to be some palpable intervention so you feel something physically. We swallow the pill and then we feel something. But how do we interpret and appreciate, or not, what we feel? That depends largely on the social context. ∎

What Science Can't Tell Us
John Horgan

John Horgan is a science journalist and director of the Center for Science Writings at Stevens Institute of Technology. A former senior writer at *Scientific American* magazine, he has also written for *The New York Times*, *National Geographic*, *Time*, *Newsweek*, *The Washington Post*, and *Slate*. His books include *Rational Mysticism: Dispatches from the Border Between Science and Spirituality (2004)*, and *The Undiscovered Mind: How the Human Brain Defies Replication, Medication, and Explanation (2000)*.

Neuroscience still hasn't given us a unified theory of the brain or mind....you have almost an anti-progress: the more scientists study, the more confused they become about how the brain & mind work.

WILL HALL Your books *The Undiscovered Mind* and *Rational Mysticism* focus on what science can't tell us about ourselves and the limits of science. What about psychology?

JOHN HORGAN For example, you constantly have proclamations that Freud is dead, and claims that modern science shows Freudian theories of the mind don't work. But, obviously, if Freud were really dead, we wouldn't have to keep announcing that he's dead. In fact, his theories are just as believable as any other theory of the mind, in spite of all the progress of modern neuroscience and genetics.

WH How can that be? Don't today's neuroscience theories prove superior to the Victorian-era ideas of psychoanalysis?

JH In spite of all the progress of modern neuroscience, genetics, and all these other fields attempting to explain human behavior, there hasn't been a theory powerful enough to displace Freud once and for all. There certainly is a flood of data in neuroscientific research, and new powerful instruments of observation. We've uncovered all these neurotransmitters in the brain and discovered all these different genes that regulate the development of the brain. But neuroscience still hasn't given us a unified theory of the brain or mind.

Freud could successfully propose his unified theory of the mind and behavior a hundred years ago because there was so little real, hard, empirical data to contradict him. Nowadays any unified theory you propose would have to account for the tremendous variety of often contradictory findings about how the brain works. So you have almost an anti-progress: the more scientists study, the more confused they become about how the brain and mind work.

WH This is apparent in the media. Almost every day some new researcher makes a bid for fame by saying, "We've discovered that this gene plays a role in bipolar," or that "this neurotransmitter is behind a mental disorder." Then something totally different comes out the following week. And the following. The message is always "more research funding is needed, there's a breakthrough right around the corner."

JH This is especially true of psychopharmacology. Prozac and the whole class of SSRIs were supposed to represent a great step forward in treating depression based on neuroscience and brain research. Despite these claims, what the clinical drug trials actually show is that all these drugs aren't really any more effective at treating common disorders than the older class of presumably less scientific antidepressants, the tricyclics.

They also aren't any more effective than plain old psychotherapy, including psychoanalysis. So you have this impression of progress that's actually not in accord with what the clinical data show.

My critique of antidepressants was very controversial when *The Undiscovered Mind* came out in 1999, especially because I have lots of friends who are taking antidepressants and have sworn that they have made a tremendous difference in their lives.

WH People feel the drug works for them, and then they want to believe the science behind the drug is solid. It's like a self-mythology almost. So popular writer Malcolm Gladwell claimed in a 1999 *New Yorker* magazine essay that Ritalin isn't addictive; and Sigmund Freud even claimed in 1884 that cocaine isn't addictive.

JH A lot of people still swear by psychoanalysis, or cognitive behavioral therapy. Peter Kramer's book *Listening to Prozac* was a huge bestseller back in the early '90s, and helped create this wave of enthusiasm for Prozac and other antidepressants. As a science writer I have to go with what the data actually tell us. These drugs aren't some great step forward. I was absolutely hammered in the press for my views in 1999, and *The New York Times* review said my debunking of antidepressants was absurd. But today the studies have come more to light and this is more accepted. I was just ahead of the curve.

> I was absolutely hammered in the press for my views in 1999, and *The New York Times* said my debunking of antidepressants was absurd. But today the studies have come more to light and this is more accepted. I was just ahead of the curve.

WH Now at least we have *Scientific American* in 2009 comparing Ritalin to cocaine. It's hard to believe *Listening to Prozac* was such a bestseller, it posed the philosophical question, "Now that scientific breakthroughs like Prozac mean we can control our moods, what are the

implications of 'designer personalities?'" But that's asking a false question, because he swallowed the whole marketing message and phony scientific claims of Prozac's powers uncritically.

This gets to the issue of how drugs are effective. Tell us about the placebo effect.

JH The placebo effect is at the heart of the mind-body riddle. How does the mind influence the body? Physicians have always dismissed the placebo effect, and pill studies actually try to exclude people who respond well to placebo ("placebo washout"), but modern research shows that placebo is very real. For example there is very little difference between the response of people to antidepressants and to placebos. There's even a psychiatrist at Brown University who recommended that placebos should be the first line of treatment for people with mild to moderate depression, given that all psychiatric drugs have side effects.

> As a science writer I have to go to what the data actually tell us. These drugs aren't some great step forward.

There is a treatment that's been used for heart disease: the insertion of a stent into a cardiac artery. And someone thought, "Let's carry out a controlled study of this, and see how it holds up compared to placebo." So people who actually received stents were compared to those who simply had a surgical incision made in their chests, but nothing was actually inserted into it. And the people who just had the incision did just as well afterwards as those who actually had the stent inserted into their chests! In this case the procedure was immediately discontinued because everybody realized that the success rate was due entirely to the placebo effect.

WH And placebos work even on animals?

JH There was a study where researchers gave a bitter solution to rats, which contained a drug that made them very susceptible to various kinds of diseases.

They trained the rats to associate this bitter taste with the illness. Then when they gave them just the bitter solution, with no drug in it, more than half of the rats still got sick, and some even died. Their brains had trained them to expect they would become ill. So this isn't just some psychological, psychosomatic effect. It is very physiological and tangible and animals share it with us. There is a tremendous interest in placebo right now; particularly how the placebo effect is modulated by the immune system.

WH What about genetics? We're often told of the discovery of the schizophrenia gene or the bipolar gene is right around the corner. Some people even debate having children because of fears of genetic inheritance that has no basis in science.

JH Starting in the late '80s there was a wave of claims about specific genes for alcoholism, schizophrenia, manic depression, compulsive behavior, and male homosexuality. I started gathering material for a big article on it for *Scientific American*. And what I found was that, in every one of these cases, you had an initial paper that was announced with great fanfare in *Nature* or *Science* or some major journal. And then there would be all this other publicity, with *The New York Times* running a whole series of front-page articles on these findings. In every case, follow-up studies would fail to corroborate the initial research. But you wouldn't read about those failures to corroborate.

It was all based on a false premise. In every case, you never get the kind of corroboration that you need to be sure that the claims are correct.

WH Why is there's such enthusiasm for genetic explanations?

JH Genetic explanations of human behavior are assumed to be associated with the right wing and with the Nazis. But the eugenics movement originally, in the late 19th and early 20th centuries, was heavily populated with intellectual liberals who thought that eugenics was the future liberation of humanity. So eugenics has been mainstream all along.

Recently, genetic explanations of mental illness are seen as a way of absolving parents from blame. And some gay activists embrace genetic explanations to defend against the idea that homosexuality is just a choice.

So genetic explanations are attractive to all sorts of different groups. But I keep coming back to the science. Is the science there? So far, it isn't.

WH Blaming genetics for obesity is certainly a way to hide the economic interests behind poverty, food, and lifestyle. But what do you make of identical twins studies for mental illness?

If you looked at these Minnesota twin studies more closely, you find some of the twins supposedly separated at birth actually had contact throughout their lives. Some had incentives for exaggerating strange coincidences, and some of them were getting movie deals. These kinds of stories led to a false picture of the role of genes in our lives.

JH I looked very closely at twin studies done by the University of Minnesota. They've published some of these astonishing claims, which make it sound as though genes determine virtually everything that we are. In one case, you had these two guys who had been raised by different families in different states. But they both ended up as firemen. They both ended up married to women with the same name. They both named their kids with the same names. They had dogs that had the same names. They both liked Budweiser. All this crazy stuff.

This is just wonderful fodder, again, for science writers, but to me the message is very creepy, just the worst kind of genetic determinism. It suggests that genes don't give us just the general propensities for behavior; they determine our lives in every particular.

What I discovered was that if you looked at these Minnesota twin studies more closely, you find some of the twins supposedly separated at birth actually had contact throughout their lives. Some had incentives for exaggerating strange coincidences, and some of them were getting movie deals. These kinds of stories led to a false picture of the role of genes in our lives.

WH Babies seem to have some intrinsic temperament. But the question is, how does it express itself? Someone may have vulnerability, sensitivity, openness, or creativity as part of their personality at birth. But is it genetic, or a result of the mother's environment, or trans-generational? Whether it turns into something that's socially defined as schizophrenia or manic depression depends on many intermediary factors.

JH The nature/nurture debate is so old. And it's always the same answer: there's a complex interaction between genes and the environment. Genetic determinists are holding sway in science right now, but environment is just as important as ever.

WH Determinism used to see genes as a blueprint, but that is no longer true. In the recent theory of epigenetics, genes can be turned off and on by the environment. And acquired traits can even be inherited, in defiance of what we have believed about Darwin being right and Lamarck being wrong.

JH The apparently linear process of DNA becoming proteins in a developing organism has really fallen apart. The interactions of genes are just immensely complicated. This explains why simplistic genetic explanations of human behavior have failed. And why genetic therapies for disease have been a disaster so far. Things are much more complicated than anybody had expected. That's a real paradigm shift within genetics right now.

WH The "Decade of The Brain" campaign was great marketing for research careers and pharmaceutical companies, but a bust scientifically. And the mapping of the human genome didn't unlock the key to curing diseases.

The confusion is between what is the brain and what is the mind. There is a correlate with biology, and a correlate with chemicals and electricity, happening in the brain. If you cut off someone's brain the mind goes. But then again, if you unplug a TV the program goes off, but that doesn't mean you can understand a TV show by analyzing electrical circuits. There's something about the mind that is irreducible to the brain. That's the real question when we're talking about mental health, or psychiatry.

JH Australian philosopher David Chalmers calls this "the hard problem," explaining the mind and subjective experience, sometimes called qualia by philosophers, in physical terms. On the one side you've got neurons and brain components like the amygdala and the frontal cortex: physical objects and physical processes. And, on the other side, you have perception and memory and emotion: subjective constituents of our minds. The question is how do you go from these physical components and processes to these subjective phenomena? And this is an ancient question; it reaches back to the ancient Greeks.

This is the "explanatory gap": the gap between the physical and the mental. It's the most complex problem that scientists have ever tried to solve. It makes particle physics look like a child's game.

WH And the brain is extremely plastic, neurons are shaping themselves, changing, dying, growing and making new pathways. That's very different from the idea of a straightforward DNA strand blueprint.

JH That's right. In some sense, the neural code of each of us must be unique, must be shaped by our unique experiences and our unique physiology. And not only that, but our neural code changes constantly, in response to new experiences. So neuroscientists are chasing a moving target

On the other hand, there have been some tremendous practical advances. You've probably read about those experiments where monkeys and humans have chips implanted in their brains that can detect neural signals which are then used to move a cursor on a computer, or control robotic arm?

The eugenics movement originally was heavily populated with intellectual liberals who thought that eugenics was the future liberation of humanity. Eugenics has been mainstream all along.

WH I have read about those studies, and they frighten me. I don't think these are just efforts to improve the lives of people with disabilities!

JH The major sponsor of this research, right now, is the Pentagon. The Pentagon clearly has an interest in cra-

In claims about specific genes for alcoholism, schizophrenia, manic depression, compulsive behavior, and male homo-sexuality, follow-up studies would fail to corroborate the initial finding. But you wouldn't read about those failures to corroborate.

zy science fiction possibilities like cyborg soldiers. I've been told by people at the Defense Advanced Research Project Agency that's precisely what they're interested in. So you should be frightened... ∎

The Gene Illusion
Jay Joseph

Jay Joseph, PsyD, is author of *The Gene Illusion: Genetic Research in Psychiatry and Psychology Under the Microscope* (2004), *The Missing Gene: Psychiatry, Heredity, And the Fruitless Search for Genes* (2006), and *The Trouble with Twin Studies: A Reassessment of Twin Research in the Social and Behavioral Sciences* (2014). (This essay is drawn from his previous writing.)

The failure to find genes in psychiatry and psychology is now decades old. Buried in the avalanche of sensational claims reported in the media, we find more realistic evaluations by prominent molecular genetic researchers. In 2005 Kenneth Kendler wrote, "The strong, clear, and direct causal relationship implied by the concept of 'a gene for ...' does not exist for psychiatric disorders. Although we may wish it to be true, we do not have and are not likely to ever discover 'genes for' psychiatric illness." Stephen Faraone and his colleagues observed in 2008, "It is no secret that our field has published thousands of candidate gene association studies but few replicated findings."

In a 2009 article published in the *Journal of the American Medical Association*, molecular genetic researcher Neil Risch and his colleagues recognized the failure of gene-finding efforts in psychiatry and psychology. He wrote "Despite progress in risk gene identification for several complex diseases, few disorders have proven as resistant to robust gene finding as psychiatric illnesses."

Although these disorders have long been assumed to result from some combination of genetic vulnerability and environmental exposure, direct evidence from a specific example has not been forthcoming. In a 2010 article published in the prestigious journal *Science*, three Nobel Prize winning researchers and their colleagues recognized the "frustrating lack of progress" in understanding the genetics of mental disorders.

Although most researchers continue to believe that genes do exist and await discovery, commentators Jonathan Latham and Allison Wilson of the Bioscience Research Project concluded in 2010 that the "dearth of disease-causing genes is without question a scientific discovery of tremendous significance" and that, on the basis of this discovery, "most disease, most of the time, is essentially environmental in origin." A 2012 study, co-authored by many of the world's leading schizophrenia molecular genetic researchers, examined 732 previously identified "hypothesis- driven candidate genes" for schizophrenia. The researchers found no association between these previously identified genes and schizophrenia. They concluded that their negative results "suggest, but do not prove, that many traditional ideas about the genetic basis of schizophrenia may be incorrect," and that "it is possible that the next few years will lead to marked changes in major hypotheses about the genetic basis of schizophrenia."

And *DSM* Chair David Kupfer of American Psychiatric Association said, "In the future, we hope to be able to identify disorders using biological and genetic markers....Yet this promise, which we have anticipated since the 1970s, remains disappointingly distant. We've been telling patients for several decades that we are waiting for biomarkers. We're still waiting." In their assessment of decades of unsuccessful gene finding efforts, most researchers choose to emphasize optimism and deemphasize failure. As Latham and Wilson observed, "The history of scientific refutation...is that adherents of established theories construct ever more elaborate or unlikely explanations to fend off their critics."

A recent example of this optimism is a 2010 article by psychiatric geneticists Hudziak and Faraone, who wrote, "Genetic research on developmental psychopathology has grown exponentially, as reflected not only in the number of published papers but also in the power of molecular genetic and statistical technologies. Although we are only in the infancy of our field, the pathway to discovery is clear. One can only imagine the incredible progress that will be made in the next decades."

Instead of emphasizing that the findings of these published papers were not replicated, their view implies that the number of published papers *itself* constitutes scientific progress. Psychiatric geneticists have been saying this for 30 years. Rather than being in its infancy, molecular genetic studies of psychiatric disorders have produced an important finding: the genetic basis of these disorders appears to have been refuted. ■

Trauma, Not Illness
Jacqui Dillon

Jacqui Dillon is the chair of the UK Hearing Voices Network, and co-editor of *Living with Voices: 50 Stories of Recovery* (2013), *Demedicalising Misery: Psychiatry, Psychology and the Human Condition* (2011), and *Models of Madness: Psychological, Social, and Biological Approaches to Psychosis* (2004).

A new and profoundly important paradigm for understanding overwhelming emotional pain has emerged over the last few years. It has the potential to change the way we conceptualize human suffering across the whole spectrum of mental health difficulties. It is based on scientific evidence, and substantiates what many individuals with first-hand experience of mental health problems have always known: when bad things happen to you they can drive you mad.

I am not mentally ill. Never was, never have been, never will be. I am a survivor of abuse. I have had a perfectly natural response to serious trauma. To name my response as an illness is offensive.

We spend too much time talking about illness and what's going on in peoples' brains and not enough time on what's gong on in people's lives.

Trauma recovery means that accepting support is not a sign of weakness. Accepting support is an act of courage, a commitment to life, and a belief in the future.

When trauma is perpetuated by people we trusted and depended upon, society makes us ask "what's wrong with me?" Growing up, the only safe place was in my head, and imagination. Part of healing is developing a different relationship with the voices. The journey to recovery means believing that I am deeply lovable. I want the question instead to be "what *happened* to me?"

I've had to fight tooth and nail for recovery, but I am one of the lucky ones. ∎

Ecology Of Madness
Will Hall

How mind, body, and society interact is a mystery I've struggled with my whole life: I've never achieved personal change without change in my relationships and community.

Today I believe humans are fundamentally ecological: a single fabric of food, relationships, oppression, society, spirit, and environment weaves our physical bodies together.

San Francisco in the 1990s: doctors recommended medication for HIV positive people as a way to prevent AIDS. The pills, AZT, were highly toxic (and highly profitable), and many people who died in the AIDS epidemic were, in fact, killed by the drugs that doctors prescribed them.

I had a friend who was HIV positive, and took me to a conference on "psychoneuroimmunology." Speakers recommended alternatives to AZT to prevent AIDS holistically, and I had an epiphany. What if the madness I was suffering, diagnosed as schizophrenia and pronounced uncurable, meant my own immune system needed healing? The hospital prescribed medications and therapy. What if I tried holistic health instead?

Tests showed I had allergies to milk and chocolate, and I realized: on the inpatient ward every meal came with two paper cartons of chocolate milk. I was very interested in that milk. I would drink it and drink it, trading my desserts with other patients for even more milk, all the milk I could get. They had a nickname for me in the hospital, they called me the "choco-meister."

Do people crave foods they are allergic to? The doctor told me yes, and so I asked, "What are some of the symptoms?" He rattled off a long list of reactions, and when he got to "depression," "anxiety," and "neurological problems" my eyes widened. I swore off milk and chocolate.

I started connecting more dots. Today I believe humans are fundamentally ecological: a single fabric of food, relationships, oppression, society, spirit, and environment weaves our physical bodies together. I've seen acupuncturists for years, stopped eating gluten and sugar, went to a homeopath, had my mercury dental fillings removed, started taking EFA and probiotics and vitamin B, and learned yoga and meditation. After 15 years I finally got off disability payments and left my mental illness identity behind. My life changed.

I'm also sure I wasted a lot of what little money I had. Looking back, the turning points for me actually weren't learning about psychoneuroimmunology, changing my diet, getting allergy tests or taking supplements. The key moments were the connections I made, the risks I took to form friendships, the steps to overcome isolation, and all the ways I gradually learned to take back power in my life.

Can holistic treatments such as food, supplements, naturopathic doctors, acupuncturists, even medical cannabis, make a difference for mental health? Of course they can. Does poor diet, driven by poverty, play a key role in mental distress? Absolutely. Physical health conditions are well known to cause emotional problems; lack of vitamin D or vitamin B can cause depression, for example, and there is growing research on the connections betweeen food, mind, and gut health. But no psychiatric diagnosis has ever been shown to always result from any biological imbalances. Yes gluten allergies, for example, are more prevalent in some people diagnosed with schizophrenia. But not all. Poverty is also more prevalent. Each person is unique.

Chronic infection, toxic exposure, pain, hormone imbalance, nutritional deficiency, thyroid conditions, adrenal fatigue… they all can lie behind a mental illness. I'm glad I had the privilege to get my health treated, and lived in a state where Medicare paid for acupuncture. The high sugar, processed and chemicalized standard American diet does make many people sick: everyone should have access to healthy food and holistic healthcare.

What if my diagnosis of schizophrenia meant my own immune system was in need of healing?

But for me there were also just as many years of holistic health with no effect as there were with treatments that seemed to work. At the same time I was seeking holistic options, I also retreated from a stressful lifestyle, stood up to my abusers, cultivated close friendships, embraced spirituality, organized my community, and dedicated myself to meaningful work: maybe that set the stage for holistic treatments to take effect?

Some of us, myself included, credit part of our recovery to diet changes and holistic health. These certainly make healthier brains, but is brain health the answer for everyone? Is brain health determined by food and vitamins, or shaped by social context? Why do so many people who follow holistic health plans still suffer from mental illness? If holistic health is the key to bipolar, schizophrenia, OCD, or psychosis, why do I keep meeting people spending money on holistic treatments or making food changes who haven't gotten better?

And when a specific person does respond to a more holistic view, what is it that makes the difference? Is it physical body changes? Or the act of choice

Maybe the most important benefit holistic health gave me was the faith to question mainstream treatments.

and empowerment? Does the change make a difference, or the deeper attitude of making a change? The placebo effect? A trusting relationship with a provider? Being part of a community that encourages empowerment? Gaining confidence to speak your own truth?

And maybe the most important thing holistic health gave me was the faith to question authority. Even when fish oil, gluten free cooking, and homeopathy don't work, they don't kill people. Navane and lithium do. My HIV-positive friend who took me to the holistic conference is alive today, with a strong immune system and a healthy diet, and no AZT. Many others are dead, after they did what mainstream doctors told them to do. ∎

Community Acupuncture
Lee Entel Hurter

Lee Entel Hurter was a main organizer with Freedom Center, directed its free acupuncture clinic, and went on to become a licensed acupuncturist. Lee is now based in Denver, Colorado.

Getting stuck in the ears with needles may not be the first thing we think to do during an episode of trauma, mania, or depression. Maybe it should be, though.

I ran the Freedom Center's weekly acupuncture clinic, one of the first of its kind anywhere. We gave many hundreds of people entirely free treatments, and I've seen firsthand the benefits for insomnia, addiction, mania, depressed states, and trauma, as well as psychiatric drug withdrawal. Sometimes acupuncture feels subtle, while other times it breathes life back into an emotionally drowning person. You can become more grounded in your body, feel like you stand taller, and maintain a deep, peaceful state of mind.

The NADA (National Acupuncture Detoxification Association) protocol is simple: 5 needles in ear points corresponding to organ meridians, administered in a drop-in, group setting. Treatment is anonymous, silent, and in a circle, which can feel safer than talking with a counselor about traumatic events or meeting one-on-one with a professional.

One example of acupuncture's power is Jenafer Andren. After sleeping pills, psychotherapy, and Baystate Medical Center failed to help her insomnia, she came to the Freedom Center clinic. In a local newspaper cover story, Jenafer told the *Hampshire Gazette* newspaper, "I don't have to take naps anymore, I don't have meltdowns, where I'm so tired I start crying. My overall health is so much better."

As acupuncture becomes more mainstream, many professionals have made it an expensive, elitist "boutique" treatment. A community approach is vital now more than ever, so that the benefits of traditional and holistic Chinese medicine can be accessed by all. ■

Is Shyness a Mental Disorder?
Christopher Lane

Christopher Lane is a professor of literature at Northwestern University and author of *Shyness: How Normal Behavior Became a Sickness* (2008), editor of *The Psychoanalysis of Race* (1998), and co-editor of *Homosexuality and Psychoanalysis* (2001).

Shyness in the 1950s was often prized as a virtue. It was seen as appropriate bashfulness and modesty.

WILL HALL How did a professor of literature get interested in shyness and psychiatric disorders?

CHRISTOPHER LANE Many of the students I teach are on medication for relatively mild problems that earlier generations dealt with quite differently. I wrote a book on what the Victorians thought about antisocial behavior, so the question for me became, Are medications being used today to eliminate a large range of emotions? That led me to the American Psychiatric Association archives to determine exactly why 112 new disorders were added to the third edition of the diagnostic Bible, the *DSM*, in 1980. The statute of limitations on many behind-the-scenes documents had just expired, and what I found was quite disturbing.

WH What did you discover?

CL The most extreme was a proposal (mercifully unapproved) for something called "chronic complaint disorder," which aimed to pathologize people who grumble about the weather, taxes, or even race track results. The claim was a person with this disorder would say "oy vey" and "inflict their persistent and consistent complaining in a high-pitched whining fashion, which is especially noxious to the listener." Other proposals which got a lot more discussion were for "chronic undifferentiated unhappiness disorder," and "social phobia," which included symptoms such as "fear of eating alone in restaurants," "concern about hand trembling when one is writing a check," "and avoidance of public toilets or restrooms." Those criteria are still in the *DSM*.

The *DSM* writing process was tilted towards psychiatrists already predisposed to biological explanations. Isaac Marks, emeritus at the University of London and a world-renowned expert on anxiety, described it as consensus arranged by leaving out the dissenters. Those who disagreed were not invited to subsequent meetings.

WH You are describing a very political, not scientific, process, back room deals and negotiations of prestige and reputations, all under the influence of the pharmaceutical companies.

CL *DSM-5* co-chair Darrel Regier says they made mistakes in the past but today are only dealing with science. It sounds great, but simply isn't true.

Robert Spitzer, the main architect and designer of *DSM-III* who got 112 new disorders classified, told me that if a drug company is pressing the FDA to approve a new drug, there is a sort of synergy between that drug company promotion and the ease with which a new disorder can enter the diagnostic manual.

For example, Eli Lilly needed to extend its patent on Prozac and continue to profit. So it relabeled the drug as Sarafem and pressed to get "premenstrual dysphoric disorder" in the *DSM-IV* so doctors could prescribe it. Sarafem is basically a lavender-colored version of Prozac. Millions of dollars were spent in advertising to promote that disorder. There

Two-thirds of patient support groups are funded by drug companies. They recruit photogenic members to address the media, and anyone who challenges them is told "you're denying my suffering!"

actually was a big fight over that inclusion, with resignations from major *DSM* committees.

WH Tell us about shyness and "social anxiety disorder."

CL Shyness in the 1950s was often prized as a virtue. It was seen as appropriate bashfulness and modesty. I don't want to idealize shyness; there are all kinds of problems associated with it, particularly for women. But there has been a massive shift in the way that we *think* about shyness.

Shyness is an extremely common personality trait. There's a 50% chance that anyone will consider themselves shy or identify as such. I discovered that the symptoms for "social phobia" overlap so closely with shyness that they are almost interchangeable. Astonishingly, some of the *DSM* discussions about how to diagnose social phobia actually centered on whether people took their cars to work or preferred public transportation, whether they were avoiding other people or the car was simply more convenient because you had a bad commute. Mind boggling!

So the whole definition of the disorder totally overlaps with a very common behavioral trait. GlaxoSmithKline spent over $93 million in one year on a public awareness campaign to encourage people and especially doctors to re-label shyness as "social anxiety disorder." Not a campaign for their drug directly, they wanted people to second-guess themselves and question whether ordinary shyness was in fact a disorder. They put questionnaires up on the

DSM-5 co-chair Darrel Regier says they made mistakes in the past but today are only dealing with science. It sounds great, but simply isn't true.

web and distributed brochures, where people could check on a scale 1 to 5: "Are you anxious about people in authority"? "Do you dislike going to parties alone?" "Do you dislike speaking in front of your colleagues at work?" Then if you have enough checks, you are supposed to go to your doctor and say, "It looks like this is what I'm suffering from."

WH And this direct-to-consumer advertising is new?

CL In 1997 the FDA relaxed its rules, and pharmaceutical company advertising went from $595 to $843 million. Then by the year 2000 it averaged $2.5 billion. Today it's estimated at well over $5 billion annually.

WH And as advertising spending goes up, so do diagnosis and prescriptions?

> GlaxoSmithKline spent over $93 million in one year on a public awareness campaign to encourage people and especially doctors to re-label shyness as "social anxiety disorder."

CL Absolutely. And now the real "growth area" is bipolar disorder. Antipsychotics or neuroleptics prescribed for bipolar disorder are still on patent and are major revenue-earners for the drug companies. Drug companies have been trying to link bipolar disorder with depression and say that you need a drug that will meet both problems. It's entirely due to pushing the drugs still on patent: they are the money-makers.

The shift to sell neuroleptic antipsychotics is very cynical. Joseph Biederman of Harvard Medical School, in promoting "pediatric bipolar," is indirectly responsible for putting two-year-old children on these drugs, many of whom have died, such as Rebecca Riley who died at age 4; she had been prescribed Seroquel, Depakote, and Clonidine since age 2. Biederman hid his significant pharmaceutical consulting income while he was writing articles and appearing in the media promoting his idea of pediatric bipolar. What is a four-year-old doing being prescribed very dangerous drugs never approved for the treatment of childhood bipolar disorder?

WH What else did you discover about marketing shyness?

CL A public awareness campaign called "Imagine Being Allergic to Other People," showed a young man staring into a teacup saying how alone he felt. There was a 1-800 number to call, but no indication the ad was paid for by a drug company. GlaxoSmithKline had been sponsoring a group called "Freedom From Fear" to do the campaign; it was set up by Madison Avenue-based PR company Cohn and Wolfe, which has clients from VISA to Hilton Hotels.

WH So GlaxoSmithKline was posing as a charity?

CL Two-thirds of patient support groups are funded by drug companies. They recruit photogenic members to address the media, and anyone who challenges them is told "you're denying my suffering," or "you are minimizing a very serious condition." They are directly financed to rebut any criticism of overmedication and diagnosis.

WH Suffering becomes a human shield to exempt you from criticism.

CL Some people chafe when they hear they have bought into a certain perception; the economics behind all this, though, is very real. Labels can be comforting and reassuring, and we need to remember that suffering does exist. But the question is how do we interpret it? As a mental or psychiatric condition? Or, as in the case of shyness, as a relatively benign behavioral trait that some people even enjoy as an eccentricity or quirk, simply a feature of their personality.

And when people do find behavior limiting, there are a huge number of non-psychiatric ways of addressing it. I'm often contacted by concerned parents, and I recommend a book called *The Shy Child* by Philip Zimbardo, written before Prozac, Zoloft, Effexor and Paxil came on the market. It is packed with great advice about how to draw someone out if they are introverted and how to encourage them to participate. It's important that you don't label; you don't represent it as a crisis, you don't make someone more self-conscious by saying "this is the defining feature of your personality."

Joseph Biederman of Harvard Medical School, in promoting "pediatric bipolar," is indirectly responsible for putting two-year-old children on these drugs, many of whom have died, such as Rebecca Riley who died at age 4; she had been prescribed Seroquel, Depakote, and Clonidine since age 2.

WH What about people who feel helped by psych drugs?

CL 80% of Paxil's effectiveness has been shown to be due to placebo alone. Of course that leaves the remaining 20%, but on the basis of clinical trials, with the side effects and discontinuation problems factored in, none of these antidepressants should have received FDA approval.

Glaxo even sent around an internal, confidential memo warning that 20% of patients in Paxil trials were experiencing quite severe withdrawal symptoms, which it didn't tell the FDA about. Paxil is unique as an anticholinergic as well as an antidepressant, which means it affects the central nervous system (CNS) and brain's fight-or-flight responses. The drug presents a false neuronal picture to the central nervous system, and brain receptors assume that they are in less demand, and down-regulate. When people come off the drug, there aren't sufficient receptors in the brain to cope. So people cycle through really extreme moods.

There is a lot of litigation surrounding Paxil. There are Paxil withdrawal cases going through courts right now about high levels of suicide, obsession with suicide, aggression and anxiety. Physiological effects from the drug include risk of stroke, renal failure, blood platelet aggregation problems... And you realize, wait, this drug is being prescribed for people who feel anxious about going to parties, who dislike eating alone in restaurants.

WH Wasn't Paxil promoted in the wake of 9/11?

CL Just a month after the World Trade Center attacks, GlaxoSmithKline ran TV ads featuring a woman saying, "I keep fearing that something awful is going to happen." So of course there was a spike in prescriptions for "generalized anxiety disorder," which, as *DSM* Task Force chair Robert Spitzer confirmed to me in an interview, is a *DSM* catch-all for everything that couldn't go elsewhere.

WH How did the *DSM* even get started?

CL The first *DSM* from 1952 evolved out of a number of military memos from US Armed Forces psychiatrists who had observed behavior that they categorized as "passive aggressive." Servicemen in the Second World War, and then in the Korean War, who were not following orders to the satisfaction of their officers became the basis for "passive aggressive person-

The way we think about illness underwent massive transformation. We've gone from saying "you are anxiously neurotic about certain things" to saying "you are a person with social anxiety disorder."

ality disorder." The APA took that and reproduced it verbatim in *DSM-I* and *DSM-II*, the first two editions. They started diagnosing civilians, in particular housewives who were "procrastinating and dawdling over the laundry and doing the shopping," language that is still in the *DSM*.

The one person in charge of *DSM-II*, Sir Aubrey Lewis, made a key change. He deleted the word "reaction" from a number of the descriptions. Previously you had "schizophrenic reaction," or "paranoid reaction," and so on, based on particular responses to key life events that happened. One word was deleted and it became simply "paranoia."

WH So looking at context is erased by the stroke of a pen.

CL It becomes an ontology: "your condition." An illness that then defines you rather than a behavior to which you might be susceptible under various conditions of stress. The way we think about illness underwent massive

Physiological effects include risk of stroke, renal failure, blood platelet aggregation problems... And you realize, wait, this drug is being prescribed for people who feel anxious about going to parties, who dislike eating alone in restaurants.

transformation. We've gone from saying "you are anxiously neurotic about certain things" to saying, "you are a person with social anxiety disorder."

WH It's incredible how this one book shapes culture so dramatically.

CL And it's done in secret: committees sign a confidentiality agreement not to circulate drafts of proposals, working notes, minutes, or how votes went. There is now a limit of $10,000 for income from the drug companies. The *Washington Post* actually determined that *every* expert working on the *DSM* criteria for depression had ties to a pharmaceutical company. More than half of those working on the remaining disorders had similarly compromising ties. Basically the profession has generated an insurmountable conflict of interest.

WH The regulation of the medical industry has been captured by the people it's supposed to be regulating.

CL Absolutely and regrettably so. ∎

Autism Liberation
Ari Ne'eman

Ari Ne'eman, the founding president of the Autism Self Advocacy Network, is diagnosed on the autism spectrum and involved with disability policy nationally.

We don't believe in recovery for autism. It's trying to make us something that we are not.

WILL HALL How are you challenging "normal" and medical treatments to make people conform to mainstream standards?

ARI NE'EMAN When I was twelve I was diagnosed with Asperger's Syndrome, a form of autism. There is huge diversity among people, but common to autism is difficulty with social communication and perception, fixated or focused interests, as well as repetitive behaviors. When you have difficulty interpreting nonverbal communication such facial expressions, you can miss out on important aspects of a conversation that are more than just words being exchanged. Metaphors, social niceties, and nonverbal behaviors are all a second language to me.

So I was and still am very much out of step with what is considered normal behavior or interests. Small talk and other forms of social communication, which are often less substantive but crucial to succeeding in the social world, were a very significant challenge for me. After a great deal of effort I did pick up these skills, but one always prefers to communicate with others who understand your personal perspective. That's why it is so important for young adults with autism to connect with the larger autistic community.

WH That's interesting to think of relating to "normal" people as relating to a different culture and learning a second language.

AN There are also advantages to being on the autism spectrum. Focused thinking, categorization, and specific interests have proven to be very helpful, especially in fields like engineering and economics. My focus was always public policy, and I was very different from other students: I was the one kid bringing in the newspaper to read in second grade. I faced tremendous bullying and difficulties with peers and teachers just because we had a hard time understanding each other. It was also assumed that my diagnosis or disability meant opportunities for high level success, like going to college or having a career, wouldn't be available to me. But I wanted to have the same opportunities as those in the mainstream, so I had to fight against perceptions and expectations.

When I entered high school I was bussed an hour and a half north to an out-of-district school that was very academically inferior to the local school five minutes away. It was more a daycare than an academic setting. That was the expectation for kids with neurological differences.

It's common for other people to tell you they know your needs better than you do. That is very dangerous.

WH My own out-of-normal-range behavior got me put into a "special" grade five classroom, but luckily I was returned to a regular class. So you were segregated from other students and denied opportunities you really needed and deserved, all in the name of treatment?

AN Across a broad range of disabilities it's common for other people to tell you they know your needs better than you do. That is very dangerous. The message of the disability rights movement is "nothing about us without us" and there is a reason for that. I had to fight to get the education to unlock the future I wanted, and it was a very difficult process. But what is more

Metaphors, social niceties, and nonverbal behaviors are all a second language to me.

frightening is that many people absorb and internalize the idea that they are inferior. That's very damaging to people's potential.

WH The similarities with mental health are clear. Was there an effort to train you to become more normal, was that part of the special schooling?

AN Yes. In autism treatment there is a tremendous focus on behavior, and when I say behavior I'm not just talking disruptive behavior or objectively problematic behavior, but behavior in general, when that behavior is viewed by society as not socially optimal or normal. I was told very often "Ari, you need to start looking people in the eyes. You shouldn't concentrate on your interests. You need to learn to engage." Yes there is an advantage to understanding these things, just as there is an advantage to teaching people English as a second language when they are in an English speaking country. But there is a huge difference between teaching someone how to communicate in the standard way and teaching that way as the *only* way.

I remember being told in social skills classes, "When people are happy they smile like this." They would show a very broad, kind of stereotypical smile. Actually people don't ever look like that. Teaching the social via hard and fast rules of behavior, as opposed to the reasons behind behavior, has limits. It often actually worsens people's ability to understand the world around them.

WH So do we learn a second language to gain access to mainstream culture and enrich ourselves, or do we learn a second language to denigrate our first language and get rid of the culture we come from? That's why we are the ones who should be designing programs intended to help us: we understand the difference.

What about people whose experiences with autism are different than yours, such as people who don't have your verbal ability?

AN Autism is incredibly diverse, and no one individual can speak for the entire spectrum. The Autistic Self Advocacy Network has many different kinds of people involved. Often autistic people who have trouble communicating are presumed to be "low functioning;" I don't like that terminology, I think it feeds into a hierarchy that is often self-fulfilling. Or we are seen as unintelligent, and presumed to have no potential, and even considered to not be aware of the world around us. But in reality no effort is being put into empowering us.

When people are given the ability to communicate, including through augmentative and alternative communication and assistive technology, it becomes very clear: they have a tremendous amount of potential. They have definite opinions about the world around them and about how they want to be treated. Augmented and alternative communication is a civil rights issue.

WH What kinds of technology?

AN Such as the picture exchange communication system, pointing to images, or something more developed like the keyboard and voice synthesizers people see Stephen Hawking use. An assistant who understands social communication and can translate for the person is also helpful.

Sometimes oral speech difficulties come up in times of high stress, so there is growing attention to autistic adults and children getting into tragic misunderstandings with law enforcement officers because of traits such as not looking people in the eye or acting in socially inappropriate ways. That's also a parallel with the mental health community.

> **There is a huge difference between teaching someone how to communicate in the standard way and teaching that way as the *only* way.**

WH What about the biological basis for a diagnosis of autism? Autism findings in genetics are as equally inconclusive as for schizophrenia, but the politics are very different from the mad movement.

AN Most of us agree with the scientific community that autism is neurological in origin: we agree that our brains are different. Where we don't agree with many professionals is on how we should respond to our difference. We don't see anything wrong in being different. We might need different educational services, for example, but that is just reflective of the diversity of our society. We don't think there is any more problem with neurological diversity than any other kind of diversity. We are striving for equality of opportunity, the opportunity to be successfully employed, to succeed in living in our communities, and to have all the same opportunities as any "neurotypical" person.

WH Yet the language of biological brain difference in psychiatric diagnosis has historically gone along with expecting change to be impossible, that recovery can't happen. It becomes a self fulfilling prophecy, and people become disempowered.

The message of the disability rights movement is "nothing about us without us" and there is a reason for that.

AN In the autism community we don't believe in recovery for autism. This idea of recovery, that we need to be fixed and that we can grow out of it, has been heavily pushed by parents. It's trying to make us something that we are not. The difficulty isn't the autism label, the difficulty is the stigma attached to that label.

WH With bipolar and schizophrenia, parent advocates funded by pharmaceutical companies have been on the other side, opposing the possibility of recovery for years. Patient activism changed that. The parent-child conflict is familiar though.

AN Just like the gay rights movement, the neurodiversity movement needs to teach the world to stop looking at us as broken people in need of fixing. It's a problem to turn us against who we are. I think this is one part of the broader civil rights advocacy that our society needs.

WH **The question around madness becomes, How can we reject dehumanizing medicalization, and celebrate and embrace differences, while also opening the door to change and recovery? I do want to overcome some limits in my life caused by mental difference, just as you want people with autism to have communication support and educational opportunities. But some difference needs to be accepted and accommodated, such as being gay, shy, deaf, or passionate, hearing voices, or having visionary states.**

AN People with autism do face severe problems that aren't just a result of discrimination. I encourage professionals to take a neurodiversity framework, and ask whether a particular behavior or trait objectively causes difficulty, such as self-injury, or if the trait is only a difficulty because how society views it. Sequencing behavior (lining things up), having focused interests (which is in our minds actually one of our biggest strengths), not looking people in the eyes... these things are socially stigmatized, not objective problems.

WH **Those of us who hear voices or go through unusual sensory experiences are asking is there anything intrinsically wrong with that? Or is it our relationships to it, and the social response? The Hearing Voices Movement emphasizes voices as an unusual but normal human trait. So both the mad and autistic movements embrace difference, but have different politics on the claims of biology and genetics. It reminds me of the controversy around the claim some gay activists make about a "gay gene" as a strategy to affirm diverse sexuality.**

I wanted to have the same opportunities as those in the mainstream, so I had to fight against perceptions and expectations.

AN Our feeling has been very clear that we believe we are born autistic. The science to describe brain differences is still developing and autism is still diagnosed behaviorally, but the science shows that autistic brains are different from neurotypical brains and this is predominantly for genetic reasons. At one point it was believed that autism was the result of poor parenting, and that was shown to be false. That myth caused a lot of damage.

WH The legacy of parent blaming and the reaction to it are similar. And diagnosis based on behavior rather than physical difference raises the same questions about objectivity, but your movement has reached different conclusions than the mad movement.

AN One concern we have with genetics research is the possibility for pre-natal tests. That worries us because of what happened to people with Down Syndrome: there is a 92% rate of

I faced tremendous bullying and difficulties with peers and teachers just because we had a hard time understanding each other.

selective abortion when prenatal test shows Down Syndrome. With all the fear and the public stigma around the autism spectrum, we might see something very similar if we saw an autism prenatal test. So we have bioethics concerns.

WH Gay liberation activists have raised that fear as well, that the search for a gene determining homosexuality might backfire. Down Syndrome has very clear genetic and physical markers though, while the gay gene research has, like most genetic research, failed to reach its hype. Latest neuroscience shows brain structure is changeable by learning and environment, and the expected genetic causes of illness haven't been discovered. So "biological difference," brain, gene, or otherwise, is more complex than hardwired destiny.

And there would be less abortion of people with Down Syndrome if they were more welcomed, had a valued place in the community and media, and we heard positive things about the fact that they live high quality and happy lives.

Our movement talks a lot about the right to not be interfered with, but we need to emphasize the right to decent health and mental health services.

Is there also an element of pharma profiteering around autism?

AN There is the beginning of that, but it isn't to the same extent as in the mental health world. They recently started promoting Risperdal as a treatment for aggression in autistic people, and we are very concerned about the possible side-effects there. We see it as a form of chemical restraint. There is also a tendency to overmedicate autistic people, although more as a means of control instead of "this is going to treat people."

We also have a common cause against restraint and seclusion, and against aversives. Aversives are the use of pain as a means of behavior modification, something we view as very abusive. It is basically torture, and we have been trying to fight that. We are not tolerating it on the part of our nation's worst enemies, so why should we be tolerating it on the part of children and adults with disabilities?

We are seen as unintelligent, and presumed to have no potential, and even considered to not be aware of the world around us. But in reality no effort is put into empowering us.

WH And what are some of the historical and cross cultural perspectives on autism?

AH Many individuals have been viewed in positive ways. Mathematician Alan Turing would have been diagnosed autistic today. But there are also examples of an incredibly negative view, such as the "changeling" mythology in medieval Europe. They said fairies came in the middle of the night to place a fairy in an infant's place. The child would be withdrawn and wouldn't respond to its mother, a fairly accurate description of autistic traits. It was simply an autistic child going through what is normal development for an autistic child. But Martin Luther said that a proper response to this was to drown that child in the river. So there is a history of violence against folks who display autistic traits, that still carries over to this day. ∎

Unmaking Diagnosis
Gary Greenberg

Gary Greenberg is a therapist, contributing editor at *Harper's*, and writer for *Rolling Stone*, *The New Yorker*, and *The New York Times*. He is the author of *Manufacturing Depression: The Secret History of a Modern Disease* (2010) and *The Book of Woe: The DSM and the Unmaking of Psychiatry* (2013).

The APA and the *DSM* simply have too much power. They are a private guild, basically a corporation, and they literally own these mental disorders as intellectual property.

WILL HALL You write that the *DSM* is to psychiatrists what the Bible is to Christians.

GARY GREENBERG The *DSM* is not only a convenience for therapists and insurance billing, it determines what drugs get approved, it determines courtroom questions like whether someone is incompetent to stand trial, it determines involuntary commitment, and it is used in schools to determine who is eligible for special services. It is a foundational text, like the Constitution is to the United States: it gives the institution of psychiatry its authority. It is a hugely important book.

The modern *DSM* was psychiatry's attempt to rescue itself from a terrible crisis they found themselves in the 1970s. Some embarrassing studies showed that psychiatrists, given the same patient, would disagree with each other more often than they would agree about what mental illness the patient had.

Rosenhan's famous "On Being Sane in Insane Places" study also made a big splash, where graduate students who showed up in emergency rooms complaining that they were hearing the word "thud" in their heads were promptly admitted, all of them, to different hospitals diagnosed with schizophrenia. And in some cases, they had trouble getting back out.

> Now suddenly I am wondering, "Have I lived my life with an unnecessary amount of suffering because there is something wrong with my brain?"

And then after years of protest in 1973 the American Psychiatric Association (APA) voted to delete homosexuality from the *DSM*. This was also troublesome: can you really *vote* a diagnosis off the island? Is that science? So psychiatry was, and not for the first time in its existence, under siege. They had to come up with a way to diagnose people reliably, so they did a number of *DSM* revisions with different criteria.

It worked brilliantly. By revising the *DSM* in the 1970s psychiatry went from a backwater held in disregard by many doctors, and became mainstream. Psychiatry regained the confidence of insurance companies and government. But while the new *DSM* showed that doctors could agree that a group of symptoms added up to this disorder, they still hadn't proved that the disorder existed.

WH Not only did you write about the *DSM*, you yourself went down the rabbit hole of diagnosis.

GG I spent time at Harvard medical school as a subject in a clinical trial; a guinea pig. Thankfully it involved fish oil, not actual psychotropic drugs (and it turns out I was on the placebo anyway). I signed up for this research trial about minor depression, but when the psychiatrist did the intake interview he concluded that I had major depression.

WH How did he do that, exactly?

GG He gave me a test called the Structured Clinical Interview for *DSM* Disorders (SCID), with questions like "Have you been sad for two weeks?" It's not rocket science, it's a check box. Theoretically if you spend an hour with the person doing it, you can come out with a *DSM* diagnosis.

As this doctor was interviewing me, I realized he was asking questions keyed to the criteria in the *DSM*, but he wasn't really paying any attention to *me*. He was paying more attention to the paperwork. Not only did I find that insulting, but as a therapist and clinician myself I wondered, How can you do this? How can you simply attend to the criteria and not attend to the patient?

WH Did getting told you had a major psychiatric disorder mean anything personally to you?

GG It meant surprisingly a lot. Even though I was very skeptical, it still had an effect on me to be told "You qualify for this disorder." The idea that depression was a chemical imbalance really took hold. I do struggle with moodiness, I mean ask my wife, she will tell you! I can be moody, I can get pretty low. Now suddenly I am wondering, "Have I lived my life with an unnecessary amount of suffering because there is something wrong with my brain?"

WH That is a huge question people face. "Is this something that should be medically treated, because it is a physical limitation and I don't need to live with it?"

GG The brain, just like any other organ in the body, can go bad. It's the most complicated organ in the body, so you might even say it's more likely to go bad. The problem is that at the moment, psychiatry can't distinguish between people whose trouble is caused by something going on in their brain analogous to diabetes, cancer, or something like that, and people whose suffering only resembles organic pathology but isn't. And so they simply gloss over the distinction.

I did a lot of research into where this idea of depression as a bio-chemical imbalance came from. I discovered that it is a very carefully constructed myth. Doctors are so bound and determined to find organic pathology and biochemical imbalances behind depression that they just assume it is there, and therefore they see it.

The idea that serotonin deficiencies caused depression, which comes from the fact that the drugs affect serotonin metabolism, is absolutely incorrect. Everybody knows that. It's not serotonin deficiencies, it may not even be serotonin metabolism. The brain is way too complicated for these simplistic explanations.

Consciousness is impossible without certain biochemical events. But what does that mean exactly? I know the biochemical event is a neces-

The *DSM* suggests that if unhappiness persists for more than two weeks you have a medical illness. That is social intolerance for unhappiness and an expression of the way we value optimism. And obviously optimism is tied to buying things and spending money.

sary condition, but is it the *sufficient* condition? Maybe the brain is serving something else. Maybe there is such a thing as the mind.

More importantly, we don't even know what those brain events are. Nonetheless, at this moment, as you and I are talking, I guarantee you somewhere a doctor is telling a patient they have a chemical imbalance in their brain and that is why they should take their Abilify or Prozac. And then that very same doctor, if he goes to a medical conference and a colleague asks him, "Hey what about that chemical imbalance," he will certainly say "No. We don't know if there is a chemical imbalance." Because they don't.

And it is a myth that medications correct the chemical imbalances. If they did, you would expect more robust efficacy from these drugs. But they aren't very effective.

Pediatric bipolar is probably the biggest psychiatric scandal of our generation. It is virtually impossible to diagnose a child with bipolar because bipolar requires episodic mania, and most children haven't lived long enough to have episodic mania, it is very rarely observed in children. So prior to this idea about pediatric bipolar there was very little of it. But the *DSM* offers you this incredibly generous loophole called "NOS," or "not otherwise specified," and that is what children are diagnosed with.

When you get a diagnosis, particularly a lifelong disorder like bipolar disorder, it changes the way you think about yourself, your identity. When you tell somebody "this is what you *have*," you are also telling them, at least sometimes, "this is what you *are*." Asperger's in the *DSM-V* was eliminated, and the APA was surprised when people wrote in and said "How dare you take away our identities."

WH We lack language to describe mental difference. In a hyperspeed media culture people need to speak in soundbites and labels about themselves. So psychiatry steps in with an official, authoritative language.

GG Illness has become one of our favorite ways to understand difference. Illness also turns difference into advantage: you have a ticket to social resources. Sympathy, money, treatment, and research all get distributed to people whose differences can be understood as diseases.

WH And poverty sometimes drives people to embrace an illness identity because of disability benefits. Which is why many of us are looking at a basic income guarantee as a social policy for everyone.

GG I don't have any way of solving the gatekeeping aspect of medicine. And the whole question is complicated because we have a for-profit healthcare system.

A lot of what people are after is just being accepted and understood. To be able to say "I'm not just awkward, I have Asperger's syndrome." And that is better than a person just feeling they are stupid or worthless. But to let medicine make these determinations is to invite a number of problems.

If you call something a disease, someone is going to try to cure it. And there is the burden of having to think of yourself as sick, no matter how well it is put and or how little stigma is attached to it. That has implications.

Can you really vote a diagnosis off the island? Is that science?

The people who create the labels, the APA and the *DSM*, simply have too much power. They are a private guild, basically a corporation, and they literally own these mental disorders as intellectual property. That is a huge public trust, but it is privately held.

WH So there is a deep connection between the culture of individualist, competitive capitalism, and the power of the *DSM*?

GG You can look at the *DSM* not as a list of mental illnesses but as a manual that tells us who we are supposed to be, as a moral text. The pathologies the *DSM* describes generally occur when people don't go along with the fundamental economic and social assumptions of our society.

So, for example, our society is devoted to the pursuit of happiness. The *DSM* suggests that if unhappiness persists for more than two weeks you have a medical illness. That is social intolerance for unhappiness and an expression of the way we value optimism. And obviously optimism is tied to buying things and spending money. But maybe it is oppressive to require people to be happy all the time!

WH So the *DSM* is smuggling moral values into claims of science and objectivity.

GG Yes. The *DSM* is not just a text that says "Here is one profession's idea of what the good life is." The *DSM* is a text that actually allows a profession to *enforce* their idea of what the good life is on everyone. And that's where it becomes problematic.

WH But isn't the *DSM* also designed to say who we should be sympathetic towards and give resources to when they can't work?

GG The idea that a medical label, when it isn't stigmatizing you, gives you social resources is a sad commentary on how we distribute social resources like money and sympathy. We are in thrall to the idea that suffering is the result of something that medicine can treat. Medicine has certainly figured out how to treat an awful lot of suffering. But the idea that all our suffering can be found in biological pathologies and treated with magic bullet drugs is a very oppressive idea, a very limited idea.

WH How does therapy fit in to this?

GG Therapy is what we have left now that religion has been more or less obliterated. It's what we're stuck with and we have to make the most of it. Therapy provides the opportunity to sit down and focus on questions that we otherwise don't have time, energy, or inclination to focus on. Questions like, "what's the meaning and purpose of a life," "why do I treat people in the way that I do," "how should I treat people," "how

I realized he was asking questions keyed to the criteria in the *DSM*, but he wasn't really paying any attention to me. And that's where it becomes problematic.

should I treat myself," "what should my relationship be with the rest of my society." You have essentially the relationship that ministers or rabbis or priests used to have with their parishioners. Somebody you can go to and pour your heart out to and get back acceptance, understanding and insight. Now does any of that have anything to do with healthcare? I really don't know!

WH A minister has their values, morals, and theological beliefs right there on the table. But a psychotherapist often claims a place of science and objectivity.

GG Yes, the ideology is concealed unless the therapist reveals otherwise. As a therapist I tell people what I believe in personally and why. But I don't tell them, "this isn't healthy for you to do" as if it were objective or derived scientifically.

WH Tell us about the wars behind the *DSM-V*.

GG It's clear there are politics taking place behind the scenes. But the big picture of how the *DSM* becomes a moral document stays pretty hidden. The public controversy will likely only show that this particular crew of psychiatrists who created the *DSM-V* are a uniquely incompetent bunch. I don't believe that is the entire explanation for what went wrong, but the stupidity, incompetence and outright idiocy of some of the things that they did is astonishing.

While the new *DSM* showed that doctors could agree a group of symptoms added up to this disorder, they hadn't proved that the disorder existed.

72% of antidepressant prescriptions are written without a diagnosis. In the previous *DSM-IV* it said a person who is sad and bereaved for less than two months can't meet the criteria for depression. But the new *DSM* eliminates that bereavement exclusion. On the face of it, how stupid is that? The public is already skeptical of psychiatry, and now if you lost your wife two weeks ago and you meet the criteria for major depression, you now have a mental disorder? There's nothing to stop a doctor from providing medication to a person without diagnosing them. You don't need a diagnosis of depression to prescribe. So why turn bereavement into an illness?

The only reason they are eliminating the bereavement exclusion that is to get rid of an embarrassing thing. Because if that exclusion for a mental disorder diagnosis is in the *DSM* in the first place, people raise the question "What about unemployment? What about foreclosure? What about divorce?" And the answer is that there is no reason not to have those other stressors in there as well. But they can't go back to

The *DSM* is a text that actually allows a profession to enforce their idea of what the good life is on everyone.

the old days when they cared about why you had your mental disorder. So they're stuck between a rock and a hard place. They should've left it alone because the solution is worse than the problem. It was just stupid.

The APA didn't provide me any information at all when I was writing my book. That only meant I had to look a little harder, because there's a long public record of psychiatry out there. But at an institutional level they decided the way to deal with me was to not deal with me at all. That's an example of the hostile, paranoid thinking that goes on at the APA. ∎

The idea that all our suffering can be found in biological pathologies and treated with magic bullet drugs is a very oppressive idea.

Exporting Mental Illness
Ethan Watters

Journalist Ethan Watters has written for *The New York Times Magazine*, *Spin*, *Details*, *Mother Jones*, *Glamour*, *GQ*, and *Esquire*. He is the author of *Crazy Like Us: The Globalization of the American Psyche* (2011).

In Japan they created a whole market worth billions. They had to convince people not only to take the pill, but that they had a disease they didn't have before.

WILL HALL Your book puts culture, not biology, at the center of understanding mental illness.

ETHAN WATTERS Every generation of psychiatrists makes the case they've moved beyond culture, that they are seeing psychiatric disorders in their universal form. But even the briefest look across history shows that culture shapes expression of mental illnesses. One's own beliefs, the expectations of the people around you, healers, family members...

In the Victorian Era you had thousands of women experiencing leg paralysis or blindness, then in the modern era that simply went away. Ian Hackings wrote the book *Mad Travelers* about young men who used to travel in fugue states across Europe with no sense of their identity, no sense of who they were. Every generation has its idea about the human psyche that deeply influence the unconscious mind. Culture shapes the expression of mental illnesses. Because America is so good at exporting our ideas, today we are homogenizing the way the world experiences mental illness. Not just the categories, but the illnesses themselves.

WH So we use this word "disease" or "illness" but it means something different. And difference might only become "disease" in a cultural context.

> Every generation of psychiatrists makes the case they've moved beyond culture, that they see psychiatric disorders in their universal form.

EW It's hard for Americans to understand, we hear a word like "psychosomatic" and we think it's about faking it. But mental illnesses exist in a different category than infections or cancer. We're never going to understand these conditions except as a combination of genetics, biology, sociopsychology, and culture.

WH Even "physical" illnesses have big social and cultural determinants, but it's especially true of so-called mental disorders.

EW Types of post-traumatic stress disorder, for example, originate from different cultural beliefs. A Civil War soldier came home with Da Costa's syndrome, a pain in the chest and a kind of severe homesickness. A First World War soldier had shell shock, motor ticks, and paralysis. Those soldiers were not faking: their unconscious was responding to beliefs about the mind at the time. Expression of mental illness is directly affected by how you think about it, and how people around you think about it.

WH You write in your book about the "discovery" in Hong Kong of what gets called anorexia.

EW In Hong Kong, anorexia was very rare disorder. It didn't exist in the medical literature. Psychiatrist Sing Lee researched hospital records in the 1980s and found a few examples, but they didn't have the aspects of fat phobia, body image dysmorphia, dieting, or a desire to lose weight that are common in America. He was documenting a very rare Chinese form of self-starvation.

But then in the mid 90s the ground shifted suddenly. A young woman on her way home from school collapsed and died on a downtown Hong Kong street: she was clearly anorexic. She died in such a public way that

Depression in Japan is a remarkable example of GlaxoSmithKline and other drug companies going in and intentionally influencing where an entire culture draws the line between normal and pathological.

the press had to tell what this illness was, and so the Hong Kong media turned to perceived experts in the West. They basically imported the idea of anorexia and said, it's young women, and it has these symptoms. Then only after that point do you see a rise in the American form of the illness in Hong Kong.

So certain symptoms are accepted as legitimate and others are not, and the unconscious mind is drawn towards the symptoms that most effectively communicate your distress. Anorexia was not in Hong Kong's "symptom pool," then a decade later it was and drew more women to that behavior.

WH You're saying anorexia was not just there already and then discovered? It exists as a result of Western experts educating people through the media to have an expectation and preconception, and then they start to see themselves in a new way? That's how cultural beliefs are exported?

EW That's exactly right. The prime creators of the symptom pool are the healers and doctors. They declare if something is a legitimate symptom, creating the symptom pool and the language of suffering for one moment in history. And now we are seeing that symptom pools can drift across cultural borders, especially when the US has the sort of psychiatric influence it does around the world.

WH **So Hong Kong's culture and society, like most countries, becomes more like the United States, and homogenization occurs, including adopting a US view of what constitutes a disorder. Then people respond to that and we see a rise in that condition.**

EW Anorexia is actually very difficult not to see when it's there because the symptoms and consequences are so remarkable. So this wasn't a case of Hong Kong simply not recognizing anorexia that was there already.

WH **And this cultural homogenization also creates a market for US based products.**

Expression of mental illness is directly affected by how you think about it, and how people around you think about it.

EW The idea of depression in Japan is a remarkable example of GlaxoSmithKline and other drug companies going in and intentionally influencing where an entire culture draws the line between normal and pathological.

WH **So previously in Japan depression didn't exist? We tend to think of "depression" as objective, biological, and trans-cultural.**

EW There was a severe and rare form of "endogenous depression" found usually in psychiatric hospitals. But Japan has a cultural embrace of sadness. It's written into songs and music, it's part of the religion. There is a belief that sadness can be a place where you find moral guidance. It is not an emotional state to be afraid of, run from, or try to cover up, as we often do in the West.

WH **It reminds me of the Victorian era's culture of valuing melancholy as noble and poetic. What did GlaxoSmithKline do in Japan?**

EW GlaxoSmithKline spent hundreds of millions of dollars co-opting the profession of cross-cultural psychiatry. Remarkable scholars were romanced by the money and attention, the luxurious conferences and travel. Dr. Laurence Kirmayer, one of the leaders of the field, told me about this from the inside. He watched firsthand how GlaxoSmithKline threw a tremendous amount of money at Japan with the idea of not only marketing a pill, but marketing depression itself.

GlaxoSmithKline learned from cross-cultural psychiatrists and shaped a campaign for change. Before, Japan viewed only very rare and severe forms of sadness as pathological, and everything else was degrees of nor-

GlaxoSmithKline spent hundreds of millions of dollars co-opting the profession of cross-cultural psychiatry. Remarkable scholars were romanced by the money and attention.

mal. Now Japanese psychiatrists believe the American form of depression, that more than a few weeks of sadness is pathological.

GlaxoSmithKline spent a great deal of money in Japan for the approval process for their antidepressant drug, Paxil. They also spent money for advertising and to create what appeared to be grassroots depression support groups.

We are seeing that symptom pools can drift across cultural borders, especially when the US has the sort of psychiatric influence it does around the world.

They created a whole market worth billions, with the result that many people in Japan now classify themselves as depressed and have a prescription for Paxil. There was no market there before. They had to convince people not only to take the pill, but that they had a disease they didn't have before.

Cultures have deeply sophisticated and long held beliefs about the human mind. We need to have greater respect for cultural traditions and how they work before we go blasting in there with multi-million dollar ad campaigns promoting the American way of thinking about sadness. It's akin to biologists documenting changes in a rainforest and seeing how, like species, cultural differences are quite literally disappearing before our eyes.

The more you can tolerate and accept the behavior, the greater the likelihood that individual will do better over time.

WH What happened after the Sri Lanka tsunami in 2004, with the influx of trauma counselors?

EW One anthropologist said to me, "Meaning matters when it comes to psychological trauma." Our initial fight/flight and adrenalin response might be universal, but the very moment after the trauma we begin to assess what happened to us. We look for how to understand the trauma and how to express our distress. That moment onwards is shaped by culture.

In western culture we have an ego-centric view of self. In Sri Lanka there is a socio-centric view: self is intimately tied to one's place in the group. A Sri Lankan will likely see trauma not as existing in their mind, the way we think of PTSD, but existing in the damage done to the social group, in their ability to fulfill their role in that social group.

Western counselors rush into a disaster zone like Sri Lanka with no knowledge of that different conception of mind, no knowledge of the language or the rituals for healing, and no knowledge of the history of civil war there. It makes no sense for a Sri Lankan to seek healing in private in the way that's very common in the West. To suggest they take time away from their responsibilities and their social group not only makes no sense at all, it is a form of the very symptom and alienation most troubling to them.

WH So what would be the way to help in those situations?

EW We need to assume that cultures know that bad events have psychological consequences, and not treat PTSD as if we were telling them about a newly discovered disease. We may not understand a culture's own ways of healing and dealing with trauma, it may be hidden in family structures or their own conception of the human mind, but we should always assume the culture's own ways are present. Our responsibility is to help get the society up and running so they can do their own healing.

Certain symptoms are accepted as legitimate and others are not, and the unconscious mind is drawn towards the symptoms that most effectively communicate your distress.

WH Individualistic diagnosis and treatment in a collectivist society doesn't work.

EW Not only does it not work ,you can actually step on metaphorical landmines. Prior to the Tsunami, Sri Lankan villages had socially proscribed ways of talking about past war, to avoid flaring up violent cycles of revenge. Often in little villages the family of a murdered victim was living next door to the family of the murderer. Families had very real reasons to hate each other, and there was this pressure to talk only euphemistically about past violence.

Into this delicate balance came Western trauma counselors with the idea that healing requires finding emotional relief by talking about violence. This made sense as a Western idea, but had potential to spark incredible cycles of revenge in Sri Lanka.

WH This parallels concerns about how western "development" aid can often be damaging.

EW Imagine a reverse situation. If, after 9/11 or Katrina, healers from Mozambique starting knocking on doors saying, "We are here to help you, we want you to do rituals to sever your relationship from the dead." Would that make sense to us? Of course not. Yet we have no problem doing it in reverse, because we think things like PTSD are culturally neutral and universal.

WH Schizophrenia is also assumed to be universal, but the outcomes are very different depending on the culture.

EW A World Health Organization study suggested people with schizophrenia in different cultures had remarkably different outcomes, with people in developing countries doing much better than people in the first world. Robert Whitaker looked at the role of medications in explaining that, I wanted to explore a cultural perspective.

I followed anthropologist Juli McGruder through Zanzibar, who was sitting with families to understand their language and their concept of schizophrenia. The idea of spirit possession often accompanies the illness in Zanzibar. McGruder discovered that this idea resulted in keeping an "ill" individual within the group. There was no stigmatizing. It was considered normal.

WH People don't become "patients" or "consumers" and aren't then placed in treatment or otherwise separated from the rest of society.

The idea of spirit possession resulted in keeping the "ill" individual within the group. There was no stigmatizing.

EW In the West we believed that normalizing a biological notion of mental illness, making it akin to someone having diabetes, decreases stigma. Research shows the opposite is true. People who adopt the genetic and biological narrative about mental illness tend to interact less with people that are diagnosed as mentally ill. They also think of them as more permanently broken and dangerous than they do when they have a different narrative, such as that it's caused by something in their childhood.

WH Campaigns that say "it's a biological disease like any other" actually increase stigma.

EW McGruder's work concluded that the spirit possession narrative not only kept the ill individual within the group, it also lowered 'expressed emotion,' the intensity of feelings that surrounds the illness. Across cultures, research shows that families with high levels of expressed emotions, who are critical and overly involved, will have higher relapse rates and do worse over time.

WH If you don't see the experience as something inhuman, to separate from or be afraid of, people do much better. That's a theme in successful treatments, such as Open Dialogue and Soteria House.

EW These different views allow for an acceptance of behavior that would be weird for an American family member to accept, when someone has a psychotic break or descends into some sort of distress. We have a very Westernized notion of wanting to treat it, to figure it out and fix it. Yet the literature very clearly shows that the more you can tolerate and accept the behavior, the greater the likelihood that ill individual will do better over time.

> The prime creators of the symptom pool are healers and doctors. They declare if something is a legitimate symptom, creating the symptom pool and the language of suffering for one moment in history.

WH The US is a multicultural society, and even people from a more mainstream tradition are often exploring and borrowing from other cultures they come into contact with. What are the implications of your work in the West?

EW We need to alert mental health professionals to not simply apply western notions in every case, and to be aware there are different cultural narratives and beliefs that might be very valuable.

When McGruder, the anthropologist I followed in Zanzibar, returned to the US, her husband had a psychotic break. Try as she might to take the lessons that she had learned in Zanzibar and employ them to benefit her husband, she simply couldn't do it. It's easy to export a drug or the *DSM*, but it is very difficult to import notions or ideas that are deeply layered in a culture.

wʜ So this is about a deeper social and institutional fabric, not just a set of personal values or a technique. How is your book being received?.

A Sri Lankan will likely see trauma not as existing in their mind, the way we think of PTSD, but existing in the damage done to the social group, and their ability to fulfill their role in that social group.

ᴇw Psychiatrists and professionals have almost unanimously agreed with the fundamental points of my book. Interestingly enough though, they rarely see it as a fault of their own. They'll say things like "You're absolutely right. This is really a problem, but it's true of the guy down the hall or the guy down at the other institute. When *we* go into a culture, *we* really know what we're doing." ∎

Community Development
Pat Bracken

Pat Bracken is a psychiatrist and clinical director of the Mental Health Service in West Cork, Ireland. He was previously an academic at the University of Central Lancashire's Institute for Philosophy, Diversity, and Mental Health. He is the co-author with Phil Thomas of *Post-psychiatry: Mental Health in a Postmodern World* (2006) and author of *Trauma: Culture, Meaning and Philosophy* (2002).

The answer is not more therapy, the answer is us as a community re-establishing a powerful sense of purpose.

WILL HALL Tell us about your work in traditional cultures.

PAT BRACKEN I worked in a notorious part of Uganda, the Lorero triangle. About 500,000 people lost their lives there in the 1980s under a "scorched-earth" government counter insurgency policy. I went with a small organization caring for people who had been tortured, but I quickly realized I myself could do a lot of harm bringing diagnostic systems, treatment ideas, and a "Western" philosophy of mind into a developing country. They were very vulnerable to outside experts telling them what to do. I became horrified to see Europeans who would arrive after a six-week counseling course and say: "I'm gonna counsel people who've been tortured or raped." Many of these people were completely ignorant of local cultures, way of life, and history.

It's a generalization but African societies are by and large very strong. They've been through a hell of a lot of things, and they have a lot of wisdom and strength in their own communities to find ways to move forward. What they wanted from people like myself wasn't therapy and it certainly wasn't psychiatry. They wanted practical support, to rebuild the school and rebuild the roads so people could get to the market. So we started to think of our job as assisting that process, re-establishing a way of life, promoting indigenous ways of healing, and helping people to restore the routines of ordinary life that would ultimately serve as the foundation for their recovery.

WH I think this applies to richer countries as well, a community development approach rather than an individual treatment model.

PB Yes. And people did want witness for what went on, for the violence that happened. But you can't do the witnessing without the practical support, questions of trust are extremely important. Only after we'd established a relationship and people felt we were on their side would they tell us about things that happened. There's no shortcut to trust, though that's the Western way, to quickly just try to get people to talk.

WH So in your view the diagnosis of PTSD is questionable?

PB Yes, because I think it individualizes our suffering and decontextualizes our experience. Current models of PTSD assume that trauma works on a person's cognitive schemes to produce particular symptoms. Therapies are essentially various techniques aimed at speeding up our processing of the trauma. Many of these models are incredibly simplistic: they tend to ignore how our experience of suffering is wrapped up in our culture and our social worlds.

I think we should be more focused on how trauma can destabilize our sense of meaningfulness in the world, and we should work to re-establish a sense of continuity and a background context in which suffering can be understood. That can be done in ways that don't fit our categories of mental health work and therapy. Some good individual and counseling work can be done, but meaningfulness is about our actual connection with one another, not something we hold in our heads as individuals. Mental health is hope about moving forward, and that can happen through all sorts of things: faith, religion, art, creativity, politics, sport, and community activism. There's a whole series of routes.

People can make it through enormous suffering if they believe there is meaning and purpose to it.

WH What kinds of things would support that process?

PB I was able to visit a number of "child soldier" projects in West Africa. What these kids needed more than anything else was to get away from the focus on their experiences in the military and instead start living a life involved in their community. That means training and job opportunities and a clear economic and practical path away from military life. I was disturbed to see a number of organizations doing intensive counseling work with kids, which just seemed to hold them in the frame of that experience. This had the effect of solidifying their identity as a "child soldier" more than anything else.

That mirrors what happens in Western psychiatry, where we take episodes of emotional distress and put names and labels on them and fund programs around them. There is a good motivation behind that, people want to do something. But there are dangers to it. I have learned over the years: knowledge is dangerous and the theories we use are dangerous. We should use them carefully and lightly.

WH How key is religion in creating meaning?

PB People can make it through enormous suffering if they believe there is meaning and purpose to it. Christianity and Islam have a strong history of martyrdom and often an underlying theme of religious belief is the turning of awful suffering into meaningful suffering.

In Uganda I met a former political prisoner who had been arrested, stripped naked, humiliated and beaten quite badly. He told me it was the best thing that had happened to him in his life. He had not been very religious before, but while arrested he had a profound sense of identification with Jesus and his suffering. When he was released he became a lot more active in his church and his life became more deeply meaningful for him. I've heard those kind of stories from very many people.

I'm not religious myself but I do believe religion holds a culture together, gives it strength, beliefs, and purpose in life. In the Western world we're weak on that.

WH In most cultures the healers are the most prominent spiritual figures, but in the West psychiatrists are among the least religious of the medical professions. My suspicion is the process is the same, just in place of the awe of religion, psychiatrists just instill religious awe for the *DSM*, pills, and disorders.

PB I wrote about this in my book on trauma, and it's a generalization, but there is some truth in it: in the West we are largely a "post-Christian," "post-religious" culture. And so we have a particular vulnerability when it comes to trauma and its effects on our sense of meaningfulness. If this is the case, then the answer is not more therapy, the answer is us as a community re-establishing a powerful sense of purpose.

For me it's about opposing the superficiality of contemporary capitalism and raising a political agenda, not an individual therapy agenda. A lot of very good individual therapeutic work happens with people, but we need to think more socially and we need to think more communally.

> **What they wanted from people like myself wasn't therapy and it certainly wasn't psychiatry. They wanted practical support, to rebuild the school and rebuild the roads so people could get to the market.**

WH You mentioned traditional healers in Uganda, is there a danger that traditional alternatives might also have oppressive qualities and be harmful?

PB My experience of traditional healers in Africa is that some of them are charlatans who were exploiting people, charging a lot of money for bad treatments. No question. But some of them were decent people doing their best for people who consulted them, treating them well and giving them a way forward. They had historical and cultural knowledge from their tribe to explain people's distress. That gave people continuity with the past and a sense of identity. Healers were providing remedies and help on a surface level, and on another level also rebuilding community beliefs and connection with gods and rituals.

It's about opposing the superficiality of contemporary capitalism and raising a political agenda, not an individual therapy agenda.

WH Tell us about the Sharing Voices project you helped start.

PB Black and ethnic minority communities in the UK have always had a problematic relationship with mental health services. More people end up being detained, they get more drugs, and more ECT than the white British community. The traditional response was the development of transcultural psychiatry, that psychiatry would become more sophisticated so it could intervene more effectively and appropriately in those cultures.

That's about building psychiatry its expertise up. This is fine but it is not enough. The Sharing Voices project in Bradford is based on the idea that communities themselves often have the answers to problems. We believed that the immigrant communities in Britain were strong and that our job was to support them, learn to listen to them and to help them to ask questions and find solutions. Let's go back to them for some of the answers, not build up psychiatry. It's a community development approach to mental health. So there's music, writing, spirituality groups, and a sense of support for people not becoming labelled as being mentally ill.

For example, A number of Pakistani women were supported getting Muslim prayer groups going for difficult times in their lives. They found a way through faith and community with other women, without going into the psychiatric hospital or clinic. Sharing Voices has become very powerful in Bradford and is now used as a model for other developments in the UK.

My experience of traditional healers in Africa was that some of them are charlatans. No question. But some of them were decent people doing their best for the people who consulted them, treating them well and giving them a way forward.

WH It reminds me of work done with the Freedom Center, where we built the community, not services provided by professionals, with free classes and clinics open to all. You've also been developing, with Phil Thomas and others, the idea of post-psychiatry.

PB Postpsychiatry sees standard mental health as primarily a technical approach. But the most important aspects of mental health work are the non-technical: values, relationships, meaning. In the journals of psychiatry, 90% of the articles are about some kind of technical issue: diagnostic categories, the biology of distress, cognitive psychology... And the solutions are technical solutions: drug treatments, ECT, and specific psychotherapy techniques. Progress in technology is at the center; meaning, values, and relationships are secondary and marginalized.

We need to think more communally and we need to think more socially.

Post-psychiatry says we need to reverse that: put values, meanings, and relationships back at the center. It would also put research defined and led by patients/ex-patients and service users themselves right at the center.

What people need is not technical interventions in their lives, but holding a human space where our encounters with madness, distress, and

Mental health is hope about moving forward, through all sorts of things: relationships, faith, religion, art, creativity, politics, and community activism.

alienation can be worked out in a meaningful environment, where people are treated with dignity and respect, and their experiences are valued and listened to.

With the emergence of the worldwide service user/patient movement over the past twenty years, for the first time ever in Western history we have the possibility for dialogue between people who experience states of madness and people who are trying to help them. That's an exciting prospect for me. ∎

Depression & Oppression
Alisha Ali

Alisha Ali is an associate professor at New York University and co-editor (with Dana Crowley Jack) of *Silencing the Self Across Cultures: Depression and Gender in the Social World* (2012).

Most research is geared toward medication, the brain, and individual pathology. Social context and economics are ignored. Our study runs counter to that, and suggests depression implicates society as a whole.

WILL HALL Blaming serotonin imbalance for depression (the "monoamine hypothesis") has been discredited; tell us about your study that looks at the role of poverty in depression.

ALISHA ALI The feelings associated with depression, extreme sadness, low sense of self-worth, lack of motivation, are connected to poverty, and poor people are more often diagnosed with mental illnesses, including depression. But real-life experiences of people living in poverty are not represented in the research literature. There is a belief that poverty doesn't matter, because depression is a "brain problem."

WH And so research participants tend to be privileged white college students, or patients at well-funded clinics.

AA In our study we looked at people in poverty who met the criteria for depression (we used the standard *DSM* criteria as it was necessary to speak to the existing literature). They were enrolled in a micro-credit loan program that trained them for small collective business ventures. Members share accountability for loan payback and receive better interest rates. These programs have not been used much in the US, but have been very successful in so-called developing countries and have a repayment rate well over 90%.

WH People who were both poor and depressed got collective microloans for businesses. What was the impact on their depression?

AA Micro-credit loans are very effective, and participants were successful in becoming economically self-sufficient. When we looked at their depression levels before the loans and then after, there was a significant decrease in their depression.

WH Did they receive any other kind of treatment or mental health care that might have affected the outcome?

AA No. Less depression was specifically linked to the financial empowerment from being in the successful micro-loan program.

WH So the approach is anti-poverty instead of antidepressants. And this was a National Institute of Mental Health funded study, the gold standard in research. Are there any other studies like this?

AA The research worlds of psychiatry and community economic development are rarely combined: we looked for other studies, but our research is unique. Most other research is geared toward using medication to treat depression, which means focusing on the brain and individual pathology. Social context and economics are ignored. Our study runs counter to that assumption, and suggests depression implicates society as a whole.

Our political and social systems are based on silencing marginalized individuals so they don't have the wherewithal to creative positive change. The mental health establishment itself becomes part of that system.

WH In mental healthcare thinking we lose the common-sense understanding that poverty is depressing.

AA When people have something we call "depression," (or, if you don't want to use that term, feelings of anguish and persistent unhappiness in their lives), there are many options that might be more effective than medication and which the person might feel good about doing. Changing lives from an economic point of view is very different than taking a pill. The first is empowering. The latter, to many, is disempowering. When people become more self-sufficient, it builds resources that provide scaffolding for themselves, their children and future generations. Compare this to a reliance of medication. Not only are there side effects, but you have a daily reminder, in the form of a pill, to think of yourself as a defective individual with a problem inside of you.

WH This highlights the cultural assumptions that go into our understandings of depression.

AA Depression carries stigma, meaning you are somehow personally ineffective in moving forward in your life. I interviewed a woman who had suffered with extreme sadness and lack of motivation for years. She was given a diagnosis of depression and internalized this label. When I asked her about aspects of her life where she could make a change, she said, "I'm a depressive. I'm not a person who can do that." She had internalized this label as central to her identity as a person.

Our political and social systems are based on silencing marginalized individuals so they don't have the wherewithal to creative positive change. The mental health establishment itself becomes part of that system, in effect controlling and keeping people where they are. So this is connected to oppression and social inequality.

WH What about guilt? When people receive a label that says, "it is not your fault, it's a chemical imbalance in your brain," it can be incredibly relieving. The message is that you lack personal ability to ever control things, and so you are not to blame.

AA Most of my interviewees saw their depression as yet another defect. Not only were they socially incompetent, unable to maintain relationships or a job, but now their brain is also defective. When medications do work, it's like taking a pain pill when you have been hit on the head by a falling brick. The pill might make you feel better, but the cause of the pain was external.

In these beliefs there is a collusion between drug companies, psychiatrists and patients as well, who deeply want to be liberated from their self-blame.

WH It redirects away from social change, and it reminds me of Michel Foucault's view, that social control can be internalized by a kind of inner surveillance, trained by helping institutions.

Changing lives from an economic point of view is very different than taking a pill. The first is empowering. The latter, to many, is disempowering.

Your work also looks at racial inequality. We know mental health services are underutilized by people of color, which is a civil rights issue of equal access to care. So "reducing stigma" and increasing access is emphasized in ethnic minority communities.

AA The drug industry needs profit to succeed, and this requires targeting as many people as possible. Anti-stigma programs to increase access to services are very popular with pharmaceutical companies. They encourage people to seek medical help in the current system, which grows the market for pills. And they also normalize medication by promoting the idea depression is an individual defect.

WH Jonathan Metzl says professionals need "structural competence" about the social forces that drive mental suffering.

AA This is not to say many psychotherapists aren't well intentioned in wanting to be "culturally competent." But the real need for change rests not only in the individual but in culture as a whole. Instead, people learn to talk about their problems in ways that are in effect marketing the drugs to everyone they meet.

WH Anti-stigma campaigns become sophisticated tools to overcome obstacles to market reach. The story is, "I was suffering but finally overcame the stigma to get services. I was saved by treatment with medication." People become sort of walking pill advertisements. I want people to get help too, but the advertising and pharma-funded support groups twist that into marketing.

AA Being on medications is today so widespread in part because the medication is less stigmatized and more open and accepted.

WH We again see how understanding mental health reform defies simple equations and sound bites. You've also worked with immigrant women of color, tell us about that.

AA They face the same challenges other patients experience, but in far more extreme ways. For patients already marginalized because you are not white, English isn't your first language, and you're not familiar with the system, there is more power differential between you and the person providing services to you. Add the cultural gap and patients are at great risk.

One woman I interviewed had been assaulted in Colombia before immigrating. Her male psychiatrist tried to be "culturally sensitive" by telling her Colombia is "very much a rape culture." At first she felt relieved of blame, but months later, after he made several other derogatory comments about her country, she realized he was really pretending to know the culture. When her anger came out towards him, she was even more severely stigmatized: social workers, nurses, and the psychiatrist saw her as a "problem patient" resistant to diagnosis.

WH Doctors are trained to treat sickness, not communicate with people. Is cultural derogation a common theme?

AA Yes, usually by white male psychiatrists pretending to understand a person's culture. For example, an African woman learned the aunt who raised her from birth had died, but she wasn't able to go home for the funeral. Her husband brought her to the emergency room because she was crying uncontrollably, and she was admitted to an inpatient facility. The next morning she told the nurses she felt better and thought she could go home. She explained that during the night she heard her elders whispering in her ear that her aunt was fine, and because of this she had made peace with not being present at the funeral. But the staff wrote in her chart that "an aggressive treatment plan is recommended for these auditory hallucinations." She is not the quiet, calm patient who has experienced a recent death in the family that they might see from their own cultural background. She is very dramatic, talks with her arms, moves her hands, raises her voice and wasn't just crying she was screaming. She was expressing in a way that made sense to her as normal. But to the medical staff it was abnormal, and they used it as a reason to confine her.

WH What is a normal experience in one culture can be seen as a hallucination and a symptom of a broken brain in need of medication in another. Pathologizing anger is also common.

AA Women especially are expected not to show anger, it's seen as "inappropriate." This becomes a means of controlling people and

> Women are expected not to show anger, it's seen as "inappropriate." This becomes a means of controlling people and keeping them in their place.

keeping them in their place so that they are not able to engage in forms of resistance. Foucault wrote about psychiatry equating mental illness with moral degeneracy, and using confinement and treatment to protect soci-

When we looked at their depression levels before the loans and then after, there was a significant decrease in their depression.

ety. This containment for the sake of social safety means people who are incarcerated in prison and people in psychiatric institutions have astoundingly similar life conditions that brought them into these institutions.

It's more readily explained by understanding oppression, discrimination, and poverty than it is by looking at a scan of a person's brain.

Oppression, when we unpack that word, means a higher risk of violence, a greater risk of poor nutrition, higher chronic stress, all of which affect the body and the brain. We now know that the brain is physically shaped by experience, and repeated trauma changes the way that the brain looks on a brain scan. And yet the whole idea of mainstream psychiatry is that someone's brain is defective by nature, that there are predispositions and genetic inheritance and given differences between a normal person's brain and abnormal person's brain from the beginning. But why can't someone start normal and then become abnormal through the impact of oppression? We know this is possible, because we know that social influences can change a person's biology. The brain and even our genes are physically shaped by experience.

WH Science has viewed the poor and criminals as innately biologically abnormal since the days of phrenology and eugenics. Now the word "predisposition" and "risk factors" carry the same message. What are some other examples of race dynamics?

AA For many immigrant women, their psychiatrist is the one person they see outside their own family, and comes to represent the culture of their new country. They start to have what psychologist Dana Jack calls externalized self-perception, which is seeing oneself not through your own eyes, but through they eyes of others.

And there can be a massive split between how the women talk about their experience and the way psychiatrists view them as patients. For example, a Caribbean woman was labeled as "depressed" following the loss of her husband. She described how although her psychiatrist was compassionate and tried to understand her culture, he couldn't. In her chart the psychiatrist wrote, "upon admission the patient reported having no current sexual partners, despite being dressed in a sexually provocative manner, as is often the way with women from the Islands." That was one of the first sentences in his notes that went into her medical record.

WH It is especially disturbing that such a view was written openly in the guise of professional assessment.

AA Researchers actually did a careful study on the *Diagnostic and Statistical Manual Casebook*, a textbook that gives fictitious case examples in order to illustrate different mental disorders, and is used worldwide to train psychiatrists, nurses, social workers and therapists how to properly diagnose people. When they looked at these case examples, they found that women of color were significantly more likely to be described in sexualized terms like "sexually provocative."

> Anti-stigma programs are very popular with pharmaceutical companies. They encourage people to seek help in the current system, which grows the market for pills.

WH If that's in the official school training manual, it's probably just the tip of the iceberg of what is happening in clinics.

AA The psychotherapeutic setting is not some kind of value-free, decontextualized scientific space. It is a microcosm of society's bias. Stereotypes are perpetuated with every new generation in psychiatry who refer to the Casebook and are teaching the Casebook. Changing this requires more than simply training psychotherapists to be more culturally competent. It requires more than ending stigma so that people of so-called other cultures can embrace the idea that they, too, might be mentally ill and need medication. It requires stepping away from the foundations of psychiatry, and looking to non-medical alternatives that deal with real issues. It means no longer pathologizing individuals as an excuse to avoid addressing social ills.

WH The entire mental health framework needs to be rethought in as community development, to think not in terms of mental illness, but in terms of empowerment and connection.

AA We need to move away from diagnostic labeling and the public education campaigns around it. With diabetes and cardiovascular disease there is a strong link between raising medical awareness and improving people's lives. That is not what happens with depression and mental illness; the medical model doesn't work for these experiences. The labels themselves can be damaging. An approach that relies on medical labeling and the expertise of someone outside the community takes away from the strengths within the community. We need to look at *existing* strengths communities have to change the conditions of their lives.

But why can't someone start normal and become abnormal through the impact of oppression? We know this is possible, because we know social influences can change a person's biology. The brain and even our genes are physically shaped by experience.

WH Such as micro lending programs that help people gain financial independence.

AA The people I interviewed have a history of unemployment and going through the prison system, and they are afraid their sons might go into in the prison system. Expanding programs like micro-lending requires an investment, but the savings in the long run come from keeping people out

It means no longer pathologizing individuals as an excuse to avoid addressing social ills.

of the cycle of poverty and incarceration. From a simple economic point of view, preventive approaches save money and make more sense. This is what psychiatry and psychology are really supposed to be about: enhancing conditions so people feel fulfilled and productive in what matters to them. That creates a positive legacy for the next generation. ∎

Black Politics and Schizophrenia
Jonathan Metzl

Jonathan Metzl is a professor at Vanderbilt University. A Guggenheim fellow, he has written for medical, psychiatric, and popular publications, including *MSNBC*, *The Lancet*, and *NPR*. His books include *The Protest Psychosis: How Schizophrenia Became a Black Disease* (2010), and *Prozac on the Couch: Prescribing Gender in the Era of Wonder Drugs* (2003), and he co-edited *Against Health: How Health Became the New Morality* (2010).

Black Power activists in Detroit were swept up into the mental health system after protesting. They ended up in psychiatric hospitals and diagnosed with schizophrenia. Political protest in the '60s became coded as mental illness.

WILL HALL Your book describes how the evolution of schizophrenia diagnosis intertwines with the politics of the 1960s. How did you get interested in this?

JONATHAN METZL In my first book *Prozac on the Couch*, I looked at how years of ads for depression and anxiety medications represented drugs as white middle class "mothers' little helpers." It was amazing to me the invisibility of people of color in those representations.

WH And the psychiatric portrayal of black Americans has always been culturally bound. Where does that begin?

JM In the 1860s the American surgeon Samuel Cartwright coined the diagnoses "drapetomania" and "dysaesthesia aethiopis" for black slaves who ran away from their masters. Cartwright said that because blacks are physiologically better off in slavery, then they must be insane if they're running away. He advocated whipping and other kinds of "treatments" for this disease.

   This was clearly racist, but it was picked up by psychiatric authors over the course of the next 30 or 40 years. So there is a clear history of diagnosing black bodies as insane for reasons that have largely to do with political or social factors.

WH Wanting freedom was considered a mental illness?

JM Yes, and at the time this was given credence in medical literature.

WH And how does racism persist up through the modern era?

JM We've supposedly learned the lessons of the past, like the Tuskegee experiments from 1932 and 1972, where blacks were denied syphilis treatment and allowed to die in the name of research. But there are many less obvious present-day examples. Today African-American men are anywhere from four to five, six, even seven times more likely to be diagnosed with schizophrenia

In one of the medical charts I looked at, a women was diagnosed just for creating a public disturbance and embarrassing her husband.

compared to other groups.

WH Instead of being diagnosed with anxiety, depression, or something less severe.

JM Yes, and what's interesting is that this isn't just coming from white doctors. Clinicians of color are just as likely to over-diagnose black men with schizophrenia. These are structural attitudes about race.

WH And prior to the protest era of civil rights and Black Power, how was schizophrenia defined?

Cartwright said that because blacks are physiologically better off in slavery, they must be insane if they're running away. He advocated whipping and other kinds of treatments for this disease.

JM Psychiatry in 1952 described schizophrenia as a relatively mild personality condition that led to splitting of the personality. You would see it in popular culture: women's magazines talked about the schizophrenia of being a housewife. There was a famous 1948 Olivia de Havilland movie called *The Snake Pit,* where three days into her marriage a white woman ends up developing schizophrenia, manifested in her inability to recognize her husband. Different kinds of magazines, newspapers and films all assumed schizophrenia was an illness of white female docility, and also sometimes white male genius.

WH And one of the main symptoms for schizophrenia in women was losing interest in being a wife or a mother?

JM Yes. In one of the medical charts I looked at, a woman was diagnosed schizophrenic just for creating a public disturbance and embarrassing her husband.

WH So psychiatry is labeling women who aren't conforming to gender expectations and then locking them up in hospitals. This is social control to keep the gender status quo in line.

JM Certainly. At the time people thought they were performing state of the art science, but when we look back historically it becomes very apparent what was happening: in the mother's little helper era, 70-75% of Valium prescriptions were written to middle-class women.

WH So originally it was housewives who were being diagnosed schizophrenic, and schizophrenia wasn't inherently feared or associated with violence and aggression, but then a change took place?

JM The main story of my book is about Black Power activists in Detroit who were swept up into the mental health system after protesting. They ended up in psychiatric hospitals and diagnosed with schizophrenia. Political protest in the '60s became coded as mental illness. Criminality and hostility became increasing described in the *DSM*, where they were absent before.

The second version of the *DSM* came out in 1968, an important year of protest. The new *DSM* added aggression, hostility and projection to the criteria for schizophrenia, used male case studies instead of female, and now said things like, "patient is hostile, he blames other people for his problems." Angry black men are depicted as suffering from new forms of schizophrenia, manifest by aggression and violence. The diagnostic code language changed, and lo and behold, you see increasing numbers of African-American men diagnosed with schizophrenia.

WH You give an example of a medication advertisement that reflects this.

JM I came across an ad for Haldol, a major tranquilizer used for schizophrenia, in the *Archives of General Psychiatry*. The ad appeared right after the aftermath of riots, and shows an angry, protesting black man in the street, shaking his fist at the viewer. The text says "Assaultive and belligerent? Cooperation begins with Haldol."

WH So psychiatry diagnoses black protesters as mentally ill. In the same era political dissidents in the USSR are also being diagnosed as mentally ill, and treated with the very same drug: Haldol. The memoirs of Soviet dissidents describe the drug as torture.

Your book focuses on a hospital near Detroit, which was a center of the Black Power movement and the Nation of Islam, as well as labor unrest and the auto workers movement. There were also big riots there. One story you tell is of Abdul Rasheed Kareem.

JM Kareem came from a military family, started out life in the housing projects of Detroit, and got into some trouble as a youth. He went to Vietnam, and while visiting his family on leave he was in a fight with some white strangers as he was walking to his house. He was swept up by a police raid, and severely abused while in prison.

He had a prison conversion to the Nation of Islam, and became an active protester, angry and hostile. He starts to develop mental symptoms: he starts to hallucinate and becomes delusional. They ship him to Ionia State Hospital for the Criminally Insane.

WH He has a lot of really good reasons to be angry.

The diagnostic code language changed, and lo and behold, you see increasing numbers of African-American men diagnosed with schizophrenia.

JM Absolutely. And it was an ethical dilemma for his doctors. He fits the criteria for what their profession tells them is the illness, so what do they do? Do they say, no this is a social construction, and refuse to help him? Do they see if they can treat him? Is the problem the doctor? Is the problem the system? Is problem the diagnostic manual? Is the problem the patient?

WH So there actually were doctors who said, "Wait a second here, maybe he's got good reasons to be angry, maybe he's not just crazy?" There was some kind of debate?

JM I've done oral histories with a lot people in the hospital and there was a tremendous amount of debate about whether they were doing the right thing or not. They faced a dilemma. What were their options at the time? They couldn't really let him go, because they were already under court order. The system trumps the individual very often in cases like this. I don't think that's an excuse, but change means seeing the institutional and structural context in addition to the problems of individuals.

WH **That is eerily reminiscent of the situation today, where so many people working in the mental health system are questioning it and calling it broken, but also say they are constrained by the larger structures and can't do anything differently.**

So what finally happened to Kareem?

JM The court ordered him to remain in the hospital until restored to sanity. His relatives tried again and again to get him released, and in my book I reproduce a series of heartbreaking letters from family members to doctors. He finally ends up, like many of these people, "lost to follow-up." I assume he was transferred out to another facility, and very often people died in the hospital. So not a happy ending at all.

We've supposedly learned the lessons of the past, like the Tuskegee experiments from 1932 and 1972, where blacks were denied syphilis treatment and allowed to die in the name of research. But there are many less obvious present-day examples.

WH **Or hopefully he managed to get away for psychiatry and just didn't have any more contact. And is his story just one example of what happened to many black men, not just in Ionia Hospital, but in many hospitals around the country?**

JM In my research, we looked at about 800 randomly selected charts. As increasing numbers of African-American men were brought to Ionia in the '50s, '60s and '70s, the hospital became a black facility. It went from being roughly 15% African-American in the 40s to being about 70% in the '70s. And the community became increasingly concerned about the possibility that people might run away, and what they might they do in the community. In 1977 the hospital literally becomes a prison: the mental health system was taken over by the corrections system and became what's called the Riverside Correction facility, a medium security prison. So here really is Foucault's worst nightmare: one system taking over the other, and the goal is social control. Hospitals become prisons literally overnight.

Although this was the era of supposed deinstitutionalization, a lot of the black men that I talked to were not deinstitutionalized, they were not let go on the streets. Instead they were either recast as prisoners or were farmed out to other prisons and ended up coming back to Riverside Correction facility a couple of months later.

WH Your book describes how Malcolm X, the black nationalist leader, was seen as paranoid schizophrenic and insane for his views.

JM As schizophrenia became an illness that was increasingly associated with angry black male protest, you see national examples of FBI profilers, leading psychiatrists, and others diagnosing black protest leaders as schizophrenic.

That's just one part of the story; the rhetoric of schizophrenia and the associations with violence also played out in Black Power discourse itself. People like Malcolm X, H. Rap Brown, Stokely Carmichael, and even Martin Luther King Jr. were talking about race and schizophrenic violence. There was a real debate: is this an illness of dopamine and the mind, or something caused by society and civilization? Is this the result of racism? Some were saying we don't have to fix dopamine in black people's minds, we need to change the system. If we don't do that, violence is going to be the result. So there was a real debate about who was causing illness and what the implications were.

This isn't just coming from white doctors. Clinicians of color are just as likely to over-diagnose black men with schizophrenia. These are structural attitudes about race.

WH There is a real mental derangement that takes place, connected with anger and rage, but is it truly an illness or a response to oppression?

JM In the late '60s the whole society was grappling with the question "What does it mean to be normal, what does it mean to be crazy?" The country was erupting into violent conflict and there were social problems being protested and a war in Vietnam. There was a huge social discussion about madness, sanity and what the nature of the current crisis was, both for the individual and society.

Today African-American men are anywhere from four to five, six, even seven times more likely to be diagnosed with schizophrenia compared to others.

WH You pointed out that black men are much more often diagnosed as schizophrenic than whites, which of course means more use of force, more discrimination, and less hope for recovery. We also know that people of color are put in restraints, locked in hospitals against their will, and overmedicated at a higher rate than are whites. At the same time there is a greater neglect of services and support: blacks are underserved by the system. How should we engage this complex disparity?

JM The medical system is actually pretty aware of these racial disparities. People within the black activist psychiatry community argue that overdiagnosis of schizophrenia is because black men are being driven crazy by racism, so of course they're going to have schizophrenia more than white men. On the other hand, in the realm of biological science psychiatrists argue that culture shouldn't matter, and schizophrenia should occur in all people equally because of deep biological structures that cause it, so the problem is in the bias in the diagnosis.

The way that all this is usually dealt with is so-called cultural competency training: train doctors to be more culturally aware and sensitive to the racial or ethnic backgrounds of patients, so that they'll be less likely to put them in the wrong category.

So here really is Foucault's worst nightmare: one system taking over the other and the goal is social control. Hospitals become prisons literally overnight.

But while on the one hand this is a good thing, it also doesn't impact the issues I'm talking about here, about race and diagnosis. The diagnostic code itself has a racialized history, and the treatment system is embedded in a racialized system. So even though we should continue training doctors to be culturally competent, we should also teach them to be *structurally* competent. Psychiatry needs to become more engaged in the larger political issues about mental health disparities and pharmaceutical company influence in more progressive ways.

It's really important to look at the '60s as a case study: fitting something in the category of mental illness automatically meant that we didn't have to pay attention to the meaning of it as political protest. The minute you feature a black protester in a Haldol ad, then who cares what he's saying. He's insane. ■

Prison Madness
Terry Kupers

Terry A. Kupers, MD, MSP, is a professor at The Wright Institute. He provides court expert testimony on the psychological effects of prison conditions. He is author of *Prison Madness: The Mental Health Crisis Behind Bars and What We Must Do About It* (1999) and received the Exemplary Psychiatrist Award from the National Alliance on Mental Illness.

Today there are more people with mental illness inside prisons than confined anywhere else; state hospitals are small by comparison.

WILL HALL The US has changed dramatically since the survivor movement began: hospitals are no longer the main institutions of medical confinement. Tell us about the prison crisis.

TERRY KUPERS The US incarcerates people at a much higher rate than any other country, there are about 2.5 million people behind bars (according to the Prison Policy Initiative), and many more under prison control through probation and parole. This far surpasses our closest competitors: the Soviet Union before it broke up and South Africa before the end of Apartheid.

WH The United States has less than 5 percent of the world's population, but almost a quarter of all the world's prisoners. That's even more prisoners than China today, which we consider a much less free country. In fact, there are more black men under prison control today than ever were slaves in the US.

What is driving prison growth?

TK The War on Drugs is central. Starting in the 1970s, individuals using illegal drugs were incarcerated, which is foolhardy as a treatment intervention because we know that if you go to prison with a substance abuse problem, when you come out you will still have a substance abuse problem. Add on longer punishments, "three strikes" laws and mandatory minimum sentences, and the prison population keeps increasing. Crowding leads directly to violence, suicide, and psychiatric issues.

WH And there's been no decline in drug use as a result of the War on Drugs, which President Nixon launched as a form of political repression just as the Black Power movement was reaching its height. Tell us about how prisons are also a race issue.

TK When you walk into a prison, it's shocking; you see the racism of our country. 50% of prisoners are African-American. Another 20%-25% are Latino and Native American. If you go to the solitary confinement units, the punitive segregation, they're mostly people of color. Desirable programs that provide training and vocational skills have disproportionately white prisoners.

WH You've written that today's prisons are a throwback to the snake pit mental asylums of the 1940s with their rampant abuse, horrible conditions, injustice, and torture. What do prisons do to people's mental health?

TK Resources going into our mental health system declined steadily since the 1970s, while prisons expanded. Today there are more people with mental illness inside prisons than confined anywhere else: state hospitals are small by comparison. There is a disproportionate number of people with emotional problems among the homeless, who tend to get locked up. We know from studies that prison crowding increases violence, mental breakdown, and suicide. So the imprisonment binge has exacerbated and created serious mental illness.

There was an historic wrong turn with the "tough on crime" approach to crime begun in the '70s, which dismantled rehabilitation and education programs. Robert Martinson wrote a famous research study claiming that rehabilitation didn't work, which was seized on by conservatives and became one of the most famous papers in criminology. When 4 years later Martinson himself wrote that his own study was flawed and he had gotten it wrong, that actually rehabilitation does work, his recantation was ignored. So the punishment approach grew and prisons expanded, which added to crowding, and combined with idleness because there are no programs. In California, basketball courts were filled with bunk beds three high, so you'd get 150-200 men in what used to be a gymnasium. They can't be supervised, there's just too many people. The result is a lot of violence, a lot of rape. By the 1980s, prisons were out of control. There were a lot of what were called 'riots' that were often actually protests by prisoners demanding more humane conditions. The Prison Rape Elimination Act was passed in 2003, and mandates a "zero tolerance" attitude towards rape. Even so, rape is very prevalent and sexual abuse occurs quite a lot.

> # There was a wrong turn with the "tough on crime" approach to crime begun in the '70s, which dismantled rehabilitation and education programs.

WH Prison authorities and the media dismissed political protests as just dangerous rioting, presumably without demands or meaning?

TK Correct. Authorities could have addressed the real problem in the '80s, but instead of reducing crowding and supporting rehabilitation programs, they resorted to solitary confinement, often in supermax security segregation units where prisoners are alone nearly 24 hours a day. The 80s began these supermax prisons and now over 40 states and the federal government have built them. There is no programming, no rehabilitation, almost no educational opportunities. Think about being locked in a space the size of your bathroom for years with no human contact. This causes or exacerbates mental illness.

WH Tell us more about the impact of isolation.

TK Anyone will break down and go through anguish and despair. It's an "attribution error" to blame the person's innate proclivities for the breakdown rather than blame the extreme conditions they are put in. This is shown again and again in the research. The Stanford Mock Prison Experiment done in the early 1970s by Philip Zimbardo and Craig Haney divided ordinary student volunteers into roles as prisoners and guards. After two days they had to stop the experiment because of the sadism and cruelty that broke out. And that was with Stanford University professors watching! In prison, nobody is watching and the abuse goes on for years.

WH I do believe we need to hold people responsible, but we can do it by also addressing the social context, as with restorative justice. We tend to say the violence comes from the prisoner, that "you are the problem, you are a psychopath, you are bad." Or we blame bad guards. But it's really the conditions themselves.

Authorities could have addressed the real problem in the '80s, but instead they resorted to solitary confinement.

TK When I started going into Pelican Bay state prison in California and supermax prisons, I was told these prisoners are the worst of the worst. But when I started interviewing them, I discovered that wasn't the case. Some of them were average people who had run into trouble. A stunning proportion were suffering from serious mental illness. These individuals tend to have trouble following directions and falling in line. In prison, they are then punished with solitary confinement.

In his book *Asylums*, Erving Goffman described a person being brought to a hospital against his will. When the person would argue and be uncooperative or protest, the authorities would say "See, he really is abnormal and disturbed." On the ward no one listens to him, his clothes are taken away and he has no way to express himself. So he gets angry and hits someone, and they say "See, we were right to admit him." They put him in isolation and he acts more bizarrely, for example writing with feces on the wall. Goffman saw that when you take away their self-expression, people become more and more extreme in their efforts at expression. This is happening in the supermax prisons today, where people are screaming, cutting themselves, writing on the walls with feces. And people don't hear about it because it so difficult to visit prisoners.

Crime is the new face of racism. Seventy-five percent of people in prison for a felony did not commit a violent crime, yet our society uses fear of violence to justify extremely harsh sentences.

WH Is it true that supermax prisons contain a disproportionate number of prisoners who were protesting conditions?

TK Guards can write a ticket for anybody for anything. Prisoners who sue the prison system for denying them their rights often end up in a supermax. Such punishment tends to be retaliation. There are also disproportionate numbers of political prisoners in supermax prisons, prisoners who have a very high level of consciousness about what's going on, including religious leaders and Muslims.

WH How are things made worse by sleep issues?

TK Sleeping in these situations is extremely problematic, particularly when someone is up all night screaming, for instance someone with mania. Then the other prisoners can't sleep either. Deprivation of sleep makes every condition worse.

WH Isolation also means loss of social contacts key to mental health.

TK Prisoners need quality contact with loved ones throughout their prison term if they are going to do well when released. This requires good visiting and educational programs. But prisons are far from urban centers where prisoners, particularly the prisoners of color, come from. It's almost impossible for their families to see them, and the state doesn't help at all. Family members are harassed, searched in extremely abusive ways, and barred from visits. Rather than promote social contact to help prisoners succeed when they are released, the opposite is done.

WH What does research show about rehabilitation and offering more support to people who commit crimes?

TK Research shows rehabilitation works. But politicians and people who make money building prisons and supplying food or guns to prisons have a self interest in keeping prison populations large. They are the ones who claim that rehabilitation programs don't work.

WH This is all connected to deep prejudice and fear in society.

TK Crime is the new face of racism. Seventy-five percent of people entering prison for a felony did not commit a violent crime, yet our society uses fear of violence to justify extremely harsh sentences. If you brutalize people in prison, they will fail when they get out: they won't have the skills necessary for anything other than prison. This is especially true for people with mental illness.

WH One of the most shocking situations that affects mental health is sexual abuse.

TK Sexual abuse in prison is endemic. Among men, it tends to be prisoner on prisoner because staff do not provide a safe place, so one group of prisoners can victimize another. Among women, the abusers tend to be the staff themselves. It is hard for women to come forward because the retaliation is massive.

WH What do you mean by retaliation?

TK If a woman complains that an officer is sexually abusing her, she can be ticketed for a minor offence. Even if it's bogus, it will then keep the woman from visiting her children, and it might get her sent to segregation. Worse, she may be sexually abused again as retaliation for reporting the initial sexual abuse.

WH And prisoners often have their own histories of abuse to begin with.

TK A huge portion of prisoners had been massively traumatized as children prior to incarceration. When they experience more sexual abuse, for example forced strip searches, the repeated trauma makes them suffer more. In the men's prisons, there are gangs or groups of people who look out for each other. A perpetrator doesn't want to rape someone with tough friends, so they pick on the loners. And people with mental illness are more prone to be loners.

WH What prison reform strategy would work?

People with substance abuse problems don't belong in prison. We should be offering them treatment programs or a good job that might motivate them not to do substances.

TK We have to work at all levels. Our public schools are failing, which sends people into drugs, crime, becoming homeless and getting arrested. We're not providing adequate access to public mental health care, so people fall through the cracks and get arrested. We also need to stop sending so many people to prison in the first place. Historically, the juvenile system also provided education, counseling, and rehabilitation; today this is no longer the case. Children are being put on trial as adults in ever-increasing numbers. Finally, people with substance abuse problems don't belong in prison. We should be offering them treatment programs or a good job that might motivate them not to do substances. People with more money have lawyers, so they stay out of jail, while low-income people and people of color are less likely to have adequate legal representation. Draconian sentencing reflects this income split. Individuals caught with crack, which is more used by low income inner city people, receive a sentence ten times than if they were caught with powdered cocaine, which is used more by middle class white people.

WH Actually, a greater percentage of whites than people of color in the US use illegal drugs; for example, a 2011 Substance Abuse and Mental

Health Services Administration study showed the rate of cocaine use is twice as high among whites as blacks. And a greater percentage of whites are drug dealers than blacks. But in a low-income community, it tends to be on the street so it's more visible, unlike in the suburbs or in downtown offices.

If you brutalize people in prison, they will fail when they get out: they won't have the skills necessary for anything other than prison.

TK We must stop crowding prisons and stop sending substance abusers to prison. We need to put rehabilitation policies back together. Where people do need to be in prison, we have to ensure they receive humane treatment and that we address what got them into so much trouble to begin with. A positive development occurred in Mississippi, where I was an expert witness in a successful lawsuit against the state for its prison conditions. This led to Mississippi reducing the number of prisoners in its supermax prison, and as a result, violence across the entire Mississippi Department of Corrections dropped. That disproved the rationale for their supermax strategy.

WH So there are precedents for a very different approach to crime, such as the restorative justice movement.

TK Yes. In England, Grendon prison provides therapeutic communities where prisoners meet to make decisions for themselves rather than being told what to do every minute of every day. Participants at Grendon have a much lower violence rate while incarcerated and when they get out have a much higher rate of succeeding. And there are places where restorative justice approaches are being tried, including mediated dialogues between perpetrators and victims. Restorative justice consistently results in a much better sense of resolution and greater community reintegration than the punishment based, "law and order" approach. ∎

Indian Country
David Walker

David Walker, PhD (Missouri Cherokee) is a psychologist, writer, and musician who has consulted since 2000 with the 14 Confederated Tribes and Bands of the Yakama Nation. He is the author of *Tessa's Dance* (2012) and *Signal Peak* (2014), and has written for *Ethical Human Psychology & Psychiatry* and the *Journal of Clinical Psychology*.

Today labels of "horse-stealing mania" and "feeblemindedness" have been replaced by "bipolar" and "ADHD."

"Historical trauma" among American Indians and Alaska Natives is a metaphor for the intergenerational effects of genocide, cultural destruction, and forced assimilation. These same oppressive forces echo through Indian Country today: the biomedically-dominated US Indian Health Service (IHS) mental health system descends directly from the American eugenics movement.

From 1899 until 1933, the Hiawatha Asylum for Insane Indians in Canton, SD imprisoned "insane'" Indians, often until they died. "Indian lunacy" determinations captured native people who were displaced or resistant to federal policies. In the 1920s, US psychologists began using highly biased tests to prove the inferiority of children forced from their homes and removed to federal- and mission-run boarding schools. Today labels of "horse-stealing mania" and "feeblemindedness" have been replaced by "bipolar" and "ADHD." IHS use of diagnostic labels and first-response psychiatric medicating (chemical restraint) are just contemporary versions of coercion, indoctrination, and thought reform.

To influence change, for years I've tried to provoke a reexamination of this history and its contemporary manifestations. My few scholarly publications seemed doomed to dusty university shelves. So I dramatized the difficult journey of a Yakama Indian girl and her curmudgeon mixed-blood IHS psychologist in two indie novels: *Tessa's Dance*, and its sequel, *Signal Peak*. I'm honored they've been

"Indian lunacy" determinations captured native people who were displaced or resistant to federal policies.

well received by the Yakama Nation community and have won several awards. And I wish I could answer my spiritual brother, Dr. Eduardo Duran (recognized internationally for his work on historical trauma), who asked me about my novels, "What in any of this is fiction?" ∎

Psychology of White Racism
Tim Wise

Tim Wise was named one of "25 Visionaries Who are Changing Your World," by *Utne Reader* and has lectured on anti-racism internationally. He is the author of six books, including *Dear White America: Letter to a New Minority* (2012) and *White Like Me: Reflections on Race from a Privileged Son* (2008).

White people don't want to look at their racial privilege. Instead, insecurities, about their own immorality or drug use or lack of discipline or inherited advantages, are thrown onto people of color as projections. Stereotypes aren't just inaccurate: stereotypes are made out of disavowed truths about yourself.

For example, whites get defensive about affirmative action and believe people of color enjoy unfair advantage. But it's whites who have been enjoying a massive unfair advantage, a historical system of getting ahead: alumni admissions preferences; Federal home loan segregation; easier hiring and promotion; greater freedom from police brutality; less criminal prosecution and sentencing. Our whole society is affirmative action for white people.

Instead of seeing privilege, whites claim to be "color-blind." I treat everyone equally, they say. Julian Bond explained it best: color blindness is blindness to the consequences of color. Yes racial groups are fictional biologically, but race is real socially.

Dr. Martin Luther King was very clearly pro-affirmative action. He said you can't have equality leaving from the same starting line when the marathon began 300 hundreds earlier. The nation has done so much against blacks; now has to do things in their favor. Blacks need compensation: a promissory note is in default.

We need to see each other instead as a multiplicity of identities: race, gender, class ... that give us different privileges and oppressions. We don't solve the race problem by acting neutral. Blindness to privilege's consequences is a recipe for maintaining injustice. ∎

We need to see each other instead as a multiplicity of identities: race, gender, class, that give us different privileges and oppressions.

Afro-Caribbean Black Mental Health
Philip Morgan

Philip Morgan worked for over 15 years in human community development, including as project coordinator for Tower Hamlets African and Caribbean Mental Health Organization (THACMHO) in London. He established *The Spiritual Health and Well Being Experience* on Galaxy Radio and is today a consultant and teacher.

Part of healing is to reclaim and understand history.

WILL HALL What was your experience with the mental health system?

PHILIP MORGAN Well, I've got a strange kind of history...

I come from a broken family, I didn't grow up with a mother or father, and as a child I was very sick and had several chronic illnesses, asthma and eczema which was very bad from head to toe. I was often described as being leprous.

As a result of those things and not having any parents, I became extra marginalized. I also couldn't attend normal school due to having a hearing problem and various other learning difficulties. So I was in special schools up until the age of 8 or 9 and in the care of social services and the state throughout my childhood.

Growing up as a child I always questioned things, and I realized that the normality that existed in society was not really normal at all.

In 1993 I was evicted and was homeless for

5 years. Prior to that I had a breakdown, felt unable to cope, didn't go out or communicate, and got evicted.

I didn't want to go back into the system due to memories from my childhood of being institutionalized. So I avoided seeking any form of psychiatric help. I went through a period of a year where I barely spoke to anyone. I had some crazy times. Eventually I did see some psychiatrists who worked with homeless agencies. They were sympathetic to the concerns of vulnerable people and suggested that counseling might be helpful. So I went for counseling for a couple of years. They referred me to a housing agency where I was able to get accommodation and rehoused. That helped me calm down, refocus and come out of my shell a bit. Because of that shell, I had been very subdued.

WH Given your fear of institutionalization, was it difficult to get help?

PM In my experience, when you go to any kind of government or medical institution, the first thing they want to do is give you drugs. Most of the time they're unsympathetic to your needs and concerns. I had seen people who have gone through the system and when they emerge they're completely different people. So I avoided the system as much as I could.

WH So it was helpful for you to not be medicated?

PM Yes. I had a doctor prescribe me some pills that I took a few times. But the moment I took the pill, my brain said "there is something wrong here." It's like my spirit was questioning my actions. I decided that if I felt depressed, I had to face it straight on, rather than suppress the feelings and perhaps create more of a monster later down the line. So I stopped taking the pills.

WH Beyond being in institutional care and being marginalized your whole life, what else pushed you into that breakdown?

PM There were a lot of things. I had financial and girlfriend issues. I was living in the inner city, and there were a lot of junkies. Even though I'm a large man, I felt scared to leave my house. I lost a lot of material possessions. I couldn't deal with anything because I was trying to work, but the work available for me at the time was very low pay. I started studying social sciences and was good at it, but what I was thinking as a social scientist was too radical for the institution. I failed my exams. That also led to depression.

I went through a period of a year where I barely spoke to anyone.

WH Tell us about your work with Tower Hamlets African and Caribbean Mental Health Organization, which began in 1996 out of concerns that a disproportionate number of African and Caribbean people were being detained at Saint Clements Psychiatric Hospital in London.

PM THACMHO is run by the members, all of whom have had some kind of negative mental health experience with mental health services and or life in general. We do events like last night's panel in Brixton "Satisfy Your Soul: The Disintegration of Self Through the Illusion of Materialism." We were able to get Caribbean meals into the hospital, pushed for more medication information, and promote the social rather than the medical model. Part of healing is to reclaim and understand one's history.

Our first project examined the lives of five Africans who lived near the Tower Hamlet bowers during the late 1700s and wrote about their experiences. We created a tour based on their work. We then wrote a book about them called *Power Writers* because we believed that they had power. Their power came from their writing. The subtitle of the book is, *And Their Struggle Against Slavery*. The slave trade was abolished in 1807. We think that the power writers were the real abolitionists because their written work encouraged others to work towards ending the slave trade.

WH This occurred at a time when people believed Africans and Caribbeans were incapable of having human feelings, thoughts or ideas.

PM Precisely. Blacks were not allowed to read, write, or allowed access to any form of knowledge. Society wanted to keep these people underground. Through work of the power writers, people realized they could read and write, and at a time when many white people were unable to do so. It was really an outstanding achievement.

WH How does publicizing these experiences help black mental health today?

PM It helps people realize that African History is not just about slavery. It's also about personal achievements by those facing extreme daily adversity. Today's black people can identify with this. I feel different about myself knowing my history isn't all about slavery; my people have achieved monumental things. It makes me feel better about the history of African and Caribbean people, and makes me more prepared and able to look forward to the future.

WH Can you talk about the holistic approach to your work?

PM Oppression doesn't just occur in psychiatry. It's widespread in terms of the food we eat. We encourage our members to come off medication but also eat healthy and avoid recreational drugs. I know many who took no drugs until going into hospital and being medicated. When they came out of the hospital they now had a drug mindset. It is then easy for people who have been in psychiatric care to become hooked on recreational drugs.

WH How does generational trauma play a role in mental health?

PM "Post-traumatic slave syndrome" is serious; the experiences of the past become intergenerational. For example, it was very common for slave masters to beat their slaves. Many slaves inherited that particular action and beat their children. This got passed on. I remember being beaten as a child, and know people who still beat their children. It's not just about the physical beatings but the effects that follow: being scared to resist, scared of change, or scared of challenging authority for fear of suffering the consequences. We need to think about how we live out our histories and then address these issues.

> I had seen people who have gone through the system and when they emerge they're completely different people. So I avoided the system as much as I could.

WH What project is THACM-

HO currently working on?

PM Our latest project documents African history at the Tower of London. African people lived and worked at the tower as slaves, servants and soldiers. In addition, some of the crown jewels, gold, and arms in the tower also came from Africa. These are divided into museums all over Britain. We talk about Africa's contribution as a whole. What the Greeks learned and imparted was brought from Egypt and Ethiopia. The teachings of Plato, Aristotle, and Archimedes are the foundations of our knowledge, and they came originally from Africa. ■

Post-traumatic slave syndrome is serious: the experiences of the past become inter-generational.

Remembering John Brodie
Inez Kochius

Inez Kochius is a Freedom Center and Madness Radio volunteer who supported her friend John Brodie. The article *"A Vt. Drowning Sets Off A Story of Revelations,"* about John Brodie's death, appeared in the *Rutland Herald* on April 9, 2006.

I am blessed that John Brodie was in my life.

At 36, John was a Princeton PhD and already a world-renowned string theory physicist; the *Journal of High Energy Physics*, for example, published his essay *"D-branes in Massive IIA and Solitons in Chern-Simons Theory."* He was also a psychiatric abuse survivor, whose non-ordinary mental states were repeatedly met with forced treatment in hospitals.

On the night of his death, John was not violent or suicidal, or breaking any laws, but was behaving in a strange way: knocking on doors at 11pm. Confused and frightened neighbors called 911, and when police arrived a harmless situation escalated into a tragedy. John was terrified of the police and the threat of forced hospitalization. He ran away in a panic, fleeing into a freezing river. He drowned.

John's death is a great loss to the world.

In John's memory I ask people to stop the oppression and the torture of forced treatment. We can all start by making a conscious effort to change our thinking, abandon our fears, show love and gentleness, and accept and embrace each other's differences.

The police have *no* place in mental health care. The police are an armed force: frightening, violent, and intimidating with their guns and uniforms.

I still miss John, and the injustice is beyond words. To me John did not accidentally drown, he was driven into the water: by all of us. ∎

Death by Cop
Jenny Westberg

Jenny Westberg's writing has appeared in *The Oregonian*, *Portland Mercury*, and other media. She is the Portland mental health examiner on Examiner.com, a board member of the Mental Health Association of Portland, a Portland Hearing Voices facilitator, and co-creator of the Women Survivors of Sexual Trauma support group.

In the U.S. each year police kill an estimated 1,200 or more persons.

James Chasse died after a brutal police beating in 2006. He was not committing a crime. He was not even suspected of a crime.

Portland cops chased him down, tackled him, shot him repeatedly with a Taser, beat him, and kicked him, ignoring his pleas of "Mercy! Mercy!" When an ambulance came, officers sent it away. A photograph taken by a horrified bystander shows Chasse hogtied, face-down and broken, encircled by police officers chatting and drinking coffee.

Finally, in the back of a patrol car, struggling for breath, bleeding from his mouth, and with his head covered with a blood-soaked "spit sock," Jim went into convulsions and died. He was 42 years old.

James Chasse was an artist, a musician, and a poet. But all that mattered to police was that he was a "schizophrenic."

Chasse's family sued. And city attorneys countered with a nauseating blame-the-victim strategy: they wanted to tell the jury that "Chasse's preexisting physical and mental condition, his resistance to the officers' lawful orders and his inappropriate conduct is [sic] what caused his death." The City lost that legal battle, and eventually settled for $1.6 million.

But the killings continued. In 2010, 25-year-old Aaron Campbell, a black man in emotional crisis after learning of his brother's death, was fatally shot by police as he tried to surrender. He was unarmed. The killing so shook the city that *The Skanner*, a leading Portland black publication, advised residents in crisis *not* to call 911.

Two months later Jack Dale Collins, 58, was ordered by police out of a park restroom where he was cutting himself. Seemingly dazed, he did not respond to commands quickly enough, and so the officer shot him dead. Just two weeks before, Collins had walked into the Central Precinct police station and asked for mental health help.

And again that same year, Keaton Otis, a 25-year-old African-American, was at a traffic stop when police shot him so many times that another cop, arriving on scene, said it "sounded like World War III." Otis' mother said they too had been trying to get him help for mental health issues.

More deaths from police violence: Craig Boehler, age 46. Darryel Dwayne Ferguson, age 45. Marcus Lagozzino, age 34. And others...

As the bodies fell, the US Department of Justice (DOJ) opened a civil rights investigation, and the following year they issued their findings: the Portland Police Bureau was indeed violating the civil rights of a protected class. There was a "pattern or practice" of using excessive force against persons with psychiatric disabilities.

Police shot him so many times that another cop, arriving on scene, said it "sounded like World War III."

But in response the City of Portland failed to present a satisfactory plan for amending police conduct. So in 2012 the DOJ sued the city. After months back and forth, the parties reached a settlement agreement, including a large number of police reforms. But then, only seven weeks later, the city announced its intention to go back to court and appeal the court's ruling.

Even with reforms, the casual prejudice and routine maltreatment of persons with differences or diagnoses goes on, and not just in Portland,

The Skanner, a leading Portland African-American publication, advised residents in crisis *not* to call 911. everywhere.

In the US police kill an estimated 1,200 or more persons each year.

In every city, every day, police are targeting the most vulnerable: the disabled, the poor, the homeless, the voice-hearers, the ones in crisis. Blacks and people of color are especially at risk.

Remember your mad brothers and sisters. Memorialize them. Print their names, print the names of the officers who killed them. The grim practice of "Protect and Serve" predation flourishes in silence and shadow. Shine the light on the moral chasm that allows killing with impunity. Our lives have value. ∎

Ending Homelessness
Marykate Conor

Mary Kate Connor has been working with issues of homelessness as a service provider and an advocate in San Francisco for more than 30 years. She is the founder/director of Caduceus Outreach Services, and a psychiatric survivor.

It's about money. If you can't make money for someone, if you are not a commodity, if you are not a voting bloc, then you don't have any value. You become reviled, hated, and dehumanized.

WILL HALL When did you start to see something was wrong in the world around you?

MARYKATE CONNOR It was at the height of the Vietnam War, a war that had been going on for my whole life. My single mother was very involved in the movements for non-violence and peace, and I remember feeling incredibly helpless and hopeless about it. I'm also a survivor of sexual abuse in childhood and violent sexual assault, and I think all this culminated in having a complete dissociative experience, where essentially became two different people as a response to trauma.

I remember floating above my body like I was on the ceiling in the corner of the room, looking down at the violence happening to me. I couldn't feel anything, I couldn't feel my body at all, and I was watching it from a great distance. That's how I survived, it is something people do as a survival mechanism. But after you make that split with yourself it is very difficult to return to the person that you were.

WH What was happening?

MC I was 14 years old, and was becoming psychotically depressed. I didn't know what was going on, I just knew that I was pretty crazy. I was so out of my body and out of my mind that I would wake up and find myself in places and I had no idea how I had gotten there or where I was, or who I was sleeping next to. I was suicidal all the time. Fortunately I had a progressive mother, and she got me to a great therapist who was very patient. But at a certain point the therapist told me she wanted me to go to the hospital, because I needed to be in a safe place. This was 1970, and things were pretty grim in hospitals, so I was terrified. We made a deal, I said I would go, but only on a strict no-drug order.

> There is no separating people's lives from the health of the community. And the community was very ill. It was ill because it was impoverished.

WH Why did you ask for that?

MC I grew up next to a big VA hospital, and when I took the city bus to school I saw guys coming and going from there. They were the classic shuffling zombies. We got to know each other, and they talked with me about what was going on with them. That's the first time that I heard of medicine injections that last for a whole month, shots of Prolixin. It was terrifying to me.

WH Did your therapist honor that "no drugs" deal with you?

The answer is not providing mental health treatment in prison. Prison makes people sick, it is not an environment that people will ever get well inside of.

MC Yes. There was a huge mix of people on the unit, adolescents, veterans, old people, drug- and alcohol-users. I met extraordinary people and learned amazing things, but I was not on any medicine. I felt overall how completely dehumanized we were by the staff, how they were trained to not have feelings for us. To me, that was appalling; I went to a progressive Quaker school and was taught deliberately to think and feel and question everything. What I saw in the hospital made no sense.

After two weeks, I realized that to make these people let me go I had to be "good." Go to groups and participate and make art. It was very condescending, allowing myself to be condescended to seemed to be what "getting well" was all about. I got out, and then the internalized stigma was amazing. I felt like people were pointing their fingers at me, saying, "Oh, she's the crazy girl." And actually they were: those who did know what happened to me did point their fingers and whisper about that crazy girl. Stigma is real.

The biggest lesson for me was that healing is about being cared for in a very deep and unconditional way. That was what was so taboo in this hospital; it seemed like the staff were trained in exactly the opposite.

WH So your hospitalization experience also inspired you?

MC Yes, I knew that this was the work that I wanted to do. I ended up working at a really amazing, strange, completely wacky residential treatment center for young people, most of whom had been locked up on back wards for the majority of their lives. It was called St. George Homes, but it wasn't a Christian place, it was based in Jungian depth psychology as well as creating a healing milieu.

WH So this was one of the early community programs?

MC Yes, and some of these young people had been in places like Napa

State Hospital since they were 3 and 4 years old. A lot of the kids came with a diagnosis of mental retardation when that wasn't what was going on with them at all. St. George Homes was a program in Berkeley in regular houses on regular streets, and it was an astonishing place, looking back at it, with a really intensive focus on healing.

WH How did you work with people there?

MC Every morning the community gathered and had a ceremony where people told their dreams to each other, and then the elders of the community would give the young people specific tasks to work with about their dreams. And there were a lot more mundane things like chores and cooking, but we also spent extensive time in the wilderness.

I've seen essentially the complete destruction of anything that looks like real treatment in our society. In San Francisco, from 1970 to 1978, we had the most beautiful community mental health care. Then Proposition 13 passed: the ballot initiative that decreased property taxes. Almost overnight, every single non-essential service was de-funded.

Bear in mind this was before the whole bio-psychiatry revolution, when everything was blamed on a biochemical brain malfunction. This was 1974 and John Weir Perry (the Jungian psychiatrist) was also doing Diabasis House then. It was a tremendously creative period; a lot of what we were doing worked and a lot of it didn't work, and a lot of it was really difficult. But we were experimenting, creating a real community, a safe place where healing could happen.

WH I can only imagine what our society would be like if, after de-institutionalization, we had honored the commitment to fund real community care and hadn't sold the system to budget cuts, pharma, and the biomedical dogma.

MC Ten years later I worked in San Francisco's Tenderloin doing case management, and very similar young people were being turned out of programs and becoming homeless at age 18. I saw the conditions people had to live in: programs that called themselves aftercare for in-patient hospitalization were really SRO hotels with rats and roaches, dope dealers coming to your doorway, and no one caring about you or for you.

And it struck me: there is no separating people's individual lives from the health of the community. And the community was very ill. It was ill because it was impoverished. And it was impoverished because of negative stereotypes and stigmatized perceptions of disability.

In the thirty years that I have been doing this work, I would say that 90% of all homeless people I have worked with were traumatized as children. And personal trauma turns into institutional trauma. Children are taken from their homes and placed into foster care, where they are abused, put into another foster care where they are abused again, sent to juvenile mental health, then juvenile justice jail. And a lot of those kids go to live on the street when they are thirteen, fourteen years old. All of those kids have a similar story. All because they don't have value in the eyes of society.

WH Productivity and going to work have become the measure of worth: if you can't measure up, you're discarded.

MC It's about money. If you can't make money for someone, if you are not a commodity, if you are not a voting bloc, then you don't have any value. You become reviled, hated, and dehumanized: no wonder people are traumatized. And also traumatized by the experience of homelessness, because the way homeless people are treated by housed people is itself enough to make you crazy.

WH What is the role of the criminal justice system in this?

MC I've seen essentially the complete destruction of anything that looks like real treatment in our society. A 2006 report from the US Department of Justice cited that 65% of individuals who are incarcerated have disabling psychiatric illness. What we saw in California in the 60's and early

70's happened in the rest of the country in the late '70s and '80s.

Deinstitutionalization was supposed to take the funds used to keep people in giant, expensive warehouses, and make it available to their communities for treatment and everything else needed to get well.

In most places, that didn't happen. The money never got to the communities. It got siphoned off to pay for other things seen as more important.

But in San Francisco, from 1970 to 1978, we did have the most beautiful community mental health care. Then Proposition 13 happened, the so-called Jarvis Tax Payers Revolt, which was a ballot initiative that decreased property taxes. Almost overnight, every single non-essential service paid for by the State was de-funded. The only ones that were reinstated were "life safety" services: fire, police, EMT, etc. What was deemed non-essential wasn't funded. Mental health didn't come back. And by 1996 as a result there was more mental health treatment available to people in San Quentin State Prison than in the City and County of San Francisco.

By 1996 there was more mental health treatment available to people in San Quentin State Prison than in the City and County of San Francisco.

WH Some policy makers say that what we need is more mental health treatment in prisons. What is your view?

MC The answer is not providing treatment in prison, or providing special, segregated courts and prisons for people who need mental health treatment. Prison makes people sick, it is not an environment that people will ever get well inside of, regardless of how much treatment is provided.

The answer is to reinvest each and every human being with the worth they were born with, and stop seeing 65% of the population as being completely expendable.

WH **The prison-industrial complex is key to what is wrong with our** mental health system. We need to not lock so many people up in the first place, and instead we need to provide voluntary services to prevent people from getting to the point of crisis. Our movement talks a lot about the right to not be interfered with, but we need to emphasize the right to decent health and mental health services. We always hear "there's not enough money" but there *is* enough money: it's just not used fairly. The whole country went the way of California's Proposition 13 tax breaks for the rich; we need to have equitable income policy that doesn't leave the rich 1% paying less taxes than working people.

MC What you are saying is not just a dream; it's entirely possible to do this.

WH Utah ended longterm homelessness with a "housing first" approach that gave people homes and support. And you provided an living example in San Francisco with Caduceus Outreach Services.

MC I started Caduceus in 1996: I wanted psychiatry to do pro bono service like attorneys, and come to the streets rather than having people go into a clinical environment that is completely off-putting in every way. I wanted to do this without any government money whatsoever, so no one could tell us what to do or dictate who we could or couldn't treat. And our funding

90% of all homeless people I have worked with were traumatized as children.

couldn't be cut. You cannot provide treatment where one year there is money for it and next year there isn't. If my healthcare were provided that way, I would sue for malpractice.

I also wanted homeless people to understand that there are psychiatrists who are not all-powerful and who won't lock them up. So I spent a year looking for doctors who would come to work for Caduceus for free, and not have to deal with bureaucracy, or have anything between them and the person they are working with, so they could make that powerful connection where healing takes place.

WH What services did Caduceus provide?

Our movement talks a lot about the right to not be interfered with, but we need to emphasize the right to decent health and mental health services.

MC People had a place to rest or sleep in the daytime, take a little bird bath in a private bathroom, have something to eat, and be with other people. A place where they are going to be safe, without having to give anybody their name or social security number or anything else.

People got psychiatric services 3-4 days after entering the program, compared to 6-8 weeks with City funded clinics. We did criminal justice advocacy, and represented people in court, pushing back the really punitive probation and parole sentences that are designed to help people fail and return to prison.

We helped people store their medication and figure out how to take it safely; the cops, when they roust homeless people and shake them down, take their medicine and throw it away, or arrest them for it, it's amazing what cops do. We had drop-in clinics where people can see their doctor if they want to. We did housing applications and advocacy, and brief emergency housing for people.

One hundred percent of our SSI applications got awarded on the first application. We had a welcoming, safe drop-in space for respite from the streets, with food, phones, computers, a private bathroom, art supplies, and a living room. And all of this was designed to reflect the worth and value of people, without fear, judgment, or blame for having become outcasts by society.

WH How many people were a part of Caduceus and what was the budget?

MC We served about 100 people a year with a budget of $300,000. That's $3,000 per person per year.

WH What does standard care cost?

MC It costs about $200 an hour for involuntary psychiatric treatment, so two days in a locked ward is $12,000. One month in jail in San Francisco costs $3,750; one year is $45,000.

Our services were voluntary, not jail, and much cheaper.

WH Could Caduceus be reproduced around the country?

MC Yes, if there were clinicians willing to take the risk. A model that is both professional and non-professional, but everyone is treated equally. Clinicians have to actually engage at a deep level with the people they are working with, so that they could say honestly, "I really love my clients."

WH What happened to Caduceus?

Two days in a locked ward is $12,000.
One month in San Francisco jail costs $3,750.
One year in San Francisco jail costs $45,000.
Our services were $3000 per person, *per year*.

MC In January 2011, Caduceus Outreach Services was forced to close its doors because of funding cuts. We hope to begin our new program, Caduceus Justice, soon. This program will focus on changing, not reforming, the culture and practice of law enforcement, in order to end lethal encounters between police and people in crisis. ∎

Vets Aren't Crazy, War Is
Paula Caplan

Paula J. Caplan PhD, associate at Harvard University's DuBois Institute, is a psychologist, award-winning playwright and filmmaker, and activist. Her eleventh book, *When Johnny and Jane Come Marching Home: How All of Us Can Help Veterans* (2011), won three national nonfiction awards.

It's normal to get upset when you see your buddy blown up, when you are raped by your sergeant, or when you return home to find your job was given to someone else. But if military veterans having these human reactions seek help, they are often diagnosed as mentally ill and given psychotherapy and psychiatric drugs.

Why should it be considered a mental illness to be devastated by war, assault, or other traumatic experiences? And if that is a mental illness, then what would a mentally *healthy* response be to death, moral horror, or major life losses?

Being classified as mentally ill can worsen the soul-crushing isolation of many veterans' lives, as well as fuel shame and cause self-confidence to plummet. A diagnosis can lead vets to believe wrongly that they should have "gotten over it;" isolate them behind a therapist's closed office door; and make it harder to find employment. Real physical problems are often mistakenly attributed to the imagination of a person who is allegedly mentally ill; veterans with children can lose custody; and a diagnosis can jeopardize their right to make their own decisions about medical and legal affairs.

Psychiatric drugs carry dangers of severe negative effects, including impaired emotional and sexual functioning and increased risk of suicide or violence. Shockingly, veterans are often subjected to polypharmacy, prescribed three, six, or even twelve drugs simultaneously, although drug interactions are rarely even researched.

Therapy and drugs are at the very least clearly insufficient: the suffering of veterans of past and present wars is reflected in the fact that at least 22 veterans kill themselves every day, with the highest rates among vets of World War II, the Korean War, and the Viet Nam War, those who have been isolated the longest. More than 58,000 veterans are homeless each night, and substance abuse and family breakdown rates among veterans are increasing.

Sometimes nonveterans say, "I'd love to help, but I am not a therapist, so there is nothing I can do." But when we send anguished veterans off alone to talk to therapists, we convey the message that we don't want to listen. Furthermore, we keep the truth about war, sexual assault in the military, and other realities of military service and the return home, under wraps. This fuels our nation's unhealthy and dangerous war illiteracy and military illiteracy.

What we need is massive depathologizing of the effects of military trauma. We need widespread use of alternative and low-risk approaches, including just listening to veterans through The Welcome Johnny and Jane Home Project; working with vets through the arts, meditation, physical exercise, or community volunteering; or helping them get a service animal.

Anyone can participate in a simple listening session, in which the non-veteran sits in respectful silence and listens to whatever a veteran from any era wants to say. Research at Harvard Kennedy School shows this to be healing for the veterans, and also for the helpers.

We know that listening to people, truly listening and not judging, labeling, or pushing away, can be positively transformative. ∎

Madness and Social Justice
Caty Simon

Caty Simon organized with Freedom Center, ARISE, and Poverty is Not A Crime. She co-edits the sex worker blog *Tits and Sass,* and her writing has appeared in *Alternet, Make/shift, Refinery29,* and *The Influence.*

As a sexually active young woman I wasn't wise enough to stay good and closeted in my religious community. So when I came out as bisexual at age 15, it was one of the reasons I was psychiatrically incarcerated. They immediately branded me with the label of "borderline personality disorder," a diagnosis which reads like an extreme caricature of male fear of women. As a teenager, I was threatened with hospitalization because I didn't want to take the mind-stultifying drugs prescribed to me; only to then grow up into a young adult threatened with imprisonment for taking illicit drugs which actually *did* help me cope. Throughout my adult life, I've hid my psychiatric history when I ran into official trouble, to avoid being stigmatized and further discredited as a "dual diagnosis drug user."

So my own oppression hinged on multiple axes: being a woman, a psychiatric patient, being queer, and using illegal drugs. When I joined Freedom Center in Northampton Massachusetts, it made sense for me to take a leading role in our collaborative work with social justice organizations such as ARISE for Social Justice around queer rights, feminism, low income rights, anti- war on drugs, and prison abolition work. After all, I myself was a walking embodiment of "intersectionality" in the mad movement.

We worked with Arise's Springfield Harm Reduction Coalition to call for alternatives to mandated jail diversion programs, because involuntary drug treatment goes against the principles of self-determination and harm reduction. When the state refused to dedicate sufficient funds to voluntary drug treatment services, it made arrest the only way to access treatment, and made a mockery of recovery. Drug diversion programs are also a racist and classist punishment: drug arrests disproportionately target the poor and people of color. And open arrest records and background checks alienate people from the community by complicating their employment and housing.

I was also our spokesperson for the Poverty Is Not A Crime alliance of college students, low income people, and local progressives. We worked against Northampton legislation that would criminalize "panhandling," asking for spare change on the street. When you are low income or homeless, you are dehumanized because of your class, but also because the public assumes you to be crazy and potentially violent. This is despite the fact that both homeless and psychiatrically diagnosed people are much more likely to be *victims* of violence than others. The drug war also tars panhandlers' request for money with the brush of addiction, even though most drugs in our city are consumed by affluent young adults.

Local shop owners convinced the Northampton Mayor's office to post signs city-wide discouraging giving spare change to panhandlers, claiming they were probably just going to waste it on drugs. So Freedom Center parodied the Mayor's hypocritical effort. We put up our own signs asking people not to give money to businesspeople, because who knows how *they'd* use the money? The satirical posters made it to the local newspaper and struck a chord; the Mayor dropped the campaign.

Proponents of the panhandling ban invoked the bogeyman of deranged panhandlers threatening college town student safety, so we mobilized again, inspiring area Five Colleges students to protest in huge numbers. Time after time we packed every city council meeting where the issue was discussed. Finally, legislation supporters were shamed so thoroughly they withdrew it from consideration.

The mad movement is not and should not be single issue. Psychiatric oppression, like all oppression, is always constructed along race, class, and gender lines. Our abhorrence of psychiatric incarceration and restraints should extend to efforts at prison abolition. When we condemn Big Pharma for peddling psychiatric drugs, we must also condemn the prison system for locking people up for using illegal drugs that are often chemically similar. To eliminate the roots of psychiatric abuse, we have to fight social injustice everywhere. ∎

The Urge To Die
David Webb

David Webb is the first suicide survivor to complete a PhD on suicide, and is the author of *Thinking About Suicide: Contemplating and Comprehending the Urge to Die* (2013). He has been on the board of the World Network of Users and Survivors of Psychiatry and the international representative for the Australian Federation of Disability Organizations (AFDO).

I still can't say for sure the cause of my suicidal feelings. The trigger was the break-up of a very significant relationship. I've lived my whole life with deep feelings of sadness, and when my relationship collapsed it was like the dam broke and sadness overwhelmed me. I just wanted to go to sleep and not wake up.

I'm not a violent person, I'm not a brave person. I tried a couple of times to jump off a high place and I just couldn't push myself over the edge. I don't know anything about guns. I just wanted to take a drug and not wake up, but drugs are the least reliable form of suicide.

I was also exhausted. I felt I had tried everything. I had done years of hospitals, doctors, retreats, ashrams, medication, counseling, talking therapy, I was just utterly exhausted. I just reached the point where life was intolerable and I couldn't see any alternative.

And so I tried to snuff that life out. I tried to kill myself.

Suicide was my last attempt to take some control of my life. And when you wake up after trying to kill yourself, particularly if you've been revived in hospital, it's a pretty awful feeling. There's no sense of failure quite like failing at suicide.

In the end, what set me free was what I call "spiritual self-inquiry." It's within the tradition of Yoga, but it's not a Yoga practice. It asks the question: Who am I? And then it says, you cannot find the answer by the mind, the answer is found in the silence of the quiet mind. Bit by bit, all of the pieces came together. And one of the factors was the exhaustion. I just felt there was absolutely nowhere else to go.

Finally, I had to surrender. A wonderful and beautiful word. I surrendered to the silence within me. Almost overnight everything changed, because in that silence I discovered inner peace.

And I realized this inner peace has been with me all my life. After 45 years of thinking my innermost self was this very sad person, I discovered that my innermost self was an endless, timeless sense of peace. I also felt like a complete idiot, because here I had spent all these years searching for something, and there it was inside me all the time.

For the first few months after that, it was a novel feeling to actually want to be alive. And I was curious to make some sort of sense of what I had been through. So I went to the library and got some books on "suicidology," which is an established academic discipline, there is even an American Association for Suicidology.

I was pretty appalled. The actual suicidal person is virtually invisible in professional literature about suicide. I couldn't recognize myself or my story in what all these experts were saying. It was all about brains and neurotransmitters. What the actual person is thinking and feeling have become increasingly irrelevant.

It's not helpful to reduce complex mysterious human experiences to the shallow knowledge of medical science. I believe the biological view is one of the biggest obstacles that we face in suicide prevention.

We need to stop pretending that suicidal feelings are rare. It's a very common, natural, and normal part of many people's lives. Between ten and 25 per cent of the population have their own first-person knowledge of feeling suicidal. That's not being researched into at all by experts.

I encourage suicidal people to respect their feelings, indeed, to honor their feelings as special, meaningful and significant, even sacred, because they are.

We need to not suppress these feelings, and also not to indulge them. There is a space where you can just be with these feelings. And this can be a very healing space. ■

The Cutting Edge
Ruta Mazelis

Ruta Mazelis is an ex-patient who barely survived the psychiatric system over 20 years ago. She is founder of *The Cutting Edge* newsletter.

Self injury is not necessarily always a dangerous behavior.

I come from a very abusive childhood and I started self-injuring pretty early, before age ten. I cut myself with blades, burned myself with cigarettes, or sometimes punched myself. Later in life, people at work found out, and so I was referred to a psychiatrist, which led me to get institutionalized against my will.

Whenever staff were afraid I might cut again, I was dragged off to the seclusion room and forced on medication. Finally when I absolutely knew I couldn't survive any more of these psychiatric interventions, I became a good little patient so I could get discharged. I decided I would rather die than go back to the traditional mental health system.

I figured I couldn't possibly be alone with what I was doing to myself. I started holding discussion groups. This was before the internet, so I put up little flyers that said "If you've ever felt the need to cut yourself and you want to talk about it in a place that's not going get you committed, let's meet." People would actually travel from a few states away to come talk, and *The Cutting Edge* newsletter was born.

I learned that all kinds of people self-injure, not just the stereotype teenage girl. And I met people from all over the globe who need a safe place where they won't risk their freedom if they talk about self injury.

One of the key messages we are trying to get out is that self injury is not necessarily a dangerous behavior. And it's absolutely not a suicide attempt or so-called 'para-suicidal behavior.' Self-injury actually helps people survive a really hard moment, and not go ahead and kill themselves. And in all this time I haven't heard of anybody who accidentally did kill themselves from self-injury.

I wish I could undo twenty years of smoking. That was much more destructive to my body than all the years of cutting and self-injury!

Cutting works when you don't feel you have other options. That cut releases emotional pain or psychic stress or whatever it is for that person. It serves as a release so you can just get through that moment and figure out how to go ahead. It's a useful tool for coping.

When I ask people why they stopped cutting or self injury, the most common response is "I just didn't need to do it any more. I worked through the stuff that was pushing me into so much pain." And one of the most thoughtful ways I ever heard to describe cutting is: *It's a voice on the skin.*

There's no single reason someone turns to self-injury. There are common themes we share because we are all human and we're all in pain. But it's up to everybody to figure out what it means for them and what they want to do about it. It doesn't help to judge, interpret, or tell someone what to do. Instead, say "I don't understand why you need to burn or cut yourself. But I'm here for you. I know cutting helps you somehow. And I want to help you, too." ∎

Time To Stop the Violence
Oryx Cohen

A leader in the mental health consumer/survivor/ex-patient movement, Oryx Cohen was co-founder of Freedom Center and is the director of the National Empowerment Center's Technical Assistance Center. Oryx co-produced and stars in the film *Healing Voices*.

> We are all to blame, and we are all responsible for creating healthier communities so these tragedies do not occur. We all have more power than we realize.

Usually when the acts of violence that are all too common in the United States occur, I try not to think about them, and I focus on the positives, to move on quickly. I suppose I am not that different in that respect from so many other Americans. Maybe it's because I am a parent of young children, but the shooting in Newtown, Connecticut has finally woken me up. The violence has to end. For our sake, for our children's sake, for humanity's sake. We cannot allow such horrific violence to continue.

It seems that every time a terrible act like the one at Sandy Hook occurs, the blame game begins. We blame the individual for having a "mental illness," we blame guns, we blame parents, we blame politicians, we blame the media. Blame, blame, blame. And then we get defensive. I am guilty as charged: I don't want my colleagues in the "mental health" world blamed just as much as parents don't want themselves blamed, etc., etc. The truth is, every single person that makes up this country is to blame for allowing these events to keep happening. We are all to blame.

Most people are asking serious questions about guns, and I think rightfully so. A few people are asking serious questions about the use of psychiatric drugs, and I think rightfully so. These are big political issues and I think the average person is left feeling a bit hopeless that they can do anything to make broad social changes happen.

However, we are all to blame, and we are all responsible for creating healthier communities so these tragedies do not occur. We all have more power than we realize.

I believe there are three simple (although possibly revolutionary) actions we can all take to realize our power and to stop the violence.

Stop labeling people.

Not many people are talking about the effect that labeling or diagnosing others has on the rest of the society. I believe this is where the conversation should start. Just because we live in a culture that has hundreds of different ways of categorizing people as abnormal, bipolar, oppositional defiant, autistic, etc., does not mean that we as individuals have to accept it or use that language to describe other people.

Here is what often happens when someone is labeled:

A child behaves differently than other children and this is upsetting to the adults around the child. The child receives a label that "explains" why he or she is different. Instead of reducing stigma, the label actually increases stigma (the definition of stigma is a "mark" and the label is a way of marking someone as different). People treat the child as different and stay away from them, increasing isolation and the feeling of difference. Often the child is then the victim of bullying, teasing, and being socially ostracized.

And in rare circumstances, these children, feeling that they are totally separated from the rest of their human family and have nobody to con-

We can all do a better job of recognizing the many opportunities to include everyone.

nect with about their strong feelings, do terrible things.

How about we approach every person as fully human? To me, these labels are in some ways just a socially and scientifically accepted form of name-calling. They are a form of psychological violence. If we can make a conscious choice to not use these labels in our own lives, we can go a long way to stopping the violence.

Stop bullying.

It's not surprising that many kids who are victims of bullying end up being in so much pain that they either hurt themselves or seek "revenge." We each have our own responsibility to recognize when bullying is happening and to take action.

Recent events have made me realize that I need to have more conversations with my own children about what happens at their preschool. I'm trying my best to be aware if there is a child (my own or another child) who is being bullied, teased, or ostracized. As parents we need to instill an understanding that it is unacceptable to be mean to another human being, regardless of difference.

It is all of our responsibility to do something; talk to the teachers, the administration, have conversations with the children involved; if we discover that bullying is occurring.

Reach out to kids who are different

We need to give much more outreach and support to the people who are currently being labeled, marginalized, and forced to the fringes of society.

If we open our eyes and hearts, we can notice young people who are different, extremely isolated, or extremely troubled. We know who these kids are in our communities. We need to start reaching out to them, not by saying there is something wrong with them and they need a diagnosis and they need treatment, but by reaching out in a way that embraces their humanity and welcomes them back into our human family.

There are kids in my children's school who are different and perceived that way by the other children. I'm sure this occurs at almost every school in the United States. As parents we do our best to remind our kids that it is extremely important to be nice to everyone and include them in their play, to go out of their way to talk to those kids who don't have very many friends.

Labels are in some ways just a socially and scientifically accepted form of name-calling.

Of course, kids, like anybody else, are going to develop their own friendships and "click" better with some of their peers and not with others. However, we can all do a better job of recognizing the many opportunities to include everyone. For example, our daughter had a 4th-year birthday party, and so we decided to invite everyone in her class.

After the tragedy at Sandy Hook, I'm trying to be more conscious of ways that my community, and I personally, can do a better job at reaching out to those (children or adults) who seem isolated and struggling. Recently I was playing basketball at an open gym and there were two young adults there who definitely fit the description. I was heartened to see that the rest of the guys accepted them in to their group. One of the young men was particularly talkative and friendly, in a way that some might find annoying. Some people might call him slow and I wouldn't be surprised if he was given some sort of diagnosis. But we didn't seem to care. Instead of turning our noses in the air or putting him down in subtle or not so subtle ways, we engaged with him as an equal, asked him questions, and in the end he was just another guy getting a workout.

The other young man was much more quiet and introverted. His eyes darted back and forth and he seemed very self-conscious. You could tell it was a big deal for him to be there. I was uplifted at the way we all treated him. We gave him compliments: "Nice shot!" "Great hustle out there." And of course, high fives can go a long way.

The more connected we are with friends and neighbors, the more we can be aware of those who may need additional support.

In my work with the Western Massachusetts Recovery Learning Community, it was an everyday occurrence that people in our community had overwhelming suicidal feelings, heard distressing voices, and/or were going through other extreme states. However, because we had such a strong sense of community with real friendships, access to peer support groups such as Alternatives to Suicide and Hearing Voices, and people reaching out to those they hadn't heard from in a while, the amount of violence in our community was impressively low.

As individuals and as a community, we need to give much more outreach and support to the people who are currently being labeled, marginalized, and forced to the fringes of society. We also need to do a better job of reaching out to our communities in general. We need to talk to our neighbors, our teachers, and other members of our community to actually know what is going on in our social networks. The more connected we are with friends and neighbors, the more we can be aware of those who may need additional support. Hopefully we can all take a few peeks up from our smartphones and busy lives to make an effort at direct human-to-human connection. It's necessary to rebuild our broken communities.

Of course, these same strategies apply not only to young adults, but to older adults as well. We don't need to be intrusive about it and we need to respect those who truly like to spend a lot of time alone, but I feel it is our responsibility to at least reach out.

Who knows? You might save a life. ∎

Surviving America's Depression Epidemic
Bruce Levine

Bruce Levine is a psychologist and author of *Commonsense Rebellion: Taking Back Your Life from Drugs, Shrinks, Corporations, and a World Gone Crazy* (2001) and *Surviving America's Depression Epidemic: How to Find Morale, Energy, and Community in a World Gone Crazy* (2007).

In the US we have a tenfold or higher increased rate of depression over the last fifty years. In 1987, the US mental illness disability rate was 1 in every 184 Americans, but by 2007 it had more than doubled: 1 in every 76 Americans on psychiatric disability. Our biochemistry or genes just don't change in a couple of generations.

So why the increase? Partly because the economy is what it is, some people are getting marginalized and are willing to accept making six or seven hundred dollars a month from a disability payment, because they can't be a part of the economy we have today.

There's also the pharmaceutical companies, who promote the idea anybody having a difficult time must be mentally ill and need psychiatric drugs. Selling antidepressants is a more than 12 billion dollar a year industry. And the psychiatric drugs themselves can create serious long term problems.

More industrialized, materialistic, and unequal societies create more mental illness. A study of Mexican immigrants showed that the first generation living in the US had *twice* the rate of mental illness than their parents. The rate of depressive episodes was three times higher.

A lot of people are in pain because they are just not willing to numb themselves out to how crazy and dehumanizing our society is.

People are utterly demoralized. We have to be morale builders, cheerleaders, and inspirers for each other. We don't need authorities or doctors, we need to turn towards each other and take back the authority of our lives.■

Buy Nothing
Kalle Lasn

Kalle Lasn is editor of *Adbusters* magazine, "the journal of the mental environment," and has launched Buy Nothing Day, TV Turnoff Week, and Black Spot Logo. *Adbusters* helped catalyze the 1999 Word Trade Organization protests and the Occupy uprising. He is author of *Culture Jam: The Un-Cooling of America (1999)*.

We started *Adbusters* magazine because we felt people weren't generating our culture from the bottom up anymore. It was being spoon fed to us top-down by advertising agencies, television stations, and corporations.

From little babies crawling around the TV set, we grow up propagandized by commercialism, violence-laced programming, and erotic titillations, just to keep us watching. By the time we are teenagers we're recruited into believing "you can be happy if you buy stuff." We live in a hyperactive consumerism, inundated with approximately 3000 marketing messages a day that seep into our brains whether we like it or not. This onslaught is causing stress and mood disorders, depression, and anxiety attacks.

There is a huge increase in mental dysfunction over two generations and it is not going to abate unless we start working on changing our culture rather than changing our brain chemistry.

Adbusters decided to not just be a magazine but to also launch waves of activism around the world. A lot of people get involved in Buy Nothing Day to escape the strain of living in this culture. They also join for political reasons: one of the root causes of our never-ending War Against Terror is the huge gulf between the rich and poor. We the rich 1 billion people on the planet, 20% of us, consume over 80% of all the goodies in the global marketplace. And we wonder why so many parts of the planet are breeding grounds for terrorism. ∎

Roadmap for Change
James Gottstein

James Gottstein is a Harvard-educated lawyer, psychiatric survivor, and longtime activist for change in the mental health system. He is the director of The Law Project for Psychiatric Rights.

When I told hospital staff I was a Harvard Law School educated attorney, some thought it was just a psychotic delusion.

When I was 29 I didn't sleep for days. I went psychotic: I thought the devil was after me, and I jumped out of my father's second-floor window in my underwear. After I was captured, I was taken to Alaska Psychiatric Institute in a straight-jacket, and pumped full of Mellaril.

When I told hospital staff I was a Harvard Law School educated attorney, some said it was just a psychotic delusion. Others announced I would never be an attorney again. I refused to believe them. In the hospital I was somewhat belligerent, since I was used to being free. But in spite of the heavy medication and the poor sleeping conditions, I gradually learned that I had to behave. I ceased being uncooperative at stupid daily "group therapy" sessions, and I attended the asinine "occupational therapy," where we literally had to weave pot holders.

I was let out after a month, and I soon had a job at a law firm and resumed my career. I was lucky to have escaped being made permanently mentally ill by the system. This changed the trajectory of my life: towards trying to prevent people from suffering the fate I narrowly avoided.

I founded The Law Project for Psychiatric Rights, PsychRights, in late 2002 after reading Robert Whitaker's *Mad in America: Bad Science, Bad Medicine, and the Enduring Mistreatment of the Mentally Ill*. To me, it was not just a great book, but also a litigation roadmap for challenging forced psychiatric drugging. Under the United States Constitution, people's fundamental rights to liberty cannot be legally infringed by the government unless there is a compelling governmental reason and there are no less restrictive means for accomplishing the government's goal. PsychRights' mission is to mount a strategic litigation campaign against forced psychiatric drugging and forced electroshock, and to stop the drugging of children, particularly children in poverty receiving Medicaid.

> # Under the United States Constitution, people's fundamental rights to liberty *cannot be legally infringed by the government* unless there is a compelling governmental reason and there are no less restrictive means.

I've had some victories. The Alaska Supreme Court ruled forced drugging procedures are unconstitutional to the extent that don't provide clear and convincing evidence that the drugging is in the person's best interest and there is no less intrusive alternative available. The State also held Alaska's involuntary commitment statute unconstitutional, because the statute said someone could be held involuntarily without the state proving that the person was unable to survive safely in freedom.

I am most known for releasing the Zyprexa Papers, secret Eli Lilly internal documents which showed that pharmaceutical giant had lied about how Zyprexa causes diabetes and other metabolic problems, and illegally marketed Zyprexa to children. I followed court procedures in publicizing these secrets (which made the cover of *The New York Times*), but in the ensuing litigation the court decided I had conspired to steal the documents. I was prohibited from further dissemination.

My strategy today is (1) changing public attitudes, (2) creating other choices, and (3) strategic litigation. I call this The Transformation Triangle. It's based on debunking key myths: that psychiatric drugs are the best treatment, that locking people up, drugging and electroshocking them against their will is an effective strategy, and that people do not recover after a diagnosis of serious mental illness.

In 1954, *Brown v. Board of Education* held segregation unconstitutional. That played a pivotal role in changing public attitudes, and today it is hard to find anyone that believes segregation is acceptable. By winning the Alaska court cases and more to come, I hope we can achieve a similar shift in public attitudes: from "psychiatric drugs for everyone, forever, of course," to a recognition that there should be real choices. ∎

Democratic Psychiatry
Peter Stastny

Peter Stastny MD received his medical degree as a psychiatrist from the University of Vienna and is an associate professor at the Albert Einstein College of Medicine. He is one of the leading organizers of the International Network of Treatment Alternatives for Recovery, and with Darby Penney created *The Suitcase Exhibit*, based on patient lives at Willard State Hospital.

What is the best way to deal with a person who says "I'm feeling like killing myself?" Tie them to a chair, put them on Haldol, and lock them in a hospital for weeks?

WILL HALL You've got quite a history as a critical psychiatrist.

PETER STASTNY As a medical student I was involved with "Democratic Psychiatry" in Austria: we wanted to close down the mental institutions. Austria is the birthplace of Freud, so it's like being behind enemy lines in some way.

My supervisor at Albert Einstein College of Medicine, Joel Kovel, was a Marxist psychoanalyst. That was a time when psychoanalysis was considered potentially revolutionary.

WH But isn't psychoanalysis traditionally very conservative?

PS Conforming, promoting the state, and the superego winning isn't the only possible position. The tradition is broad when you consider Wilhelm Reich, Alfred Adler, Herbert Marcuse and many feminist psychoanalysts, all of whom see individual transformation as impossible without social transformation. Franco Basaglia and others in Italy based their revolution on a class struggle, increasing worker awareness of how institutions maintain patients in the role of, well a role below slaves really. Nowadays psychoanalysis is not radical any more; most psychoanalysts are in private practice and rely on wealthy patrons who can afford it.

WH In Italy, weren't they able to abolish a lot of the hospitals?

PS They succeeded with laws prohibiting any more admissions to state institutions in Italy, and causing hospitals to close down. Then community based services developed, but not as radical as the initial impetus. In Turin or in Trieste there has been some change: in Trieste former patients became active in starting cooperative businesses. But basically people were liberated and then largely ignored. It was a top-down revolution carried out by the professional class. Today Italy hardly has an ex-patient/survivor movement.

In the US we are twenty-five or thirty years into a movement. When I first got involved the fight against coercion was very strong; now some of those voices have quieted down. Today we have former patients becoming mental health providers or "peer workers," but I have serious doubts that was actually a positive development. It's been positive for individuals, but co-optation reigns and people are not expressing positions against medication or against coercion. They're told to keep fairly silent.

WH Legal scholar Lawrence Lessig talks about "dependency corruption." You don't go against those you depend on for money. But you yourself have managed to stay true to an anti-force politics.

PS The logic that says you have to treat extreme emotional states with extreme measures is false. Extreme states can be dealt with using subtle and quiet methods: you're willing to engage but you're not going to pounce on the person, to restrain the person physically and inject them.

Instead you're saying: "I'm here, I'm willing to be present for you." In the Soteria House program, for example, just the staff's willingness to tolerate and support people in psychosis meant most people came back from extreme states without drastic measures.

What is the best way to deal with a person who says "I'm feeling like killing myself?' Tie them to a chair, put them on Haldol, and lock them in a hospital for weeks? Or continue to talk and listen to them, maybe for many hours, and come up with a way to continue living?

And if you take a poll of community psychiatrists, most of them would tell you that 90% of the hospitalizations are not necessary. I don't agree with any type of force done by a medical practitioner. Psychiatrists should not have the authority to force someone into a hospital or into treatment, those decisions should be up to society. When practicing medicine and practicing coercion are conflated you are on the slippery slope towards Auschwitz. Just as we want to separate church from state we should separate medicine from the enforcement powers of the state.

WH Your work as a psychiatrist also helps people get off medications.

PS I know a guy who has taken antipsychotic neuroleptics for years and years and he's got tardive dyskinesia, a neurological disorder caused by medication. Within a week or two when he stops his medication all that acts up terribly. He has bad muscle, mouth and jaw movements, facial grimacing, jerky hands and feet, and cognitive deterioration. He has a super-sensitivity to psychosis as well. And why? It's because of withdrawal. His brain receptors have been transformed by the medications. And therefore he can no longer live a normal life at all. And this is not a relapse, this is not his illness coming back, these are the iatrogenic disabilities that have been caused by the medications, which resurface when the medication is discontinued.

There's virtually no research or money spent on figuring out what to do with such people. There are virtually no studies on tardive dyskinesia; they used to even say it was caused by the presumed disease of schizophrenia, until the evidence became undeniable that it was the drugs causing it. The pharmaceutical company answer is: "Well, we've got a new medication that doesn't cause that." Except the new drugs *do* cause that, and also have metabolic side effects, which turn out to be a boom for pharma: now you've got people at the age of thirty or thirty-five who will not only take an antipsychotic/neuroleptic that costs whatever, but they also have to take Liptor, they also have to take blood pressure medicine, and anti-diabetes medicine, all sold by pharmaceutical companies. And it can add up to thousands of dollars a month.

WH Pharma giant Eli Lilly's big seller Zyprexa causes diabetes, and another big seller for Eli Lilly is medicine for... diabetes.

PS Isn't that something! I once gave a talk called "Unrequited Schizophilia." Psychiatrists are pursuing a Holy Grail, believing someday they're going to be just as good as other medical practitioners, just as good as neurologists, because they'll discover the biology underneath the schizophrenia label and find a treasure trove. It's just a shared delusion. ∎

When practicing medicine and practicing coercion are conflated you are on the slippery slope towards Auschwitz.

On Our Own
Sera Davidow

Sera Davidow is director of the Western Massachusetts Recovery Learning Community, co-producer of the film *Beyond The Medical Model*, and a blogger at *Mad In America*.

WILL HALL Tell us about the Western Massachusetts Recovery Learning Community.

SERA DAVIDOW We have four centers in Massachusetts where people can attend groups like Hearing Voices, Alternatives to Suicide and the after-incarceration support group. We also have a three bedroom peer respite hospital alternative, one of only fourteen in the country, called Afiya.

WH And these are all run by people who have been patients in the system. What was your experience?

SD I used self-injury, burning and cutting to help myself when I felt out of control with my emotional pain. I was given a Borderline Personality Disorder diagnosis, which is basically saying "there is something fundamentally wrong with who you are, something wrong with your personality." The diagnosis is really destructive, and hospitals certainly didn't help me feel safe or more in control.

WH And how did you move on with your life?

SD With many stumbling points! I come from a lot of privilege, and even in my worst moments I was still able to pay rent, and keep away from some other people in my life, that certainly helps. Part of it was just the passage of time. And having a child gave me a clear reason to keep moving forward.

I also started to work in the mental health system. For the first five years I didn't tell anybody what I had been through, then I decided to "come out" and share my patient experiences.

WH Were you able to keep your job?

SD Not for long! When I put my story on the internet, my supervisor and their funder started questioning my competence.

WH Not because of job performance?

SD For five years I had been promoted and told my clinical work was above many people with degrees I didn't have. Our program was very successful. So, yes, being discredited and scrutinized was directly tied to coming out as someone diagnosed. I ended up losing my job. But then I began a new role, becoming co-director of the Recovery Learning Community with Oryx Cohen.

WH It was an exciting time, Freedom Center and other groups had been organizing for years and now the system starts to hire people, including Freedom Center activists, into new recovery programs.

SD Judi Chamberlin says in her manifesto, *On Our Own*, "Look, we can provide support. We are the ones who need to be in leadership." Over the last five to ten years governments have been hiring people with experience of hospital and diagnosis and calling them peers. I think this is changing the system.

But in practice it also gets really distorted with tokenism, where traditional professionals hand-pick the people who get hired. "Peers" are selected because they share the values of the traditional system. They promote drugging and labels, and push the same attitudes and perspectives we are trying to change in the first place. It becomes a cooptation process. We are seeing this happening all over the country.

I often question if it is workable to have one peer specialist in an organization by themselves, or even five, because they are surrounded by hundreds of people trained in the traditional model. So I am not sure where all this is going to go.

I do hope we drop the word "peer." Just like "client" "consumer," "patient," "user," there's so many of these one-word labels. Ultimately we need to just be people connecting with people. ∎

Meeting Different Realities
Arnold Mindell

Arnold Mindell is a Jungian therapist and founder of Process Work and Earth Based Psychology. His most recent book is *Processmind: A User's Guide to Connecting with the Mind of God* (2010)

Cultures get very rigid, and people who go through extreme states come forward with experiences that balance the rigidity.

WILL HALL How did you go from being a physicist to being a psychotherapist?

ARNOLD MINDELL When I began to study engineering and applied physics at MIT I realized, my God, these people are not scientific; the physics community is wonderful about exploring subatomic states but they were not good at exploring the observer's nature. Psychology should be a part of physics. Then when I was at the physics department at the ETA in Zurich, I started dreaming a lot of wild things at night, and a colleague said, "You better go see this old witch here." And that's how I met Marie-Louise von Franz, Carl Jung's main student at the time, and began to study dreams and Jungian psychology.

WH Physics wasn't scientific enough? Is this the quantum mechanics idea that the observer, the scientist, influences what they're observing, so we have to study the people behind the science rather than seeing them as separate?

AM That's right. Know more about the observer. Who are we? Who is it that wants to observe something?

WH But a scientist might say, "Dreams are made up, what does that have to do the objective real world of science?"

AM The way science is defined today isn't really scientific, it doesn't study first person experience, it marginalizes it. Jung in a way was more "evidence based." He took first person experience very seriously, and said, "Watch what people dream. Watch what people feel and follow that."

WH How did you develop Process Work out of Jung and other methods?

AM The Jungian community was working with people who just sit in chairs and talk to you. I love that, but it didn't go far enough. It didn't work with people sick and dying in the hospital or jumping around with extreme states.

WH Was addressing social issues key to taking Jung further?

AM I was born in 1940 and was badly hurt as a child by other children who wanted to kill me, who decided my religion should be eradicated. I repressed this, I didn't dream about it, it was too traumatic to deal with. After I finished my Jungian analysis I realized "Wow, sitting in a chair is good, but I need to get back onto the streets. I need to learn to work in a way that's real, with people who hate each other and who love each other." So I began to work with people in conflict.

WH How do dreams go together with group work?

AM A man who had heart problems came to me, so I asked "What is your first person experience of heart pain?" He said, "I have a knife feeling in my chest that hurts terribly." And then I said "What did you dream last night." And he said, "Oh! I dreamed about a big carving knife" So I said, "Maybe you should be sharper and get more to the point?" He said he was a pastor, and that people in the church said he is too wishy-washy. So I said, "Can you get quicker to the point, as well as taking your medication for your heart problem?" He went back to his congregation and made a couple of big points the next Sunday morning sermon, and came back very happy.

WH I my own altered state experiences I've seen that what we live in is actually a dream. We think of it as objective, but what appears outside of us is actually what's inside of us. This view resonates with indigenous traditions that say there is a deeper underlying intelligence that moves everything.

AM "What is reality?" is a very central question. Most wars, inner problems, and relationship troubles are connected with the question, What's real? What's not?

People in extreme states show the experiences that other people don't want to look at.

WH One side says, "You're crazy," and the other side says, "No, no, you're crazy."

AM Somebody says, "I think you're out to get me," and the other person says, "No, you're nuts. I'm not out to get you." So what is real?

Actually, reality is *consensual*. Everybody sees the moon get eclipsed and says, "the earth came in and blocked out the moon." But that's only been reality for the last few hundred years. In Northern Europe, people used to say, "Great wolves are eating up the moon, and if people don't scream, those wolves will eat everything up."

I call that view dreaming and a second part of reality, because I know it's real. If you go to New York City you can hardly see the stars or the moon or anything anymore. Human beings are making a mess out of our environment: and we need to scream louder to stop it. So, were those early Northern Europeans nuts? Or were they dreaming?

WH You have a degree from MIT; how does quantum physics support your ideas about reality?

Science today isn't really scientific, it doesn't study first person experience, it marginalizes it. Jung in a way was more "evidence based." He took first person experience very seriously.

AM In quantum physics, things happen that can't be explained by causation. Two particles may be hundreds of miles apart but still connected through what's called entanglement. Scientists have just discovered this, but dreamers and shamans have always known it. When you go into an altered state sometimes there seems to be a synchronistic connection between you and another person.

WH People in psychotic states of consciousness are told we're out of touch with reality. In my experience, I was in touch with a different reality.

Most wars, inner problems, and relationship troubles are connected with the question, What's real? What's not?

AM When it comes to many things, such as allergies and psychotic phenomenon, medicine is really in a pre-scientific phase. Medical science doesn't understand extreme states: medication is used just to calm people down. But everyone goes through these same states at least a little bit, they're just not as statistically prevalent. Some people stay in them longer or go through them more often, but they're absolutely, unto themselves, normal states of consciousness. Calling them sick doesn't make any sense, so I call them "extreme states."

WH Everyone goes through at least moments when they're ready to give up on life, or experiencing paranoia or in some kind of other reality or, at least for a moment, something that could be considered psychotic.

AM Everyone is depressed and feels low sometimes. Everybody gets manic. Everybody thinks, "Oh, I don't care about life much anymore." That is very, very common. People in so-called extreme states show the experiences other people don't like to look at themselves. So we want to marginalize those states, and the people who go through them get looked down on and told, "You're weird and you're crazy or sick." That doesn't work for me.

WH Why do these states get pushed away? Is it fear? Is it being afraid of looking at the psychosis in ourselves?

These states could really enrich cultures, if the culture is open minded enough to understand that. That's my great hope.

AM Yes, because any given culture says, "We are this. We are not that." I remember working in Australia, and a teacher had said to one of the aboriginal students, "Stop dreaming so much. Come on, you've got to be real." Dreaming and fantasy become marginal and people become marginalized. Cultures get very rigid, and so people who go through extreme states come forward with experiences that balance the rigidity. These states could really enrich cultures, if the culture is open-minded enough to understand that. That's my great hope.

WH So suicidal feelings, mania, or paranoia have something positive to offer?

AM Spiritual, far out, playful experiences, scary experiences, demons… mainstream cultures need these more. We need to see them. The more cultures bring out their experiences and accept them, the better everybody will feel.

WH Can you give us some examples of how you work with extreme states?

AM In Switzerland, back before medication was used much, I worked with a hospital patient who wouldn't come out from under her bed. So I thought, Why not join her? So I went under a chair at a distance. Suddenly she said, "It's no good being a person." So I said, "Ok, let's stay where we are." Then, after a while, she said, "I'm in a fishbowl, I am a fish." You know, I had just finished my Jungian studies and I was sitting in a lot of chairs, and this was the first fish I had ever met, and I loved it. I didn't know anything, I never learned about this, so I just went "blub." And she went "blub, blub." And we blubbed around together.

After a couple of months she was out of the hospital and seeing me in my office. She explained to me, "My father came from a country that has done some very bad things to people, and he was involved in that. And as soon as I found out I decided it wasn't worth being a human being anymore. I didn't want to kill myself, and suddenly I found myself becoming a fish." And we cried together, and she was, you could say "normal" from there on out, a great person.

WH So whatever the person is going through no matter how bizarre or strange is potentially meaningful. You join them as if you were joining a dream, and then you bridge to ordinary reality with them.

AM She's also doing me a favor. How many times have I had the chance to play as an adult with another adult who's under the bed as a fish? She's also healing something in me. People heal us by what they do, by bringing up a marginalized experience.

In that same hospital, doctors invited me to work with another so-called impossible patient. She was at the other end of the room and said, "Don't come an inch closer." This was a woman who they told me didn't communicate. I imagined something unfortunate had happened to her. So I said, "You're smart, you're brilliant, and you know how to keep people at a distance, and that's important." And she looked at me for a moments

Spiritual, far out, playful experiences, scary experiences, demons... mainstream cultures need these more. We need to see them.

and said, "Um, Ok, you can sit down, but not too close." And so our relationship began slowly. She wasn't "non-communicative:" she was doing something intelligent that was *seen* as crazy.

WH You validated her rather than seeing her as a problem, and so she responded.

AM I followed my own imagination that something had happened to her. You have to follow your experience. Another example is a man who was jumping all around, you might call him manic, and he sat on my chair. I was still trying to behave like a normal Jungian at that time, and this man scared me. Suddenly he jumped from a sitting position up into the air and hit his head on the ceiling. I said "Hey, you can't do that with Arny Mindell. If you want me to be your friend, you can't do that because I'm too scared." He stopped and said, "My God, no one ever talked openly and treated me like a person." So I said, "I am treating you like a person, because I'm just a person who is scared!" Being in a real human relationship with him, not stepping away or holding back, was important.

> She wasn't "non-communicative:" she was doing something very intelligent that was *seen* as crazy.

WH People seen as crazy start to get special treatment, and then the people around them are acting different too, just in acceptable and invisible ways. Lots of families I work with have learned to be afraid and not assert boundaries, for example.

What do you think about medication used to tranquilize people?

AM Not everybody has enough training to work with unusual states, so I totally appreciate that many people feel "This makes it easier for me, it cools me out." But things are left over, a residue of unhappiness or misery or fear, that medication doesn't cover. Medications can't really cover up the true nature of a person.

One of the most amazing situations was a person who came to my office and kept saying, "I am the light! I am the light!" He was saying that in the middle of a big festival in downtown Zurich, and right at that exact moment he said it a chandelier crashed to the floor. Everyone was freaked out. They thought, is he crazy, or is he a magician? So I thought, that's really exciting, let me try that, and I said, "I'm the light." And he said, "No, you're crazy if you think you're the light." The role swapped you see: he was the light as long as nobody else was picking up that role. He said to me, "You've got to come down to earth," and I just said, "How am I supposed to do that?" And the he gave all sorts of tips to me, that ended up being useful in helping him. This made him into a very creative person the rest of his life. Medication wouldn't have allowed me to know him in that state.

Quantum physics predicts that entangled states occur, like what he said about the light and then the chandelier crashing. People in extreme states frequently have magical or quantum-like phenomenon happen to them. Synchronistic, spiritual connections. People have called that God. Today we don't understand this very well, so it is the job of people who go through altered states to learn how to bring these, what shall I call them, divine experiences or synchronistic experiences, closer to consensus reality. If you've had that experience, you also have the ability to eventually bring it together with everyday reality.

WH Are you urging a rediscovery of ancient wisdom in modern science?

AM I was with shamans in aboriginal Kenya some years back. They would go into a trance, and speak with whatever it was inside someone that was bothering them. They play with fantasy and talk with people like I do, using imagination to deal with imagination. Shamanism has a great deal to offer our modern day culture, which has gotten too rational.

WH So the creative techniques you use parallel the rituals and trances of shamanic healers. What about the role of power, status and rank in extreme states?

AM I worked with a child who had the habit of spitting all the time, he just spit and spit wherever he could. His parents said "What are we going to do with this bad kid?" Here is a definite rank situation: they see him as bad and want to get rid of him, and they have all the rank and power.

And yet his spitting is what brought him to me, also a kind of power. Most Swiss are very clean and neat people. So what I did was I got the parents to be less neat, and to spit occasionally. Then the son stopped spitting.

People in unusual states of consciousness may be bringing something new that the whole social context or culture needs. In Switzerland to spit occasionally wouldn't be all that bad!

WH So this spitting is a role, balancing or complementing the larger family and society context, which is too one sided, in this example being on the side of cleanliness or control. And this is related to systems theory and the Chinese philosophy of Taoism, where everything is a polarity and things are always moving towards balance?

AM The Tao wants everyone's yin and yang. We need everybody's experience to create a whole community. One of my teachers, physicist Richard Feynman, said, "An electron or an elementary particle doesn't just go down the street directly. That particle tries many, many different paths first, it may go by way of the moon or Mars." It chooses finally the most reasonable, shortest and easiest path for itself, but all the other paths were needed to be explored first. So that's how I feel about extreme states and

Calling them sick doesn't make any sense, so I call them "extreme states." Some people stay in them longer or go through them more often, but they're absolutely, unto themselves, normal states of consciousness.

about all states of consciousness, all kinds. We need everybody, everybody's way of doing things, even if it doesn't seem reasonable to us at first.

WH What sort of advice would you offer to someone whose doctor says, "This is a disorder. Let's not explore this; take a medication."

AM I would say to follow your own true nature. You know more than all of us. If it feels better to take care of yourself in a conventional way and take something to calm things down, go ahead and try it. If it doesn't work, try another path, like the electron. Just don't think there's something terribly wrong with you. Consider the possibility that what's bothering you might be very meaningful, not just for you but for me and for all of us. ∎

Madness and Human Potential
Ilya Parizhsky

Ilya Parizhsky is a counselor and parenting coach in the San Francisco Bay Area, and an emotional intelligence group facilitator in the tech industry.

Madness is a particularly rich moment, when the sensitivities, emotions, & unworked-through scenarios of our early lives become present and available.

My play date with Bennett, a 6-year old close to our family, started off "well-behaved." He was cooperative and communicated "using his words." But it didn't take long before his pent-up emotions and frustrations started coming to the surface.

With my hand in a mouth shape and speaking in a high-pitched voice, "Handy" delighted Bennett. But soon Handy didn't like that Bennett was shoving things in Handy's mouth. When Handy would spit the things out in protest Bennett would giggle and giggle, and then do it again. I thought of how often Bennett himself must have had to (literally and metaphorical-ly) swallow things he didn't want. And so eventually Bennett was stepping on Handy, scratching Handy, and playing out the various frustrations he's put up with throughout his young life. (I gently pointed out that scratching couldn't be part of the game because it actually hurts, and Bennett instant-ly understood).

I tried to match Bennett exactly at his edge of delight, and when some-times I would get the balance wrong, he didn't hesitate to let me know. So for example after Bennett wrestled Handy to the ground and stomped on him, showing more and more aggression, Handy called for reinforcements. Now there were two Handys, chasing Bennett around the house while he giggled and screamed. But then Bennett suddenly stopped mid-play. "Let's play a different game." he said. "Okay." I answered, dropping the Handys immediately. "What do you want to play?" I said, following his lead to what-ever he wanted next.

Human beings are incredible. We are organisms inherently capable of using the aware attention of others to help alleviate our suffering. So as soon as Bennett saw I could handle whatever pent up emotions he's been storing inside, he knew exactly how to make use of my presence. All I needed to do was to follow him and interpret the signals he was giving.

The next game involved the refrigerator water button. Bennett showed how to press it and spill water all over the floor, and then he checked to see if that was Ok. I stayed very delighted but told him "No, we can't spill water on the floor like that." "But I want to!" he said, and lunged for the button. I wrestled to get him to stop, making sure not to overpower him, playfully implying the message that if he squirmed and fought just the right way, he would get what he wants. He giggled a lot and tried various tricks. "If you don't touch me and stand over there," he said, "I promise I won't press the button!" "Okay" I replied with a tone of mock disbelief, and then caught him in a run just before he made it to the button. I didn't scold him, or tell him he was wrong or inappropriate, or that he shouldn't lie to me: it was clear he was working out pent up frustrations. When we were through, this play was sure to make him more cooperative.

He kept upping the ante, showing me more and more of his stored rage. This is the frustration that builds up on a daily basis when adults take young people's agency and power away. At one point Bennett was pushing me with both legs, shaking and sweating with anger. Both of us knew what we were doing, and it was delightful. The play got too intense, the feelings coming up were greater than his level of trust with me, and so he stopped again, sat up and said, "Let's play a different game." "Okay. What do you want to play?" I said, and he re-created the same exact dynamic: this time it was "I'm going to kick over the cat's water bowl!" and he gave me a quick warning before lunging for it.

Even in the most privileged and materially well-resourced families, childhoods are fraught with difficulty. Parents are set up with an impossible job and the last thing I want to imply is that it's the parents' fault that any of this happens. Because children are so incredibly sensitive, we all grow up with mountains of pent up emotions. By the time we're adults our feelings are very difficult to access and work through, because they have calcified so deeply. They make up our "personality," and our suffering.

Human beings are organisms inherently capable of using the aware attention of others to help alleviate our suffering.

With one important exception. When someone goes through a madness process, they are re-activating their life energy's capability to work on the feelings directly, making that their priority and focus. Deep work on our emotions is still possible without a madness process, but more difficult: madness is a particularly rich moment, when the sensitivities, emotions and unworked-through scenarios of our early lives become present and available.

I experienced this first hand. When I was 20, my life was miserable, but I didn't know how to do anything about it. I continued studying academic philosophy even as I felt more and more alienated from the world and shut down in my heart. And so one day my organism spontaneously initiated a process that would get me out of that way of being, and set me on a new course.

I entered a very child-like, "anything goes" state of mind. Except that I was 20 years old, and so people were not concerned when they saw me walking down the street, an adult without parental guardianship. But I sure as hell could have used someone with me, another mind in there to give me attention, because I was in a dangerous head-space. I even decided to close my eyes and walk across a busy street in the middle of the block, a child's game to "play with fate."

What ended up happening to me happens to a lot of people who enter such an altered state of consciousness. I was locked up in a mental institution. I was forced to take drugs that eviscerated my emotions, and I was told there was something deeply wrong with me that will never go away. That's exactly the opposite of what I needed. What I needed was love, not drugs. I needed someone to come with me into my world and help me make sense of it. Not by identifying mistakes in my logic and telling me what I should be thinking instead, but by listening intently, following my mind and getting in there with me.

I'm not trying to say this is an easy task, given that my version of Bennett's "I want to push the refrigerator button" game was a young man trying to cross the road with his eyes closed. But what if someone could show me they cared enough to stop me, and then listen to my protest without going away and without putting down my intelligence? What if they met my free-associating and speaking in rhymes and riddles not with a diagnostic stare but with loving receptivity and playfulness? I could have made use of their presence, and worked through the horrible isolation that led to my madness process in the first place. And I could have come out much stronger for having gone through it.

As children and as adults, we need to be reached. Not with violence, threats, and coerced conformity, but with respect, love, and intelligent presence. These are the conditions for our blossoming, being surrounded by loving people who can truly tolerate what we are, and encourage us to show even more. When we go through a crisis and are reached, we will become more intact than we were before, more connected, and less likely to be destabilized by future circumstances. We will also be more capable of living well on this planet of ours. ∎

Somebody Always Home
Stan Tomandl

Stan Tomandl, MA, DiplPW has more than 25 years experience as a therapist working with dementia, traumatic brain injury, coma, and grief. He is faculty at the Sacred Art of Living Center in Bend, Oregon; on the Board of ComaCARE in Cape Town, South Africa; and is co-author of *An Alzheimer's Surprise Party (2009)*.

My deep belief is that there is always someone there, always somebody home who can be reached.

WILL HALL This isn't talked about enough, how we treat our elders, especially the difficult states that they get into: the forgetfulness and the dementia.

STAN TOMANDL I got into this work when my own father became forgetful at about 69. He was living at home, but after taking care of him for so long my mom burned out, a common story. So she put him in a very good veteran's nursing home, but he went into a big depression. Who wouldn't? I certainly would. And I just knew that I could do more with him. So my colleague Tom Richards and I worked with that depression through psychotherapy for around nine months before he finally started coming out of it. And then, actually, his dementia, his Alzheimer's improved quite a bit. My deep belief is that there is always someone there, always somebody home who can be reached.

WH How does working on depression improve dementia?

ST There is a crossover between dementia and depression, but people often only see the dementia, and so there is no psychotherapy done. Communication is always possible. So when I worked with my father, I saw he was rubbing the sheet between thumb and fingers, a fairly common perseveration for people in those states. Following my training I took his hand, and what he was doing changed, he stopped rubbing and started exploring my arm. So I had an intuition that he maybe wanted deeper contact, and maybe wanted a hug. It was the first hug we shared since I was twelve years old. It was incredibly deep and meaningful for both of us. One of people's biggest fears inside those withdrawn states is fear of isolation.

WH But the belief about so many of our elders with dementia and Alzheimer's is that they can't communicate, they are kind of lost to us, and their movements or speech are just meaningless.

ST It's what I would call a "nocebo" effect. With an attitude that nobody is home, it is easy to go through a quick routine and leave as soon as possible, rather than trying to engage and explore with them. And so as a result of your attitude, they are less likely to respond. If instead you assume they are trying to communicate, you discover meaning.

I went to visit my dad one time and we were playing cards around the dining room table like we have done as a family for, you know, forever. But my dad can't quite get the cards straight or he doesn't get it fast enough like he used to. He used to be one of the best poker players I've ever seen. So then my mom, bless her heart, starts correcting him, thinking that she is helping. Though her intention is right, dad feels criticized. And then he actually does worse, probably just like you or I would when we feel criticized. He goes away a little farther. And so he gets a little worse at playing cards. And then she tries to help him even more. And so it's escalating...it's a double bind. If he tries he's going to get criticized, and if doesn't try he's going to get criticized even more. So what does he do? He withdraws.

WH When we look only at the biological aspect, we forget that the way we ourselves communicate can contribute and make things worse.

ST Correct. If say grandma is convinced her granddaughter's boyfriend stole her rings, it doesn't matter how many times the granddaughter insists otherwise. At some level grandma thinks the boyfriend is a thief. We have to ask, "What is the boyfriend stealing from the grandma symbolically?" Maybe the grandma is jealous because the boyfriend is taking her granddaughter's time and attention. And people of that generation tend not to bring things, like needing attention, up directly.

WH With states called psychosis, it sometimes helps to emphasize feelings and the relationship, rather than challenging what's true or "real." How does attention to symbolic meaning help move a situation forward?

ST It helps bring issues in the background out into the open. A colleague, for instance, avoided going to see his grandmother. He was scared. For people not used to aging, seeing someone with dementia can be frightening. When he finally did go see her, he couldn't engage, he stayed at the far wall, at the end of the bed, not saying anything. So the grandmother kept saying "Son, stoke the fire, it's cold in here." The room was in the 80s, really hot. So we joked about it, then after ten minutes of wracking my brain I realized the symbolism was the chill of their relationship. When we got my colleague to finally take his grandmother's hand, she stopped saying the room was cold.

WH That's beautiful. Tell us more about how you work with the body symbolically.

ST My father's posture looked very depressed: hunched over, head down, bent forward. We encouraged him to notice his body. From there we sculpted an interaction; we had an idea that he was cowering or avoiding a blow. So I told my colleague to try role play being angry at my dad, and he said "I'm going to punch you!" but playfully. My dad instantly came out of the depression and said "No you're not!" From there we were able to build communication, and the more he came out of depression, the more he began to interact.

WH When I work with people who describe themselves as depressed, it's remarkable how often we discover anger or conflict held in their body.

ST My goal is to figure out what works best. I go by feedback. I might notice if someone is holding anger and then try to bring that to the surface. If it works, it can be an entry point into a relationship. If it doesn't work, I drop it. The problem is, especially in nursing homes, there is no place to bring out anger, agitation, or strong emotions. Patients get a mark on their chart that stays there forever.

As a result of your attitude, they are less likely to respond. If instead you assume they are trying to communicate, you discover meaning.

WH This parallels the mental health system. People are labeled as violent once, and that mark stays by their name. When I finally got my psychiatric files, I read that the hospital labeled me with homicidal ideation, because I threatened to destroy the ward television set. But at the same time, sometimes people's anger or assertiveness makes them very difficult to be around.

ST Absolutely. And that's when they get medicated. A nursing home in Winnipeg, Canada did a study. Every resident received a drug review. If their agitation was stable, their dose was cut in half. If they then maintained stability, their dose was cut again, until they were off the medication. Over a three-year span, they reduced drug rates from 56% to 6%. Residents were happier and staff had an easier time caring for people who were more alert, more functional, and could do more on their own. This is not rocket science here. Just reviewing drugs, reducing medication, seeing what happens, and then going by feedback.

WH Around a quarter of all nursing home residents are given antipsychotics, and for a lot of them it's chemical straightjacketing. Inside institutions, staff need new training, or encouragement to try new things. But if you see the agitation as only biological you give up any hope of change.

ST Everyone needs to express themselves, get more meaning out of their life, and keep growing until they die. When George Wallace, a famous Canadian sculptor and painter, developed dementia and went into assisted living, he stopped doing art. He became depressed and more forgetful, and so he was transferred to a nursing home. Staff realized he used to work in his own space, which he lost when he was in assisted living, so in the new place he was given a private room, and they encouraged him to draw again. At first his drawings were childlike, but within a few months, his earlier style re-emerged. It was some of the best work of his career. Something had stripped a lot of his so-called reality away, but the essence of the deep artist remained, and then re-emerged.

WH Tell us about the dying process and the creative and spiritual states you see as part of it.

ST A friend recently died from HIV/AIDS. He took no medication, because he wanted to stay aware. He went into some far out altered states, some of them extreme, but the family was able to handle it. And he was able to relate to his family, saying "I love you" and "thank you" and "I know I am dying," without having his pain numbed. When he would say something like, "Oh, I'm seeing the ocean" his family would say, "Yeah, Dad, go ahead and look at the ocean! I'm right there with you," rather than saying, "No you are not, you're in bed in our home and you're dying." This was the first unmedicated death the hos-

> He was able to relate to his family, saying "I love you" and "thank you" and "I know I am dying," without having his pain numbed.

> If he tries he's going to get criticized, and if doesn't try he's going to get criticized even more. So what does he do? He withdraws.

pice staff had ever seen.

We tend to be afraid of pain. Rightly so, pain can be a horrible thing, and if you have too much pain as you are dying it is not productive for anything. But for example, we worked with a woman who was very near death. She started quivering and raising her hands, and her daughter's immediate reaction was to say, "Mom's in pain, I'll call the nurse." But we realized the mom didn't seem to be in pain, and so we encouraged the mom to feel whatever she was feeling. She went into a deep, ecstatic state. Her daughter explained she was very religious, and so they sang hymns together about Jesus. Ultimately, what had looked like pain was actually a spiritual, ecstatic state trying to happen. I think that this happens all the time, not just very close to death, but in any delirium.

Everyone needs to express themselves, get more meaning out of their life, and keep growing until they die.

WH What is another example?

ST My wife Ann got a call from her mother's nursing home saying, "Your mom thinks she's in Mexico." So Ann talked to her mom and said, "What's it like in Mexico?" Her mother said, "Ah, it is warm here. And everybody is so loving." And Ann said, "That's fantastic," and she took it as a symbolic clue and started being really warm and loving to her mother, "Mom, I love you. You are the best mom in the world. I am so glad to be with you," which is all very true for Ann, so she could say it genuinely. And then after a short time her mother said, "You know, I am in Mexico, but it is strange because I see pictures of my family on the wall, how did that happen?" And Ann said, "Yeah, look at those pictures, how did they get there, Mom?" Her mom was coming back to what we could call consensus reality, and Ann helped her bridge between worlds by being loving in Mexico and looking at things in her hotel room that weren't in Mexico. Finally she came back to her nursing home room in Tennessee. We could call her delusional, but by going deeper she was able to get something she really needed, something loving, and then come back. It was a journey to Mexico.

WH An important issue to address is that even though we are talking about caregiving, often there is abuse going on.

ST Yes, and any abuse requires care and extreme awareness. It's common to abuse the elder parent who abused you as a child. And this reversal of roles can be totally unconscious: a negative atmosphere in the house, or caregivers who start sniping away at an elder's bank account, or start insulting them, telling them they are crazy and other unhelpful things. If you can bring some gentle awareness that really helps, because caregivers have probably been isolated with this process for years or decades. And when the elder has no recollection of abusing the caregiver as a child when confronted, it may be up to their son or daughter to work through it internally. They have to decide when, where, and how they want to have the elder in their life.

Especially in nursing homes, there is no place to bring out anger, agitation or strong emotions. Patients get a mark on their chart that stays there forever.

WH What are your thoughts on physician assisted suicide, such as Oregon's Death With Dignity Act? It's controversial in the disability rights movement, because when people can no longer function like the majority, they are seen as useless to society.

ST Some people are in horrible situations where they might have wished they were dead, but they were being kept alive. We have medications now for things my parents' generation would have passed away from like pneumonia, pulmonary disease, or heart disease, and today they're being kept alive. Is it right, is it not right? We've reached a point as a society where we are keeping people alive, but we are not allowing them to die.

We had a 95-year-old friend who was suffering and on heart medication. She gathered her family around and told them "On this day I'm going to stop taking my medication, so please be with me." The family stayed with her for about two weeks until she passed away.

WH But that may not be the right decision if it's driven by depression, despair, oppressive circumstances, or an inner conflict.

> # We've reached a point as a society where we are keeping people alive, but we are not allowing them to die.

ST Therapists can help both the person and their family, to work with the depression and conflict, exploring what is the depression about. It is an opportunity for people to work with their deep emotions, spiritual states, and relationships. Just giving somebody an anti-depressant and telling them that they've got to live another ten years is probably going to make them more depressed.

WH **What advice do you have for family members or caretakers facing burnout?**

ST It's better to keep someone at home than in an institution, and some states even pay family members to keep elders at home. But sometimes you just can't do it at home anymore: get support to work with your own guilt about that. "I promised till death do us part and now I'm putting my loved one into a nursing home." There are very few resources in our society for all the different steps along the way: assisted living, the nursing home, the step into hospice, the dying process. Get help sooner rather than later. ∎

Christmas Vacation in the Schizophrenia Factory
Will Hall

This essay captures some of the goings on in my family of origin. It was originally published at The Icarus Project website and then at *Psychology Tomorrow* web magazine.

"*...what is usually called hypnosis is an experimental model of a naturally occurring phenomenon in many families. In the family situation, however, the hypnotists (the parents) are already hypnotized (by their parents) and are carrying out their instructions, by bringing their children up to bring their children up...*

I consider that the majority of adults (including myself) are or have been, more or less, in a post-hypnotic trance, induced in early infancy: we remain in this state until – when we dead awaken, as Ibsen makes one of his characters say, we shall find that we have never lived."

— R.D. Laing *The Politics of the Family*

The flight from Massachusetts to Georgia creeps along gray and shrouded by clouds. At several thousand feet there is a brief moment of sunlight: best wishes from a kind angel soon very far away. I am going to visit my family for Christmas.

Two hours in a car in downtown Atlanta with my father, mother, and brother, the first time we have been together in more than three years. There, there, that was open. No it wasn't. Let's turn around. Ok so keep going. Should we go back? I think I saw lights. Look what about that place? Closed. Ok keep going, there's got to be something.

I manage to text message a friend. TRAPPED

IN PSYCHOTIC FAMILY VORTEX. DRIVING EMPTY STREETS LOOK-ING FOR PLACE TO EAT. My family and I ride in circles on Christmas day. Keep going, there's got to be something.

By the time we find a table at a Chinese by-the-pound buffet, I am in, I still don't know what to call it, one of my "dissociated paralysis states." My mind and body are seized by an overwhelming force, and I'm acting and feeling in ways that earned a schizophrenia diagnosis ten years before. Every month a disability check is deposited in my account, reminder that recovery is still elusive. In the car on Peachtree Avenue, it is impossible.

The words of my mom and dad and brother claw at me. Coded tones of voice and a secret language of gestures and glances grab and pull me down. I stare blankly from farther and farther away, trying to escape, but across the growing distance something makes me listen closely. They talk about my father's work, they talk about our farmhouse, they talk about relatives. Between gaps in sentences and pauses in eye contact, voices in my head begin to yell and taunt. Nasty, cruel, and vicious. With each shouted accusation and whispered insult I wince and withdraw deeper.

How did I suddenly become suicidal? Why do I imagine jumping from a bridge or hanging by a rope to flee the screaming in my head? Why have my own life, values, friends, work, interests... all evaporated a few hours after stepping off the plane?

A small part of me speaks up, in defiance of the clamor inside: This is ridiculous. It's just a conversation with my family on Christmas, there is no reason to be like this. And as soon as I've formed them, these words fall away. They begin to repeat over and over, more and more loudly, *This is ridiculous, this is ridiculous, you are ridiculous, it's your fault, why are you so stupid.* Now they are mocking me, swept up with the rest of the angry and contemptuous hammering words. *It makes no sense. It's your fault. You are a grown adult man and you are powerless. Stupid.*

This is my family. They have a diabolical power to entrance me.

Sunk beneath a thick wall of ice, voices shouting and whispering in my head, I watch all this unfold. Is my withdrawal a shield from my family? Or is this altered state of mind, pinned down and not responding, is that the trap too? Am I protecting myself? Imprisoning myself? Am I no longer normal? If I could say anything, would it make sense Would it be listened to? Or am

I now just crazy? Yelling, cutting words condemn my failure to solve this puzzle. A whispering, sickly sweet voice reminds me how easy it would be to just end this, to find one of my father's guns or take a bottle of pills from the bathroom cabinet. Yes, that's it, that's what makes sense, just wait until you get home...

The television screen says: A policeman's job is only easy in a police state. That's the whole point, Captain.

Back in the car and all I can do is smell everyone around me. I'm frozen, silent, and hearing voices, and now I'm beginning to gag. I become more withdrawn, avoiding eye contact and not replying when anyone speaks. But even this is not enough; their odors are seeping into my body. My coping mechanism, if that what this is, is so bizarre that everyone is reacting, visibly uncomfortable, turning away. They won't ask me directly or try to understand, they are afraid of me, and the trance prevents anyone from talking openly about what is happening. So I sit there, paralyzed, and I am the full proof on display: Yes, I am the person trained by diagnosis and institutionalization. I am the lost soul mental patient, the ostracized outsider who is not like us, not participating, not part of the family, unreachable. I am mentally ill.

I am not responding to my family's craziness: I am the one who is crazy, and my family is just responding to me.

I watch my father's gestures as he speaks in more codes and secret messages. Now he is copying my texting: I have never seen him text message before. He has hacked into my cell phone and reads what I wrote. He is talking with step-children somewhere, his backup family, another sign of my own irrelevance and failure as a son. He reads my thoughts and he replies with a cypher: we talk of his world and work, intellectual property rights, infringement lawsuits, a biography he authored, his lawyer – it is all cunningly directed at me, to harm me invisibly. He is a writer, my father, and he is reading my thoughts so that he can control me. He is the judge, he is the law.

On the screen, Janet Leigh is stalked by a Mexican marijuana and speed gang. Charlton Heston is searching the Hall of Records.

I'm not going to make it. On the drive back they ask me questions: how are you, how is work, how do you like where you live. I don't answer. At least we tried, they will tell themselves, at least we tried. I am not in control of my own body, my mind, or my speech. I try to phone friends, but did I reach them? It is Christmas. Did I dial? I'm convinced that anyone I call will try to hurt me. *I think, If tomorrow things aren't better I will hitchhike to a hotel.* The plan is comforting, like all my plans to crawl away and hide. It is a better plan than suicide, maybe.

When we finally arrive at my dad's farmhouse, I collapse onto a 28-year-old mattress in the back bedroom. My father's wolves and dogs penned in the yard howl at the crescent moon. I pass out, and dream I am facilitating a support group and my friend announces she has quit heroin. I wake up. It is a vivid image, but is it ridicule, or a prophetic riddle?

The next day I manage to eat a bowl of fruit, and then I spend hours trying to be in whichever room of the house no one else is in. I'm like one of those numbered tile puzzles where you can only slide one tile at a time into the empty space before the other pieces can move. My

He reads my thoughts and he replies with a cypher.

father, mother, and brother talk with me, but I can't say anything or look at their eyes. I am conspicuously, flagrantly, exposed. I want to eat more but the stench is overpowering, so I spend the morning cleaning out cat litter boxes that haven't been emptied in a month. It is the day after Christmas and my dad has invited people over to work in the kitchen, so we can't cook. My brother sleeps until one.

From the television, Dennis Weaver scares me.

I manage to find a hiding place playing a video game on the Internet and checking my email. I am still not able to reach any of my friends, or at least the ones I don't think are trying to hurt me. Or did I even try to reach them? Then I take a nap. There is no cooking oil that is not rancid so I head to the gas station to buy some for my falafels. I am using a boxed mix that says it expired eight years ago. In the kitchen I exchange words with my mother. She sends something into me, poison wrapped in secret messages. I dissolve and disengage, and the conversation ends.

At this point my body is something else, owned by someone I don't recognize. My thoughts are not mine. I am locked in the schizophrenia factory:

trapped with my anguished family, with its confusing mixed messages and tangled dynamics, it subterranean flows of trauma and its history of violence and abuse. Who I have become, the pain and disorientation and madness I go through, cannot be understood without seeing where I came from. I don't blame my parents. Blame wouldn't do anyone any good. My madness is a mystery I bear and wrestle with, a life's work unchosen, an unspeakable affliction. This Christmas vacation visit of just a few days has brought the family mechanisms and my reactions to them out into the open. A hypnotic field as tangible and overpowering as a storm wind, tearing and pushing and sweeping my being away. My mind is spilled, debris. I am strewn between invisibility and explosion. It is happening, I am watching, I recede.

My madness is a life's work, unchosen.

I get out of the house on the pretext of finding good cell reception, and I sit in the car. I stare at my phone. I know the people on the other end told me they are my friends. They told me to call them if I have a crisis. I am looking at their names but each one is a secret sign like the ones inside the house, a trick of language, a smiling cruelty, a promise to hurt me. Did I call someone? On the other end is my poor friend's voice mail, and now all I can manage is to unleash my voices, a ventriloquist speaking through my mouth, a spite-filled disoriented outburst about how I need to hire people to comply with my treatment plan. I hang up, trembling, shocked that my effort to help myself has only made things worse.

Charlton Heston is white trying to pass for Latino trying to pass for white.

And then, just as Orson Welles' police captain Hank Quinlan is going to die in this shadowy and crime-infested maze of dusty streets and corrupt lawmakers, my own role as a stunted monster in the family drama reaches a climax. Someone answers the phone. It is wrong to reach out to friends who say they care about me. No, that is not my own voice telling me that, that is a trick. There is no allegiance and there is no love and I am selfish. Did I say that? But is that someone different, someone there, on the other end of the phone, someone who is not part of the hypnotist's trance?

The clammy gray mist starts to burn off in the warmth of that voice. There is someone there from my other life, my real life, my chosen family now. I'm not crying or raging from the emotion buried inside. I am still and frozen and lost, but now I can feel that warmth somewhere. Simple words: take a risk, you're not alone, remember who you are, remember that your whole world is not as crazy as your family.

Back inside we are watching the 1958 film *Touch Of Evil*. Film noir, dark misanthropy, shadows within shadows, claustrophobic and horrifying. It has always been one of my favorites. We sit silently in front of the television set, plates on laps, eating leftovers. My brother, my mother, and my father. And me. I watch them as they watch, transfixed on the screen. Their faces dance with faint shapes of light. My family.

A feeling in my chest surprises me, a sensation that is... my own. Mine, not from somewhere else.

I know this moment. My father looks at me and then he says five words. Five mean, hurtful words, and I am crushed. They are familiar words in a familiar tone, raw, acid, etching deep. They are unrepeatable. I stand in front of him and I know his eyes, but I can imagine only shadows of what he has seen in his life. Soldier in the Korean War, gunshot wounds, self-inflicted injuries, prison, torture, psychiatric wards, electroshock... and his own violent father, my grandfather, standing over him. To this moment of abuse towards me he brings his own history of abuse. *Bringing their children up to bring their children up...*

This time is different, though. The feeling in my chest. I look into my father's eyes and something within me stays within me. I feel myself to be both part of this drama and also outside of it. I remember my phone call. I speak back to him, defend myself simply and clearly. I tell my father, Do not degrade and belittle me; I tell him, I deserve respect. I tremble, I sink inside.

I stand instead of collapse.

And does the fog burn off, and do the dead awaken? We'll see. Now I'm in front of the television again, and eating junk food, but the film is starting to be kind of fun. The director's cut is even better than the other version I have seen – there are more lines and angles, more depths of brilliance shining through. That night in a dream I am struggling to walk, stooped over like my father. Hanging from a scar on my right side there is a flap of unhealed flesh, but it isn't bloody and gaping, it's dry. Like molting skin, as fragile and easily torn as paper. ∎

Supporting Family Recovery
Krista Mackinnon

Krista MacKinnon is the director of *Families Healing Together*, an online education and support community for individuals, families, and professionals. She practices and teaches yoga and breathwork.

The most important recovery tool families have is their relationship.

WILL HALL How did you go from psychiatric survivor to family counselor?

KRISTA MACKINNON Things unraveled for me at age 16. I used to say, "Oh, I don't remember any of my childhood trauma, so it doesn't affect me," but my understanding has evolved and I now see how early trauma played a role in leading up to things. I smoked marijuana with my friends, who would laugh and have a good time while I got extremely paranoid. I started thinking people were following me and eavesdropping on my conversations. I liked to take psychedelic drugs, but it got to the point where I would be hallucinating and seeing things even when I wasn't taking them. I got engrossed in nature and watching bugs crawl on the pavement for hours, I would piece together numbers connected to my divine mission, and I started to believe I was famous.

Most people who talked with me for two or three minutes would know that I was not my usual self. I wrote a lot of poetry, and I even included it in my application for a job at Dairy Queen, not exactly a skill-set required for working there!

My madness was spiritually complicated, and while I was acting unusual, confusing, and dangerous, I also felt very clear. Even in the darkness, I had a deeply connected feeling with myself that held me together. In what was labeled mania I found my brilliance, zest for life, courage, and creative spirit, and in what was labeled depression I found my inner quiet muse, my philosopher, and my art.

I tried to hitchhike and run away from home, and I got picked up by my friends' parents who took me to the emergency room. Hospitals do help some people, especially temporarily to aid in crisis, but for me the treatment of my madness was far worse than my experience of madness. Treatment annihilated my connection to self and spirituality, disembodied me, humiliated and numbed me. As a 16 year old young girl I was put in restraints, forcibly medicated, and told my feelings and experiences were ill and always would be. Treatment contributed to my healing in no way whatsoever.

My family talked to the doctor and went to treatment team "family meetings," as well as to support groups. Everyone told them their 16 year old daughter had a biological brain disease that required lithium for the rest of her life. It was now their job to make sure I took my meds and to always be on guard for symptoms of any kind. Nothing about recovery of wellness or how to put this behind me.

WH **What finally got you out of your altered state?**

KM Just sleeping was what I needed. I didn't believe any of it was useful, diagnosis, the medications, anything. But my family told me to take the meds or be kicked out of the house. I didn't have much choice, and so I decided: I would trick them. I stopped the meds, but to make it look like I was still on them I took just a few pills before my regular blood level tests - not something I recommend! I just flushed the ones that were extra. I'm still kind of amazed that it worked.

WH **And did you have any more altered states or crisis?**

KM No. I was a teenager, so you could say I did have extreme states, but I think that all teenage girls, and boys too, have extreme states! When my boyfriend broke up with me I cried for five days and locked myself in my room. But this was immediately considered as "She's having another episode," because everything I did was seen through the lens of my "bipolar disorder." If that label had never happened, my outbursts and emotional extremes would have just been chalked up to teenage angst.

So after I got out I was fine and I didn't have any other episodes or end up back in the hospital. But I learned not talk about what I was thinking and feeling, and when I got accepted into college at 18 I told my parents I hadn't taken meds for two years. They were shocked, but what could they say at that point? I was leaving home. And I have been medication-free since then.

WH How did you end up working as a family counselor?

KM Afterwards I just shut the whole experience out of my life because I didn't believe it, basically. But then I saw a job posting looking for a "psychiatric survivor" to work as a peer counselor. It was the first time I had every heard of that, and it occurred to me there might be other people out there who also felt mistreated and misunderstood, not "mentally ill."

WH And in your work today do you see the kinds of power struggles that went on in your family?

KM Definitely. Most young people will want to come off their meds because the side effects are absolutely horrible. Especially during high school years, the weight gain, acne, losing your sex drive... it's intolerable. But the family is taught to be an ally to the medical community, and that creates a battle. So I teach families instead to be an ally to their relative. Not to go against the doctor necessarily, but to support their relative first with solving life issues.

Parenting teenagers is already a difficult challenge. When medication becomes a power struggle it can make things worse. I emphasize that the most important recovery tool families have is their relationship. If someone wants to go off their meds they will find a different route, an alternative route, any kind of route, or do something risky like I did. So the relationship is crucial so that the young person is not left making decisions all on their own. It's not about alienating medical professionals, it's about collaborating together. A young person might not have skills for thinking through options, or diplomatic, effective communication of their needs. Families can help that.

WH People already want to come off meds and are already trying to do it. So they need to not be alone. Otherwise it's like trying to deal with teen sex by not talking about it, just saying no. Young people are transitioning to adulthood, and they can't just be controlled like children.

Are power struggles around what is "real" similar?

KM With unusual and strange beliefs the family becomes desperate. The first instinct is to say "There are no cameras in the corner, no one is following you. You are really sick!" But fighting someone's reality and trying to convince them of your reality only damages the relationship further.

In what was labeled mania I found my brilliance, zest for life, courage, and creative spirit, and in what was labeled depression I found my inner quiet muse, my philosopher, and my art.

WH It can be as devastating as trying to convince someone they weren't really raped.

KM Yes. Of course you don't see any cameras or the strange things they are seeing, so you don't have to say "Oh, yes, I agree the FBI are after you." But instead you can engage at the level of emotions and say "You are so scared right now. What do you need to feel less afraid?"

WH That is very hard to do when the unusual belief includes an accusation of a crime; families sometimes jump to defense and denial. But I've seen that if you don't challenge directly, instead listen to the emotional truth and also assume that something terrible must have really actually happened, things can move forward.

What about when families want medications to calm people down?

KM When someone has been boisterous or belligerent, with police involvement and chaos in the home, medications can finally bring peace and quiet. But that is not life. If someone is so medicated they are tranquilized, they are not really living. It might give the family a break, but now they need to work to reach a quality life, which doesn't mean being tranquilized all the time.

Families are told their son or daughter will be disabled for their whole life and never be who they thought they could be. Hopes for school and career get destroyed. So families become brokenhearted, and will even say they are "grieving" for their relative. But I say, "Your relative is not dead! A horrible thing has happened and they are figuring it out, but it is not over for them. What about questioning what doctors are saying? Maybe it isn't true that recovery is impossible. Maybe you don't have to have low expectations."

WH Parenting is also about letting go. You have to realize maybe your child doesn't want the career or life you want to impose on them, or maybe they need some time to figure things out. Every parent is afraid of the trial and error of gaining independence, and sometimes they can become overprotective and act like lifelong custodians.

If that label had never happened, my outbursts and emotional extremes would have just been chalked up to teenage angst.

KM To do well in recovery people need to be in power, actively contributing to their world. This is what being in recovery really means: going out and living life. But then there is "being in recovery," tranquilized on the couch following a treatment plan.

I help relatives understand what is and isn't their responsibility. They may have extreme worry about their son failing a job interview. But their responsibility is their worry, not the son failing. So let's talk about your worry. Boundary confusion is common, believing your know what's best and telling your relative how to live their life. It happens in young adult / teenage years anyway, but especially when there is a mental health issue complicating things.

Most importantly, family members need to be diligently protective of their own self-care, and not allow the mental health issues to entirely take over their own life. That actually doesn't help anyone. Self-care is paramount to the job of supporting others.

But any time there is physical abuse or sexual abuse happening in the family, it needs to be addressed separately first. It may be that the relationships are so damaged the family can't come together. A strength-based approach or how to have good boundaries won't work because things have gone too far. And abuse can go both ways: the person with the diagnosis might be hurtful. I encourage families to stretch and allow someone to yell and scream a little more because the expression of strong emotions might

> **Family members need to be diligently protective of their own self-care, and not allow the mental health issues to entirely take over their own life.**

be important. But you absolutely do not have to accept abuse. So, how do you know what your limits are?

I worked with one mom whose son would scream and scream at her whenever she went to his house. The next time she went, she focused on her breathing and just stood their patiently while her son screamed. Eventually he saw she wasn't responding and wasn't going anywhere, and the screaming toned down. He just collapsed in her arms crying, and gave her a hug. This was a huge breakthrough. He had come out of the hospital and had a lot of legitimate reasons to be upset, and now he saw that his mom could be an ally.

WH Do you see your work as an alternative to NAMI and DBSA and other pharma-backed family support organizations out there?

KM I have a great deal of empathy for families: they are called to be supportive and compassionate in a situation that is often personally draining, difficult to understand, and frustratingly isolating. And families also sometimes get blamed for the problems their relative faces!

Everyone connected to the traditional mental health system can easily feel oppressed, alienated, and disenfranchised. Psychiatrists feel oppressed by time constraints and pressured by pharmaceutical industries, case workers feel alienated from families, people in recovery feel denied self-determination and basic respect, and family members feel left in the dark and disregarded. I approach this by being as inclusive as possible, accepting all perspectives, and creating a safe space to discuss, connect, and grow.

The ultimate goal of the work I do is to empower the entire system. We can't do it alone. There is no us vs. them. Underneath we all share the common goal of healing trauma and suffering. The 13th century mystic poet Rumi wrote: "Out beyond ideas of wrongdoing and rightdoing there is a field. I'll meet you there" We have to figure this out together. ∎

Fighting someone's reality and trying to convince them of your reality only damages the relationship further.

Open Dialogue for Psychosis
Mary Olson

Dr. Mary Olson is on the Faculty of the Smith College School of Social Work and director of the Institute for Dialogic Practice.

In Open Dialogue 20% of the people ended up on disability, in contrast to 80% in standard treatment.

WILL HALL How successful is Finland's Open Dialogue approach in helping people through crisis using much less medication?

MARY OLSON Research that goes back to the early 80s compares Open Dialogue with treatment as usual. People experiencing a first episode of what we call psychosis were much more likely to be in school, working, have fewer return episodes, and use less medication. In Open Dialogue only 20% of people ended up on disability, in contrast to 80% in standard treatment. When I came across these statistics 10 years ago I became very interested in what they are doing differently than what we do here.

WH And this is not a single small experimental

program, this is an established hospital approach that's been around for decades?

MO In Finland it was developed at Keropudas hospital, and now there are Open Dialogue teams bringing this into settings in Northern Europe, Russia, and the Baltic States. It builds on the team-based work Tom Andersen has done, as well as the Needs Adapted Treatment approach.

WH You're a family therapist, how did you learn about Open Dialogue?
MO In the mid 90s I became interested in what was happening to family therapy in the Massachusetts Pioneer Valley where I work. Managed care, a restrictive economy, and a very strong emphasis on psychopharmacology created a new mental health system that downgrades all forms of therapy. The results have been dramatic.

WH **I like the Open Dialogue idea that family and professionals also need listening, not just the individual. And that however crazy or psychotic people are saying you are, your experience has meaning, if it's understood as a response to and a relationship with your surroundings.**

MO The original vision of family therapy was to look at people in a context, rather than simply as an individual. In some sense, whatever a person is going through is adaptive, a logical response. It's not just an arbitrary malfunctioning of a genetic script. But this doesn't mean blaming; that's what we have so much difficulty with in our culture. An experience can be meaningful, and a response to a context, without leading to condemning and pathologizing. Family therapy originally tried to introduce a non-pathologizing, systems framework, and yet it's been co-opted by a way of thinking that tends to look at things in a linear manner. It can become cause and effect, which invariably ends up with blame assigned to the individual or to the parents.

WH **Family therapy today in US social service agencies has the idea of the "dysfunctional family," where the entire family system is seen as the problem. And since these are often low income families, there's classism and discrimination, a social control side to it.**

MO Absolutely. With other forces at play the family systems approach can end up turning the family itself into a unit of pathology.

WH So Open Dialogue draws on the positive side of the family therapy tradition, the idea of meaningful contexts. One idea is the "double bind," which describes how psychosis or madness is an adaptive response to a confusing communication context.

MO In the 1950s Gregory Bateson and his colleagues formulated the double bind theory: a life-important context with conflicting meanings can paralyze the person and the people around them. There's an injunction on one level that's contradicted by an injunction on a second level.

WH So for example a parent who tells a child they love them unconditionally, but whenever the child starts to speak about what they're interested in, the parent interrupts and stops listening to them. They're getting a mixed message; on one level, I love you, but on the other level the communication says, I'm not interested in you.

MO The problem with framing it that way was is that it can then turn around and be too blaming of the parent. As Bateson's ideas evolved, he began to think about double binds across a whole system, affecting everyone, not one person just "doing" the bind to others.

For example there was recently a study of head injury patients, where the patient and family were all receiving conflicting messages from providers about how independent versus dependent on services the person should be. The research showed how the double bind affected *everyone* caught in it: it created mistrust in the caregivers, increased aggressive behavior, and made the injured person more likely to become symptomatic.

WH Tell us more about how Open Dialogue works.

MO Open Dialogue developed when traditional family therapy failed at Keropudas Hospital in northwest Finland. The families didn't want to be part of it. So Jaakko Seikkula and his colleagues started to have treatment meetings, asking, What kind of therapy should we offer this person and this family? What is going to work? And they found that this meeting to talk about the therapy was in *itself* very helpful. It became a sort of

Finnish genius of "no-therapy therapy." The meeting involved the person at the center of concern, any family members part of the crisis, anyone else the person wanted to be there, others connected to the situation, plus all the professionals.

WH So it's really a social network, not necessarily just the family?

MO Yes, and they abandoned the family therapy idea of a system that needed to be corrected. Instead, they focused more on the immediate crisis that led up to the treatment meeting. The goal of the meeting is to develop some common understanding of the problem. To do that, all the professionals need to use ordinary language, they can't use mystified jargon or labeling that can pathologize and objectify the person. Everyone has a voice as an equal partner trying to find a constructive response. There is less hierarchy, and less jargon. The focus is on what to do next. Without actually thinking of it as therapy, it turns out to be in and of itself extremely therapeutic.

WH And if a person is in a state of madness or crisis, if they are not talking, or they are expressing themselves in a way seen as weird or crazy, they're still an equal participant, still listened to?

MO Exactly. What is really so detrimental about traditional mental health care is that we place the person in crisis at the bottom of a social hierarchy, where we don't listen to them.

WH And they get talked about when they're not there, looked down on, labeled, and excluded.

MO In Open Dialogue there is transparency: all decisions about treatment, such as medication, are discussed openly, not behind the person's back. Outside conversations are discouraged. Differences become visible: professionals may disagree, take risks with ideas, and challenge each other. This is tremendously demystifying, and encourages the person experiencing madness to find words for what they're going through.

Mikhail Bakhtin, a Russian literary critic influential for the ideas of Open Dialogue, critiqued the dehumanizing and objectifying "official story" of power. Instead in Open Dialogue everyone is allowed to see the *unofficial* processes that usually go on behind closed doors. That tends to equalize power, and to support the voice of the person central to the crisis. The idea of "psychosis" disappears, because even people in high distress are respected and helped to express themselves.

Seikkula brought in two key principles from Bakhtin: tolerating uncertainty and dialogism. Both are very foreign to US society. You need to tolerate uncertainty long enough for people to find their voice and express themselves. The solution isn't imposed by professionals, but the dialogue itself generates a more common understanding, and allows a solution to emerge organically. Dialogue means a meticulous back and forth, with fine focus and attention. It gives support over time to express what people are going through, even if they start out communicating in ways that are very difficult for others to understand. People who seem to be in very extreme states begin to organize themselves differently when they are heard and respected.

> **Managed care, a restrictive economy, and a very strong emphasis on psychopharmacology created a new mental health system that downgrades all forms of therapy.**

WH Give us an example of a crisis that you've worked with using Open Dialogue.

MO I was in a meeting with a young man in his early 20s, who had been through a large number of hospitalizations. He got into a fight with a neighbor that ended up in his arrest, he was involved in the courts and had assault charges hanging over his head, and he had been on very high doses on every possible kind of medication. He became assaultive after being involuntary hospitalized, which happens to many people. (The nurse prescriber at Keropudas was bringing his medication dosage down.)

WH Sometimes forced treatment provokes violence in people, which leads to more force and heavier drugging.

MO This young man was on his way to being defined as "chronic." When they got together, Jaakko asked each person how they would like to use the meeting. The young man had a therapist who was part of the meeting and she said she said she was very concerned. The therapist said that in their sessions the young man was talking only about day to day things, what happened that week or at his job, but not about difficult things, the traumas of the past hospitalizations, his parents' divorce, or the court situation.

The original idea of family therapy was to look at people in context... whatever a person is going through is adaptive, a logical response.

Through dialogue, something new came out. It turns out the therapist was afraid of this young man. She revealed how when they met in the clinic she even made it look like other people were around so the man wouldn't know they were alone. That's how much fear she had.

Jaakko asked everyone for their response, and the mother became tearful. Open Dialogue emphasizes emotions for the transmission of meaning, and the idea is that the self is in body. I asked the mother what the tears were about, and she gave a detailed history of this family, a story she had never told.

Her son listened attentively but didn't say a lot. Jaakko asked what his father might say if he were there, which is a method often used on Open Dialogue, to ask about a missing perspective. Then the man said, I really want my parents to separate. He found his voice at that moment.

WH Someone who seems far away, in a state that would be called psychotic, found voice and expression, once the professional has expressed themselves and a family member shares a story that hasn't been told.

MO I went back to visit 9 months later and was stunned, the young man was outgoing, funny, and telling stories. His mother looked much happier. And the therapist said she was no longer afraid of this man, or concerned about what he should be talking about.

So as a result of the dialogue, he expressed something never said about this bind he feels between his parents, their conflict that put him in the middle. The therapist also overcame her fear of him, and things start to move. He went back to school, held a part-time job, and he wrote a letter about the poor medical treatment he had received.

WH Here is a family that seems stuck, with a son on heavy medications and considered violent. What happened in the Open Dialogue work that changed things?

MO The meeting was the beginning of humanizing him, improving his relation with the therapist and overcoming the fear. He began to assert himself for the first time and find some glimmer of self-determination.

WH Finding power and a voice can be a real turning point. Just listening to each other, as equals in a real dialogue, can be restorative, not just for mental health, but in conflict and community problems.

MO And once the therapist overcame her fear she was very skilled in seeing her client's strengths and talents. A door opened that he could walk through and reclaim his life.

WH A lot of people have inner resources, but treatment itself puts up obstacles to finding them. People are surrounded with messages saying their thoughts are meaningless signs of a broken mind. They become pathologized, problem people.

MO Treatment practices in the US can turn people in distress into walking zombies. Open Dialogue began to reverse that for this family and for this young man who was so heavily medicated. The therapist was also completely invigorated.

WH Was one of the ingredients the wisdom to reduce his medications? I'm not anti-medication, but tranquilizing you to the point of not being able to think or speak makes psychological change impossible.

MO Medications can really stop your ability to call on your own resources. The nurse prescriber understood that low doses are much more effective. He was on some medication when I saw him the second time, but far less than before.

WH How does Open Dialogue make room for everyone in the family if there is abuse or mistreatment going on? Are there dangers of not protecting the person? What if they need to get away from their family?

MO That's a very important point. Safety has to be your utmost value. If there's abuse, protective workers might also need to be present in the meetings. That doesn't translate well in a US context, but that's how they work in Finland.

WH And meetings are voluntary? If the person doesn't want to sit down with their abusive parent, there's no coercion?

MO No. But if there is abuse going on, it could be quite useful to empower an abused person to say some difficult things to the person that's been hurting them.

All the professionals need to use ordinary language, they can't use mystified jargon or labeling that can pathologize and objectify the person. Everyone has a voice as an equal partner trying to find a constructive response; all decisions about treatment, including medication, are discussed openly, not behind the person's back.

WH I know a lot of people who have separated from their family because of abuse, but that can leave things incomplete. Sometimes when you separate from your family you end up with them in your head, haunting you.

MO In Finnish Open Dialogue there's an environment where family members talk about the most difficult things. Finnish culture is not talkative, but when they do talk they are honest. Adapting Open Dialogue to the US context, there is a risk you would get the family into a meeting and the therapist would just make nice. But you can't just gloss it over, abuse has to be named as abuse.

WH What are some of the obstacles to bringing Open Dialogue to the US?

MO Western Finland has much lower mental healthcare costs, but they are well funded and organized in what they do. People work in teams in a way that is labor intensive in the beginning, and saves lives and costs later on. Here our mental health systems are very fragmented, and agencies don't have the resources to pay people to work in teams.

> Treatment practices in the US can turn people into walking zombies. Open Dialogue began to reverse that for this family.

WH The US has the most expensive healthcare system in the world, and terrible outcomes for mental health. By getting people out of hospitals and off disability, Open Dialogue's labor-intensive approach is cheaper in the long run.

MO Finland is also less individualistic. The US puts too high a social value on the individual, even though all the research shows that people with a first break psychosis have much better outcomes if they maintain their relationships.

WH Overcoming isolation is key, which is why the patient's self help movement is so important.

MO Our system really aids and abets a social destruction of the person and an induction into the patient role, which is very, very difficult to reverse once it's in place.

WH Those individuals also become consumers of the pharmaceuticals and mental health services marketplace. So there's an immediate incentive to keep people sick.

MO Yes, and even though medication in some instances can be helpful, no country medicates people in acute crisis the way we do in the United States. When I was visiting Keropudas Hospital someone said to me, "You know I heard in the US it's practically illegal not to medicate people diagnosed with psychosis."

WH Which is effectively true, given how professionals are so afraid of malpractice lawsuits, violating the standard of care, or being blamed if something goes wrong.

MO Finland is not a psychiatric utopia. But they are inspiring because they are humanizing what can be an inhumane approach. They do have many stories to tell about situations where they wish they'd been more helpful. There are instances in Open Dialogue where everyone feels someone would benefit from being in the hospital for a while. But hospitalization is not used to reinforce a diagnosis or to drug them until they're numb. They're not discharged into a homeless shelter, or put out to the world with a frightening label and no sense of a future. The idea in Open Dialogue is to create a network around the person so they have a world to return to. ∎

Family Homes
Carina Håkansson

Carina Håkansson is a psychotherapist and manager at Family Care Foundation in Sweden, an alternative treatment program for people in life crisis including what is called psychosis. The Foundation was featured in Daniel Mackler's film *Healing Homes*.

The family home is a kind of a foster home. Someone experiencing what might be called a psychiatric crisis is placed in an ordinary home with people who are not trained professionals, and we provide therapists to support the person and the host family. Most of the 500 people who come to us have been in many, many mental health facilities before, and are considered hopeless and the most difficult, including with criminal and violent backgrounds.

One woman came to us diagnosed with schizophrenia; she was in the system long term and was considered unreachable, a "chronic" mental patient. She hadn't been able to speak or have a conversation in a so-called normal way for the last five years. All she did was scream.

In the home the family invited her to be part of daily life if she wanted. They didn't try to analyze her, they didn't try to get under her skin. Slowly she took part in work on the farm and found some peace in daily routines. It took time and eventually a connection was formed between her and the people in the home. It turned out her screaming was because she had been extremely hurt in her life.

We try to create a place where it is possible to be a human being, with all its complexities. Those who are called "clients" have the same needs as all of us: for time, for caring, and for trust. The challenge is to remember this every day, and to create a kind of engagement that you could even actually call love. ∎

Sanctuary for Madness
Michael Cornwall

Michael Cornwall, PhD, has been a therapist since 1980. His doctoral research was on the Jungian sanctuary Diabasis House, and he leads Esalen Institute workshops on compassionately serving people in extreme states.

We took all comers, no matter how violent, wild, suicidal or out of control, because we believed unexpressed emotion is at the core of madness.

As William Blake said, "The eye altering, alters all."

For a very long season darkness was my portion. I wandered the streets at night raving inside, hearing voices, and seeing signs and portents everywhere of a culture in death throes. I felt like an alien being in a dreamscape world of shadow and menacing indifference.

Night after sleepless night I held my finger on the hospital emergency room phone number in the open yellow pages book, vowing that if one more wave of terror descended on me I would call for help.

But I never called. I knew people swept up in the system's net and then sentenced to a lifetime of shame as outcasts, so I feared the same would happen to me. I survived madness not by being picked up by the police or ending up in the state hospital. I survived because I was able to be mad in a sanctuary.

My very aged grandmother had raised me as a boy, and I went to live in her small house. She was senile and didn't know what day it was, but her loving heart was open and full of unconditional love. I would go to her when the torment was unbearable and she placed her gnarled but warm and loving hand on my head. My grandmother had no idea what was wrong with me, but she would just say 'There, there dear, you will feel better soon, you must have the flu Michael...'

Her home was my sanctuary. Weeks turned into months. Suicide seemed the only way out. But I was so terrified of death that living death was my fate. One fateful morning I saw a slim book on the bookshelf, and I opened it and read the first sentence that came into view. The words expressed merciful compassion: "Come unto me all ye who labor and are heavy laden and I will give you rest."

Unbidden, I felt a divine love, stronger than the uncanny menace and fear, fill the void inside me. That night a sense of hope told me to let go, to let myself fall into the sleep I had shunned because of fear a dark energy waited to claim me. So I let go, and fell backwards like off a tall building. I cried out in surrender and exploded in whirling lights and sounds, shuddering spasms of death. But it was not death, it was a return to life.

I was 20 years old.

That day in 1970 when I let go and trusted love and light to catch me, I made a silent vow, a vow that later became an unshakable credo. If I ever could help another through hell, I would.

I-Ward in Northern California opened in 1975 and for 8 years served more young mad people than any other alternative program that has existed in the United States. It is almost unknown today because there was no research component built into the program design. It was my great privilege to serve on staff there for several years.

I-Ward was founded by Dr. Stanley Mayerson after he worked at the Agnews State Hospital research project. The Agnews project was a National Institute for Mental Health double-blind study that showed psychotic patients who were unmedicated had better long term outcomes than those on Thorazine, and a lower re-hospitalization rate. Mayerson designed I-Ward based on what the Agnews project demonstrated and on leading edge ideas about madness at the time, including Gregory Bateson, Joseph Campbell, John Weir Perry, Alan Watts, Stanislav Grof, and R.D. Laing.

I-Ward had 20 beds and was unlocked. The building was a single story, free standing old TB ward at the edge of the state hospital grounds, with miles of open hillside behind it and a wonderful redwood grove overshadowing the building. We served everyone who came to the psychiatric emergency room nearby, and within minutes of someone's first contact with the system one of us would bring them up to the sanctuary.

I immediately felt at home on I-Ward. We did not believe in the mental illness paradigm or in diagnostic labeling: we viewed madness as a process of growth and individuation, a necessary developmental crisis of dramatic separation from the family. The county mental health system required diagnoses to receive insurance reimbursement, so we just diagnosed everyone with "brief reactive psychosis." From our revolutionary perspective, I-Ward was a pirate ship or a Trojan Horse that would transform the whole system around us.

We took all comers, no matter how violent, wild, suicidal or out of control, because we believed unexpressed emotion is at the core of madness. Many I-Ward residents would rage for hours in a padded, unlocked room, where we would hold them lovingly. We used no physical restraints, and when people would wind down they would cuddle into the arms of staff, cry softly and sometimes sob, in a deep regression of safely being held.

The first resident I worked with left me moved and humbled. The I-Ward Director, bearded and wild-haired, sporting hoop earrings and a leather pouch across his chest, told me nothing about them, just "Go find out who they are."

I walked to the dayroom, and standing atop a table was a beautiful young woman, totally nude, in ecstatic transport. Her arms were outstretched to the heavens and her face was a mask of radiant ecstasy, and she chanted over and over in a quavering, sobbing voice, "Glorious, Glorious, Glorious!"

I was so stunned I didn't know what to do. I had never seen anyone this completely possessed by madness. I remember introducing myself, which felt pretty stupid, like someone interrupting Saint Theresa. The young woman looked down at me with such sweet kindness, and again I was at a loss.

I ushered her to a nearby room where she sat wrapped herself in a blanket. She sat and continued to repeat, more softly now, "Glorious, Glorious, Glorious."

But her divine, light-filled consciousness was soon to shift to the other pole. Within a day she explained that the glorious spirit of God directed the right side of her body, but that Satan was in control of the left. She extended her left hand to me and her face was transformed into a mask of snarling malevolence.

We viewed madness as growth and individuation, a necessary developmental crisis of dramatic separation from the family.

Her voice became guttural and she rasped, "In this hand is the evil of Satan..."

She shifted back to her love filled right side, and was not frightened by this back and forth between darkness and light. But I was. There had been a suicide at the private hospital while I worked previously, and just before I arrived there had been a suicide at I-Ward. This young woman, however, was to survive her dramatic journey through madness.

She made a caring connection with me and other staff, and had space for her psyche to do its own re-organization. She would rage for over an hour at times, and the rocket fuel of un-medicated madness drove surges of emotion and archetypal imagery. She left I-Ward after 2 months, and for years I wondered what became of her. Then one day she phoned, wanting a referral for a family member with a problem. I asked her how she herself was doing, and she answered matter of factly, as if I should have known: "Oh Michael, didn't you know, I got all of mine out on I-Ward!"

What I remember most from working at the I-Ward sanctuary was one night sitting in the long hallway. The lights were dim, and towards the entrance I saw a young woman come out of her room. She looked frightened. I knew well from my own season of madness that nighttime was often the worst.

A very kind woman staff person approached immediately, and put her arm lovingly around the frightened young woman's shoulder. She leaned her head in and smiled warmly, speaking words of comfort that I could not hear at the distance.

Suddenly a golden light surrounded them both. I shook my head to rouse myself, but I wasn't slipping into a dream. Some would say I was hallucinating, but I don't believe I was: the light I saw around the two figures held an emotion that hung in the air. My heart vibrated with a feeling that took my breath away.

It was the ancient healing light that shines where the mysteries of madness occur and have occurred ever since we became human. It was the light of love. ∎

It was the ancient healing light that shines where the mysteries of madness have occurred ever since we became human.

Inside Soteria House
Voyce Hendrix

Voyce Hendrix was clinical director of the Soteria project, worked closely with Soteria founder Dr. Loren Mosher, and was co-author of the National Institute of Health report on Soteria.

A lot of people went all the way through a psychotic process without medications.

WILL HALL Were you always interested in psychology and working as a therapist?

VOYCE HENDRIX I actually thought of myself as an athlete more, I was a pole vaulter. But the military changed that. I was drafted, and that's very different from a volunteer army. The military changes you, you grow up real fast.

I remember working in communications and we had these different codes, and one day I saw one and thought, What is that? The code was "Vietnam." This was right before the war escalated, but I had done my time in the Army and so I was discharged.

I became a touring musician, traveling around. It was probably about a year on the road, and one night I remember waking up in a hotel, not having a clue where I was or what I was doing, thinking that all of these hotels are the same. I was by myself and I thought, "I can't do this anymore. This is not who I am." So I ended my music career. My girlfriend was on staff at Agnew State Hospital and suggested I try working there, so I did. That was 1965.

WH How did you meet Loren Mosher and become clinical director of Soteria House?

VH Loren did a double-blind study at Agnew State Hospital when I was there that had a huge impact on hospital culture. They assigned new psychotic patients either placebo or medication, to show people could get better without medication. This was the '60s and at the time young people were growing their hair and dressing informally. But all Agnew staff, including me, wore white uniforms and hats. Within a year of the study the entire staff wore normal clothes, and you could wear a beard. That study transformed hospital culture.

WH How did the study go?

VH Though it was a double blind study, the staff claimed to "know" who was taking medications and who wasn't, because of who got better. But at the end it was almost totally the opposite: people the staff thought had recovered because they were on medication were actually not on medication.

This was a time of great changes. My friend David Rosenhan did a hugely important research study, "Being Sane in Insane Places," where hospitals labeled graduate student volunteers with schizophrenia solely because they said that they imagined hearing a strong noise.

After the Agnew project Loren got a proposal for the Soteria House study, which he ran from 1971-1983 in San Jose California, and he invited me to be involved. I was considering quitting the field altogether, but something happened at Agnew that made me stay.

A young kid around 21 was admitted to the hospital unit at Agnew where I worked. He would sit and gesture to himself, smiling and sort of laughing. The head nurse was very upset he was making gestures, and said he clearly needed medication. We went to give him a shot and he immediately stopped what he was doing and was very rational, and said, "No, I don't want the medications, I am allergic to it." There was nothing in the chart saying he was allergic. So we held him down and gave him the shot.

It turned out he was in fact allergic like he said, and he had an aller-

People who came through Soteria had markedly better results: less criss, fewer hospital readmissions, less long term disability and much lower medication use.

gic reaction to the medications. He wound up biting a large chunk out of his arm. It was a very vivid thing to see. It disturbed me.

Something was wrong, I had learned nursing, and this didn't make sense. He wasn't doing anything or hurting anybody. The fact was that the *nurse* was upset. But we dealt with him instead of dealing with her. At Soteria, if I saw someone like this guy and I said, "We need to do something," other Soteria staff would point out that it was *me* who was upset, not him.

There were several of those kinds of incidents I saw as a traditional nurse, so when Loren was talking about doing innovative things, I took a large cut in pay and went to work at Soteria.

Loren was chief of the Center for Studies of Schizophrenia at thee NIMH at the time he started Soteria: he was in the top position in psychiatry in terms of public service, at least. And he had also spent a year in London at Kingsley Hall.

WH That was Scottish psychiatrist R.D. Laing's experimental community at the Philadelphia Association.

VH Folks with a mental health issue could live in a sort of asylum at Kingsley Hall. And no one had staff status, there were people called Friends of Kingsley Hall just to be there and be supportive. In his time there Loren saw people going through psychotic processes without medication and coming out doing better on the other end. Some people were using medications, and there were a lot of people not doing well, but overall it was therapeutic and people were being helped.

Loren couldn't explain why some people were getting better or some weren't, so he came back to the US and designed a study using some of what he saw at Kingsley Hall, adapted to the US culture. The first Soteria staff trained with Jungian John Weir Perry, and we did a retreat at Esalen, the human potential movement center.

WH How was the Soteria research designed?

VH Clients we accepted had to be on their way to being hospitalized, considered a danger to themselves, danger to others, or gravely disabled. People were very psychotic when they came to Soteria. We also didn't take people with drug or alcohol issues, which could confuse things. And we didn't take married people because they already had a greater likelihood of recovery. We focused on people who were at most risk for becoming chronic in the system, people aged 18-35 who would get diagnoses like schizophrenia, paranoid schizophrenia, or bipolar with psychosis.

WH What was the medication policy at Soteria?

VH For the study 100% of the control group at the county hospital received medication. At Soteria we did use medication, but it was only about 8% of the clients, and it was short term. There was also a third control group of people who were considered for Soteria but who were turned down because it was full, to make sure they had similar outcomes to the hospital group and we weren't taking only the clients more likely to recover clients.

> If I saw someone like this guy and I said, "We need to do something" other Soteria staff would point out that it was *me* who was upset, not him.

People who came through Soteria had markedly better results: less criss, fewer readmissions, less long term disability, and much lower medication use. Soteria clients also ended up with much better employment than the hospital group; I even ran into a former client who now works a job in high tech. And the costs between Soteria and the hospital group were about the same.

WH What else was different about Soteria?

VH What really stands out about Soteria is that we tolerated what we call psychosis. As long as people were not hurting anyone we tolerated it. And a lot of people went all the way through a psychotic process without medications.

WH To tolerate psychosis often means stretching taboos and ideas of what's acceptable. Getting naked, being idle for days and days, anger, vulgarity, weird communication styles, obsessive ranting, solitude... as a society we assume it's degrading for someone to go through such things, so we prefer to medicate them into looking more acceptable.

One of the problems with the mental health system today is we are not there. You give medication and then people are just so isolated.

VH If someone was in a psychotic state and left the house, for example, we didn't stop them. Soteria was never locked. If they walked out the door we just walked with them.

I remember one man who said, "I'm taking off, I don't want to be here anymore" and walked out. I felt really unsafe seeing him to do that, so I walked out behind him. He said, "You stay here!" And I said, "I feel uncomfortable where you are at this point." And I walked behind him for a while, and after a mile or so walking we started talking. We walked for at least four or five miles around town talking for several hours, and eventually wound up back at the front door of Soteria. And he went back in, went upstairs and went to sleep. He was over it.

WH I'm trying to imagine that happening in a hospital setting today: at one outpatient residence where I lived, I was told if I even tried to leave they'd call the police.

VH We had that commitment to people, even people we think are so delusional they're not in touch. It wasn't about technique, it was about relationship.

Let me give an example: the first resident at Soteria was very psychotic. One night she and I spent a lot of time sitting together, and I had no idea what she was talking about, but I was trying to use this technique I learned from a Freudian, Melanie Klein: I kept interpreting what she said in terms of "Good Mommy" and "Bad Mommy."

Years later she had left the system and was doing great, is a surfer, enjoying having her life together. We were talking together at a restaurant, and she says, "Do you remember that night sitting together? That was so comforting, it was one of the best days of my life."

> ## Soteria was never locked. If they walked out the door we just walked with them.

Then she says, "But you were kind of strange, you kept talking about 'Good Mommy' and 'Bad Mommy.'" Here I was thinking I was a great therapist, but she was more in touch with herself than I was at the time! It was the comfort that was important, not some psychoanalytic interpretation I was offering.

And from that point on, in my whole professional life I saw interventions and approaches as making no sense. We have an idea that people are broken and we fix them with our interpretations and techniques. It's not about that. It is about relating to people.

So working there affected me as much as it affected others. I am a very different person because of Soteria.

WH How did relationships at Soteria help people in psychosis?

VH I don't believe the brain is broken to begin with. I don't know what schizophrenia is and I don't think anyone else knows. These are labels that we have put together. A diagnosis just means a normal brain has the capacity to do all kinds of things and function in all kinds of ways. We adapt to the social system, we adapt our values and behaviors. Humans can't survive in systems where they don't understand the rules. So we create some kind of other reality and then work within that reality. That gets called psychosis. I think that's what's going on.

If you create a healthy social system, people will pick out of that social system what they need to balance themselves. I can be who I am and I can be there, and then the other person maybe can use something from me or maybe not use something from me, and thereby change who they are. But there is no way for me to do that *to* the person.

The best and most powerful thing we can do in a therapeutic setting is to be there. The brain has a capacity to change. It's like if you hurt your hand or arm and you keep it clean, 90% of the time it will heal itself.

One of the problems with the mental health system today is we are not *there*. We give medication and then people are just so isolated. That's why other countries around the less developed world, without modern treatment systems, often have better recovery. People are not institutionalized, they stay with their families, their behaviors are more or less tolerated. They can go out in the community, because the community itself is more flexible in allowing for strange behavior. And so people get through it.

WH Is there one more example or story you wanted to share from Soteria?

VH 50% of the positive outcomes at Soteria came from something we only realized after the research was analyzed: anyone who went through Soteria was encouraged to come back to Soteria and be involved at some level.

If you create a healthy social system, people will pick out of that social system what they need to balance themselves.

So what happened is that a large connected community was formed, and that helped people recover.

In 1983 when we closed Soteria we had a final get together for everyone. And just by calling three staff and two ex-residents they were able to locate 80% of folks who went to Soteria. That's how connected the community was.

WH People really stayed in touch and formed lasting friendships.

VH There was one woman who left Soteria and went back to her secretary job. Then when something happened in her family, her mother died

I think, she showed up again at the house. You would see her with everybody, hugging and laughing and talking. Then an old staff or ex-resident would start talking to her and it would come out what had happened. She did this at least four times during the thirteen years we were there, a loss, a breakup with a boyfriend, or different things. She would be with us for three or four hours, maybe sleep on the couch over night, then go to work the next day. And then years later she would come back. Without that kind of support it's more than likely she would have ended up hospitalized again.

Humans can't survive in systems where they don't understand the rules, so they create some kind of reality and then work within that reality. That gets called psychosis.

WH After I left a facility where I lived in San Francisco, I tried to contact one of the few friends I made. Staff wouldn't help me reach him. They could have used an intermediary if they were concerned about his privacy, but they didn't.

VH A lot of ex-Soteria folks became volunteers and several of them became staff. Most of the folks there as residents came back once or twice after they moved out. Soteria was a kind of a flop house! And a lot of the new residents would wind up making friends with an ex-resident who was hanging around, and so they had someone to share a room with as a way out to leave Soteria.

Soteria happened thirty years ago. People say we can't do studies like this today, because we have become so pro-medication that a project like Soteria, where we didn't use meds, is considered unethical. But the human impact of medication, the dismal recovery rates, the wasteful cost of traditional hospital care... it all says we have to look at history and at Soteria for a new way forward. ∎

Letter to the Mother of a "Schizophrenic"
Will Hall

California has gone through a long political struggle around whether to involuntary treat and drug people in mental health crisis. This essay, written in 2015, is a response to that struggle, and appeared in *Psychology Tomorrow* web magazine and *Mad In America*.

How can friendship and trust possibly come out of violence?

A few months ago I met your son. He said he would be waiting for us in the Berkeley park near where he sleeps outside at night, but at the last minute he called and was in San Francisco. He said he was at "the Mrs. Doubtfire house" with a photograph of his best friend, and that the photo showed numbers and codes predicting Robin Williams' suicide. He found the house where Williams made one of his films, and was trying to talk to the owner: it was all part of a complex plan, marked mathematically in signs and omens he was collecting.

We drove across the Bay, worried. Were we too late? Would he be arrested and end up in the hospital again, this time for trespassing and harassment, a psychotic man caught bothering someone at a private residence?

When the GPS showed we were getting near the address he gave, I started to see people milling around, a commotion, cars stopped. My first thought was that something had happened. Maybe we weren't in time, maybe he was already in trouble with the police, arrested at the house he seemed obsessed with?

At Steiner and Broadway we found your son, sitting on the sidewalk, but he wasn't alone. He wasn't the only one interested in the Mrs. Doubtfire house. The sidewalk was strewn with flowers, and dozens of other people were also there. What first seemed crazy, now seemed normal: many people, like your son, were drawn to the private residence where a Robin Williams film was made, to commemorate the actor's suicide with a pilgrimage.

I walked up to your son and greeted him, unsure how this young disheveled man would respond to me. I had been told he was considered "severely mentally ill," the worst of the worse, so beyond reach in his delusions that clinicians were considering using force to bring him

We can, and must, do better. We must think outside of the false choice between coercion or no help.

to the hospital for treatment. But as soon as we made eye contact I was surprised. There was a clear feeling of affinity and communication. He explained in rapid speech about the numbers and messages on the photo, Robin Williams' middle name, and the sidewalk code. It was all part, he said, of an alphanumeric psyche that communicates to him through signs and coincidences.

It was exhilarating and exhausting keeping up with the math calculations, anagrams, and nimble associations that flowed when he spoke. But he also at times talked normally, planned a walk up the street to a coffeehouse, explained what had happened about our delayed meeting. I lost the thread at different points in our discussion, but one thing was clear: your son is brilliant. I was not surprised when he told us he got a perfect score on the SAT. "It was easy," he explained when I asked. "Anyone can get a perfect score if they take the practice tests."

We were quickly engrossed in conversation, and when he unexpectedly wove the author Kurt Vonnegut into the pattern, my eyes widened. Just moments before our meeting I was talking with my colleague, telling my own story of meeting Vonnegut. And now here your son was mentioning the author. I was amazed by the coincidence. As your son's talk became wilder and more complex, referencing the Earth Consciousness Coordinating Office, SEGA Dreamcast, and numerology, and as he did math equations instantly to prove his obscure points, I sensed an uncanny power and clairvoyance in the air. I was in the presence of someone in a different reality, but a reality with its own validity, its own strange truth. A different spiritual view.

Perhaps I am eager to raise up your son's talents because today he finds himself so fallen. I don't romanticize the suffering that he, or anyone, endures. His unusual thoughts and behavior led to a diagnosis of schizophrenia, and seem to be part of deeper emotional torment he is struggling with. I don't romanticize because I've been through psychosis and altered states myself. I've been diagnosed schizophrenic, many years and many life lessons ago, moving on with my life only after I found ways to embrace different realities and still live in this one.

So when we met your son I was completely surprised. The "severely mentally ill man" I was told needed to be forced into treatment was intelligent, creative, sensitive... and also making sense. Like someone distracted by something immensely important, he related to us in fits and starts as he sat in conversation. Living on the street and pursuing an almost incomprehensible "calorie game" of coincidences on food wrappers isn't much of a life, perhaps. And maybe it's not really a choice, at least not a choice that most of us would make, concerned more with getting by than we are with art, spirit and creativity. But what surprised me was the connection I had with your son. Because I took the time, and perhaps I also have the background and skill, I was quickly able to begin a friendship.

By taking interest in his wild visions, not dismissing them as delusional, and by telling him about my own mystical states, not acting like an expert to control him, we began to make a bond. Tentative, fragile, but a beginning. I spoke with respect and interest in his world, rather than trying to convince him he "needs help." What, after all, could be more insulting than telling someone their life's creative and spiritual obsession is just the sign they need help? That it has no value? By setting aside the professional impulse to control and fix, I quickly discovered, standing on that cold sidewalk and then over hot tea in a cafe, that your son is able to have a conversation, can relate, communicate, even plan his day and discuss his options. Some topics were clearly pained, skipped over for something else, and he was often strangely distracted, but it was after all our first meeting, and I sensed some terrible and unspoken traumas present that were still not ready to be recognized. But to me, clearly, he was not "unreachable."

That we had a connection in just a short time made it very hard for me to understand why you or anyone would want to use force, to use *violence*, to get him into mental health treatment. A traumatic assault by medical personnel, instant mistrust, betrayal, restraint, then a complex web of threat, coercion, and numbing medications to impose compliance, possibly a revolving door of re-hospitalization, more medications, more threats and force and police... Surely creating a relationship, building trust, and interacting with compassion over time is a much better way to show concern and offer help?

> I was in the presence of someone in a different reality, but a reality with its own validity, its own strange truth.

When you think you know what is best for someone, it might seem faster to send a patrol car and force them off the streets and into a locked hospital cell. But would that really be safer? For whom? Or would it push someone farther away, undermine the connection needed to find a real way out of crisis?

You've become an outspoken public advocate of new legislation to empower clinicians to intervene drastically in the life of your son and others like him. In pushing for so-called "Laura's Law" the idea is to pressure, through force, compliance with medication and hospital care. Your son, homeless and in an altered state, is today held up as a perfect example of why force is needed. I share your desire to help people in need; that's why I went to meet your son in the first place. And I agree that our broken mental health system needs fixing, including new legislation and new services. I do want your son to get support. I want there to be more resources, more access to services, more connection, more caring, more healing. But I do not see your son, or people like him, as so "unreachable" that they cannot form a relationship with someone genuinely interested. That just wasn't the man I met that day. I don't see him as so less than human that his own voice and perspective should be ignored. I don't see strange beliefs and an outsider lifestyle on the street in any way justifying the violence of forced treatment. I don't see him as any different than any other human being, a human who would be terribly damaged by the violence of force, confinement, and assault, regardless of it being perpetrated in the name of "help."

That day I met your son I met a man possessed by a mysterious artistic and spiritual quest that others around him can't understand. He is homeless and perhaps very afraid deep down, but he is a person with feelings, vulnerabilities, emotions. Alongside the rapid fire associations that I couldn't keep up with, he was also capable of connecting. His pilgrimage to Robin William's Mrs. Doubtfire house wasn't some lone obsessive symptom, the sign of schizophrenia and a broken brain, but understandable when put in context.

The sidewalk was strewn with flowers, and dozens of other people were also there. What first seemed crazy, now seemed normal.

His ranting was not a meaninless mutter but a creative and encyclopedic stream of enormous intellect. Yes he seemed to be in touch with some other reality, an altered state that demanded most of his attention. Yes I would love to see him living indoors, less afraid, more cared for and more caring for himself. I'd like to see many homeless people in the Bay Area have the same. But no, this is not a man I would want to force into restraints, injections, and confinement. I would not want anyone to be subjected to such violence, and it is violence, as people who have endured it will tell you. I would not want to destroy my emerging friendship with him with such an attack, because I know it is friendship, long, slow, developing connection and understanding, that can truly heal people who are tumbling in the abyss of madness.

Concerned and wanting to help, wouldn't it be better for us to find the resources to gently befriend your son, to learn more about him, create trust, and meet him in his life and world? Even if this took patience, skill, and effort? Isn't this how we want others to approach us if we seem, in their opinion, to be in need of help? Don't we want our voice respected if we disagree with someone about what is best for us? How can friendship and trust possibly come out of violence?

It might seem faster to send a patrol car and force them off the streets and into a locked hospital cell. But would that really be safer? For whom?

Again and again I am told the "severely mentally ill" are impaired and incapable, not quite human. I am told they are like dementia patients wandering in the snow, with no capacity and no cure, not to be listened to or related to. I am told they must be controlled by our interventions regardless of their own preferences, regardless of the trauma that forced treatment can inflict, regardless of the simple duty we have to regard others with caring, compassion, and respect, regardless of the guarantees of dignity we afford others in our constitution and legal system. I am told the "high utilizers" and "frequent flyers" burden services because they are different than the rest of us. I am told the human need for patience doesn't apply to these somehow less-than-human people.

And when I finally do meet the people carrying that terrible, stigmatizing label of schizophrenia, what do I find? I find a human being. A human who responds to the same listening and curiosity that I, or anyone, responds to. I find a human who is above all terrified, absolutely terrified, by some horrible trauma we may not see or understand. A human being who shows all the signs of flight and mistrust that go along with trauma. A person who may seem completely bizarre but who still responds to kindness and interest, and recoils, as we all would, from the rough handling and cold dismissal so often practiced by mental health professionals. Listening and curiosity might take skill and affinity, to be sure, when someone is in an alternate reality. But that just makes it even more of a responsibility to provide that skill and affinity. Do we really want to add more force and more violence to a traumatized person's life, just because we were not interested in finding a different way?

Your son may be frightened, may be in a different reality, may spend most of his time very far away from human connection. But his life, like everyone's, makes sense when you take time to understand it. He deserves hope for change, and he deserves careful, patient, skilled efforts to reach him and to connect, not the quick fix falsely promised by the use of force.

Even under the best of circumstances mothers and sons sometimes have a hard time communicating. Many young people refuse help just because the hand that offers it is the hand of a parent they are in conflict with. Perhaps the need for independence is stronger than the need to find refuge in the arms of a parent. Perhaps children flee their parents in spite of themselves, because of some complex reality they are seeking to overcome, some developmental impulse for independence and autonomy. So maybe the help that is needed is not just for the sick individual but for repairing broken relationships. I say this because after my own recovery from what

I do not see your son, or people like him, as so "unreachable" that they cannot form a relationship with someone genuinely interested.

was called "schizophrenia" I became a counselor with families. I see again and again, and the colleagues I work with also see again and again, that by rebuilding relationships, not tearing them down with force, healing can occur. A young person whose promising life and career were interrupted by psychosis can regain hope for that possible future.

A simple look at the research literature over the past 50 years shows that recovery from what is diagnosed as schizophrenia is well documented and a real possibility, for everyone. Not a guarantee, but a possibility worth striving for. It is only in the past few decades that we forget this basic clinical truth about the prognosis of schizophrenia and psychosis, and instead predict chronic, long term illness, for everyone (and lifelong customers for the pharmaceutical companies). Such a prediction threatens to become a self-fulfilling prophecy, as we lower our expectations, give up hope, and relegate people to a lifetime of being controlled and warehoused in the identity of "severely mentally ill."

I do believe help is needed, help not just for your son, but help for everyone in the family affected by the strange and overwhelming experience of psychosis. But when parents, who are alone and desperate to change their children, resort to pleas for force and coercion, they risk sacrificing the very connection and bond that can be the pathway towards getting better.

I hear the claim that Yes, we should respect the right to refuse help, but when people are suffering so greatly and everything else has been tried, we have no choice but to infringe on freedom. This is false. We have not already tried everything we can. We have not tried everything we can with your son, or with you. There is a huge wellspring of creative possibilities, skill, and resources possible if we just direct our mental health system to try harder and do better for you and your son and the many people like you. It takes money, vision, and political willpower, but people struggling with mental illness deserve the dignity of true help, not false promises of quick fixes.

We can, and must, do better. We must think outside of the false choice between coercive help or no help. We might start by asking people who have recovered from psychosis, and there are many, what they needed to get better, and give them a leading role in shaping our mental health policies. We might start by respecting people's decision to avoid treatment, and seek to understand the decision rather than overpower the person making it. When you have been traumatized by violence from those offering help, avoiding treatment might even be a sign of sanity, not madness.

> His ranting was not a meaningless mutter but a creative stream of enormous intellect.

Maybe some of us, when we are terrified, discover different realities to hide in. And maybe some of us, when we are terrified about people we love, reach for help in desperate measures like forced treatment policies and Laura's Law. I believe that people who are afraid, perhaps such as your son and perhaps such as you yourself, need caring, kindness, patience and listening. Trying to force you, or him, to change may only drive us all farther apart.

I believe it is often the most brilliant, sensitive, artistic, and yes sometimes even visionary, telepathic, and prophetic people who get overwhelmed by madness. We need to discover who they are, and meet them as we ourselves would want to be met, rather than giving up hope for human connection.

At the cafe where we talked, the waiter was polite, but kept his eye on your son, seeing only a dirty and homeless schizophrenic, not the human being I was getting to know, not the son you love dearly. When we said goodbye I tried to imagine what it would be like, living rough on the street, facing suspicion or worse from everyone I passed. I imagine it would be lonely, that I might fall asleep at night missing my childhood home, missing my mother. ∎

I sensed some terrible and unspoken traumas present that were still not ready to be recognized.

Afterword
Will Hall

SIX YEARS AFTER I MY LAST HOSPITALIZATION I was enrolled as a student again, trying to get a degree, and struggling to regain my life. One day after class I was walking in front of the school, and suddenly I spotted one of my doctors. I hadn't seen him since he kept me locked up for three months at Langley Porter Psychiatric Institute, and I was shaken by the unexpected sighting, so nearby and crossing my path.

Memories flooded in from my time on the psych facility's fourth floor, images of the solitary confinement cell, the room where my blood was drawn for medication levels, and the nurses and doctors who observed and treated me. I felt an uncanny foreboding. I somehow knew, I was certain, that seeing my doctor again right by my school was more than just a coincidence. It meant something powerful. And I also knew that this very same doctor had told me that such feelings of meaningfulness were just symptoms of a diseased brain: believing in coincidences was "ideas of reference," a delusion that got me diagnosed with schizoaffective disorder schizophrenia in the first place. And to trust these feelings was to invite a psychotic crisis.

I was pulled between two worlds, the world where I knew what was true, and the world where my truth was just a sign of illness. As I walked away from the school and away from the doctor, I fought to hold myself together. But I was completely unprepared for what was to happen next.

I arrived at the house where I rented a room. On the table by the front door there was an accumulation of mail addressed to previous tenants, past renters who hadn't yet forwarded to their new address. And when I looked down on the top of the stack, I saw an envelope with a name on it, and the name was shockingly familiar. It was the same name as another one of my doctors, from the same hospital as the doctor I had just seen.

At this point schizophrenia patients are advised to get a "reality test," to check and defuse delusions about coincidences and letters and chance encounters being laden with meaning. We are told to alert someone that we might be on the verge of an episode, as if our perceptions are signs of a ticking bomb about to go off. But I had left the doctors and their advice behind years ago, and I held on to the belief that this was real: something meaningful was happening.

So I went to my housemate, and I told her the story. First of seeing my doctor on the street, right by the school, and then coming home and finding an envelope with the name, spelled exactly the same way, of another doctor I had. And both the sighting and the envelope on the same day.

She looked at me and her eyes widened. "Will," she said, "the man who lived here before you *was* a psychiatrist."

We both couldn't speak. What she was saying was impossible, but it was also, we knew, real. The name wasn't just spelled the same way. It actually was my doctor's name on that envelope.

I stared at her for a long time, and then I asked: *"Which room did he live in?"* And at that moment I learned I had left the hospital behind, found a place in a rented house, enrolled in school, and tried to move on with my life, but I ended up living in the same house, in the same very room, that my psychiatrist had lived in.

Like a portentous dream, the doctor's room that was now my room haunted me. At first I was filled with fear: was I being followed, tracked down by a medical professionals who not only had the social authority to confine me and declare me mentally ill, but also wielded some diabolical magic to find me years afterwards, twisting laws of time and space to suddenly reappear in my bedroom? Would I ever be free of the hospital if psychiatrists could reach through the dreamtime at any moment and enter my life? What other demonic powers did they have?

I tried to act like this wasn't happening, but I couldn't. I knew it wasn't "just" a coincidence. I was certain that, yes, there was meaning to this synchronicity. But was that certainty just a symptom of my illness?

The doctors of Langley Porter Psychiatric Institute had sprung a trap for me that day, and for a moment I thought I couldn't escape. I faced two frightening possibilities: I was trapped because they could control my life with occult powers, or I was trapped because their diagnosis was true and I was delusional. There was no way out.

THE VOICES IN THIS BOOK PRESENT ANOTHER POSSIBILITY. *Outside Mental Health* is a kind of counter-spell, an incantation to ward off fear. At first it was frightening to perceive reality as alive and purposeful, actively sending voices, signs, messages, and meaningful coincidences to communicate with me. But slowly I conjured courage, and I began to trust the way I experience the world. With that courage I discovered a vision, a vision that guides my life and shaped the book you are now reading.

Today I work as a therapist and as a mental health trainer and advocate. So what I feared is true, in a sense: I didn't leave the mental health system behind, I haven't escaped. But it's not a trap, and I'm not cursed: I have made a place outside mental health, and I don't feel haunted knowing I lived in the room of my psychiatrist. I find it inspiring.

Survivors of abuse, including myself, have justifiable anger towards those who have done violence to us. Accepting anger is part of healing any trauma, and anger can lead to action for change. But by arranging that I would live in the room of my psychiatrist, reality sent me a powerful message, a teaching about *how* to make change happen. Can we challenge a system that hurt us, and at the same time know systems are created by people just like ourselves? Can we speak out and act and also see those on the other side, even with their different power and privilege, as sharing a common humanity with us?

Oppressive systems transform when we offer them a new way forward, not when we back them into a corner. Whether we are part of systems or part of movements, whether we wield institutional authority on the inside or stand on moral high ground on the outside, we are all human. We all have the same human shadows of fear, self-interest, and power. Social movements are effective by inviting people to change together, and the greatest victory over psychiatric abuse is in regaining the full humanity of *everyone* touched by the mental health system, patient, professional, and family member alike. Changing the world becomes inspiring when it also means learning to change ourselves, where our opponent might be a reflection of what we find living in our very own bedroom.

It is a very intimate question, how to listen so deeply that we discover the other person is also within us. It invites a kind of listening that reaches deeper than words, into the very felt sense of what it is to be human. It is a sense of humanity central to the world's spiritual traditions, and at the core of the revolutionary nonviolence practiced by Gandhi and Dr. King, by Ella Baker and Harvey Milk. Sometimes it takes an uncanny coincidence to wake us up and remind us who we are. To understand and change the other we must understand and change ourselves.

OUTSIDE MENTAL HEALTH BRINGS TOGETHER VISIONS OF EMPOWERMENT. A mental disorder label means, at essence, "disempowered," and surviving madness, as these interviews and essays suggest, is about regaining the power to define who we are in the world.

But is it just the "mad" or "mentally ill" who are disempowered? Or do patients reflect the disempowerment of everyone in this crazy consumerist world we live in? Haven't we all to some degree lost control of our lives, our voices not heard and our visions cast aside?

I am often asked how I was released from lockup at Langley Porter Psychiatric Institute. Were the medications starting to have a beneficial effect? Did my voices calm down and my suicidal feelings ease? Was I more in contact with reality and better able to take care of myself?

No. I was released from Langley Porter Psychiatric Institute because the insurance money to keep me there ran out. One day I was so psychotic I needed confinement, treatment, and 24 hour observation. And then the next day I was released. Money made the decision, not the system's clinical assessment of my improvement or capacity.

And so the voices of *Outside Mental Health* teach us that responding to madness in a new way depends on far-reaching changes in our world. The problems we point to in the "mental health system" in fact originate in the society as a whole, and to find real solutions we have to trace systems upstream, to their source: disempowerment and inequality. Compared to the power of money wielded by economic elites and organized interest groups such as the insurance, medical, and pharmaceutical lobbies for example, ordinary citizens have little or no say over policymaking today. Our most intimate inner lives are fast being reshaped by huge social forces, and decisions about institutional practices affecting us are made out of reach, in a democracy corrupted by money. Patients, family members, and professionals all feel powerless to change a broken system, and in our day to day lives we are more fragmented, more alienated, and more isolated than ever before. We are disempowered.

And this is true for every human crisis we face. The medical industry's corruption of mental health policy is the same as the fossil fuel industry's corruption of environmental policy, the financial industry's corruption of economic policy, and the military industry's corruption of foreign policy. We all, not just psychiatric survivors, need to overcome our disempowerment. Without freeing our communities and our democracy from corruption by monied interests on both sides of mainstream discussions, without coming together in new ways for change, not only will the mental health system remain as it is, but we won't make headway on *any* issue of popular concern.

We can no longer afford to discuss things narrowly: the acceptable, "normal" way of talking about mental health leaves untouched the real crisis we face. To solve mental health problems we have to think outside "mental health" terms.

Outside Mental Health is an effort to make sense of what is hidden but not talked about, and to find a way to a different reality. A reality that listens to mental diversity, where we can join with each other as humans, ancestors, and spirits, and begin to challenge the normalized violence around us. The people gathered together in this book found the courage to create a more honest conversation about what it means to be called crazy in a crazy world. Their courage inspired me to believe that a different reality is possible, and I hope their courage can inspire you.

That day I saw my psychiatrist by my school, I was at first shocked and frightened. But I learned to overcome my fear, and to believe in the truth within me. I was given a message to see the other inside myself, as the way to change the world.

I believe if we all learn to listen, to truly listen, to ourselves, to each other, and to the voices within us and around us, we will discover the same powerful message, and the way out of our disempowerment. We will discover that we are all, every one of us, living in the same room. ■

Acknowledgments

MANY WONDERFUL FRIENDSHIPS and collaborations over the past three years made this book possible. I am especially indebted to designer Alex Harris, who persevered as the project grew beyond all manageable expectation, to my lead editorial assistant Rene Bermudez, whose dedication buoyed me throughout, and to Summer Brooks, who wove WordPress magic into the *Madness Radio* website. My heartfelt thanks to the many transcribers, proofreaders, translators, readers, and editors who joined the effort, including Meaghan Buisson, Janice Sorensen, Yoshi Matsuo, Nina Packebush, Dina Tyler, Annie Tucker, and Alex Maymi. Leah Harris, Chaya Grossberg, Oryx Cohen, and Krista Mackinnon sparked the crowdsourcing campaign where the book began, and our Kickstarter backers gave resources and believed in this vision. Thank you all.

Madness Radio guests contributed the extraordinary conversations that became *Outside Mental Health*, and the "mad movement" of psychiatric patients, professionals, advocates, and family members gave encouragement and solidarity. I am thankful to the many individuals and families I've worked with in my counseling practice, and to participants in workshops, seminars, and trainings I've led world-wide: their personal experiences and thoughtful reflections have deeply enriched me. An individualistic society loses sight of how creative projects arise collectively, and this book would have been impossible without a resounding Yes from my community and from the spirits, ancestors, and nature that animate it.

Thanks also goes to the guests I was unable to include. Each time I listened to the *Madness Radio* archives I wanted to add a show, and the book quickly became much larger than I ever anticipated. Difficult choices were unavoidable, but every interview is available free online.

At the risk of leaving someone out, I want to thank individually the following colleagues, volunteers, donors, supporters, advocates, and show listeners who helped make this work possible. Over the years collaborators inevitably ran into my own struggles as an interviewer, radio producer, and editor, so I want also to thank everyone for your patience as I poured myself, shadows and all, into this project. If this book is indeed part of a movement, that movement is most importantly a movement of kindness, and a movement I am very grateful to call my home.

— Will Hall

Thank you

Abigail Adams, Adam Jhugroo, Adi Hasanbasic, Agustina Vidal, Aidan Mackinnon, Aki Imai, Al Galves, Al Young, Alan Arenius, Alan Dunnigan, Albert Duran, Alex Harris, Alex Maymi, Alex Rowan, Alex Samets, Alexandra Lamoureux, Alice Lithgow, Alisa Klein, Alison Bass, Alison Hillman, Altostrata, Amra, Amy Bookbinder, Amy Morgan, Amy Upham, Amy Zulich, Angela Bischoff, Angela Shelton, Ann, Ann Silver, Anna Maddock, Anne Fletcher, Anne Weaver, Annie Robinson, Anthony Ciccarino, Anusuya Star Bear, Ari Nee'man, Arley Lindberg, Arnold Mindell, Azure Akamay, Barb Westover, Barney Plisko, Bec Young, Ben Abelow, Bert, Bert Karon, Betty Tuchler, Bill Dwight, Bob Gardner, Bobbi Creech, Bobby, Bogna Szymkiewicz, Bonfire Madigan Shive, Brian Hartnett, Brian Mackinnon, Brian McKinnon, Brian Rottinghaus, Bruce Levine, C. Beaumont, Caitlin Belforti, Carey Lamprecht, Carina Håkansson, Carole Hayes Collier, Carole Hayes-Collier, Carrie Bergman, Catherine L. Penney, Catherine Penney, Catherine Rosinski, Caty Simon, Celia Brown, Charlotte Campogna, Cheryl Alexander, Cheryl Prax, Chiaroscuro, Chico, Chris Hansen, Christa Burkett, Christopher Lane, Cindy Trawinski, Clare Simons, Colin, Colleen Sondrini, CV Scott, Dana Dart-Maclean, Daniel Fisher, Daniel Hazen, Daniel L. Ballif, Daniel Lewis, Daniel Mackler, Darby Penney, Dave Burns, David Bedrick, David Cohen, David Healy, David Lukoff, David Oaks, David Walker, David Webb, Dawn Mencken, Debbie, Delphine Brody, Derrick Jensen, Diana Epperson, Dianne Dragon, Digital Eyes Film, Dionysia Dionysus, Dirk Corstens, Dorea Vierling-Claasen, Dorothy Dundas, Dreamer, Duane Haataja, Dylan Tighe, Ed Altwies, Ed Knight, Ed Russell, Eilon Atar, Elahe Hessamfar, Eleanor Longden, Eliza Johnston, Elizabeth, Elizabeth Ann Gignac, Elizabeth Joy Zarek, Elle, Ellen Hayes, Emily Rottinghaus, Empties, Eric Nash, Eric Ruin, Eric Stiens, Erica van de Akker, Erick Fabris, Ethan Waters, Evelyn Pringle, Faith Rhyne, Fly, Forteanajones, Frances Crowe, Gabriella Coleman, Gail Hornstein, Gary Greenberg, Gentleman Bank Robber, George Badillo, George Mackinnon, Gheena, Gracelyn Guyol, Grainne Humphreys, Greg Velios, Heather Caldwell, Heinz Toronto, Helen Harrison, High Music, Humbert, Ilya Parizhsky, Indigo Daya, Inez Kochius, Ioan Mitrea, Irit Shimrat, Ivana Klement, J. Chang, Jack Biesek, Jack Carney, Jackie Smith, Jacks Ashley McNamara, Jacqui Dillon, James Weinstein, Jami Lynch, Jan McLaughlin, Jan Peterson, Janice Sorensen, Jason Renaud, Jay Harrison, Jay Joseph, Jay Mahler, Jay Thiemeyer, Jaysen Paulsen, Jen Gouvea, Jen Maurer, Jenka Soderberg, Jenna, Jenna Wikler, Jenny Westberg, Jeremy Lansman, Jill Pierce, Jim Gottstein, Jim Monsonis, Jiro, Jo Comerford, Joan Pinsky, JoDee Brown, Joe Goodbread, Johanna Halbeisen, John Bannister, John Borrego, John Frehn, John Horgan, John Judge, John McCarthy, John Rice, John Skvasik, John Stafford, John T. Heinbuch, Johnny Cashmere, Jonah Bosssewith, Jonathan Metzl, Judi Chamberlin, Judy Hurley, Julia Baber, Julia Ellis, Julie, Julie Spooner, Kalle Lasn, Karen Kieffer, Karen Psaledakis,

Karen Taylor, Karl Erb, Karyn Baker, Kate Bornstein, Kate Hill, Kate Sedgwick, Kate Williams, Kathleen Stevenson, Kayla Rosen, Keeley Malone, Keith Dragon, Ken Paul Rosenthal, Kent Bye, Kermit Cole, Krista Mackinnon, Krista MacKinnon, Krista Tricarico, Kristi Hart, Kristi Jamison, L.J. Lehr, Laura Cox, Laura Delano, Laura Duran, Laura Van Tosh, Laurel Long, Lauren Spiro, Lauren Webster, Laurie Vadnais, Laurie Ahern, Laysha Ostrow, Leah Harris, Lee Entel, Lee LePoutre, Leela Middleton, Lillian, Linda Andre, Linda Wagner, Lisa Darbyshire, Lisa Forrestell, Lisa Jakobsen, Liz Scarfe, Liza Ionia, Louis Sass, Louisa Putnam, Luis Gonzalez, M. Joy Young, Machete Mendías, Marc Comings, Marc Dinacola, Marcia Meyer, Maren Souders, Margo Adair, Margo Robb, Maria Warren, Marian B. Goldstein, Marianna Keffalinou, Marilyn Sue Hall, Mark Brunke, Mark Dinicola, Mary Hagan, Mary Jane Dean, Mary Kinsell, Mary Olson, Mary Schott, Marykate Connor, Maryse, Matt Samet, Matthew Morrissey, Maxine Sheets-Johnstone, Meaghan Buisson, Mel Gunasena, Melanie, Melanie Wilson, Melody Peteren, Metsa Niwue, Michael Cornwall, Michael Gennarelli, Michael Herrick, Michael Kalmbach, Michael Perlin, Michaela Amering, Mick Bysshe, Mike Smith, Miss Led, Mitch Earleywine, Molly, Molly Hardison, Molly Rottinghaus, Molly Sprengelmeyer, Monica Cassani, Moosa Salie, Morana Biljakovic, Myree Morsi, Myriam Rahman, Naas Sidiqui, Nadia Bomez, Nancy Burke, Nancy Chamberlin, Narousz, Nathan Foster, National Empowerment Center, Nazlim Hagmann, Neil Falk, Neil Gong, Nev Jones, Nica Noelle, Nicole Zell, Nutella, Olga Runciman, Oryx Cohen, Pablo Calderon, Pam Rainer, Pamela Murray Winters, Paris Williams, Parke Congleton, Pasha Ciubotaru, Pat Bracken, Pat Deegan, Pat Rhiannon Griffith, Patricia Kubala, Paul Baker, Paul Levy, Paula Feldman, Perry Hall, Pete Tridish, Peter Breggin, Peter Bullimore, Peter Lehman, Peter Stastny, Pheepho, Phil Thomas, Philip Dawdy, Philip Morgan, Pierrette E. Daigle, R. E. B., Rachel Waddingham, Randy Frost, Raymond Tallis, Reason, Rebecca Ross, Reet Nemoja, Rhiannon Griffith, Richard DeGrandpre, Richard Gilluly, Rita Marshall, Robert Manciero, Robert Whitaker, Rocky Caravelli, Ron Bassman, Ron Coleman, Ron Unger, Ross Ellenhorn, Roxie Mack, Rufus May, Russell Baugher, Ruta Mazelis, Sabrina Chapadjiev, Samara, Sandra Blomberg, Sandy Steingard, Sara, Sarah Edmonds, Sarah Seegal, Sascha Altman DuBrul, Scott Lahteine, Scott Steel Toe Boots, Sean Parker, Sera Davidow, Seth Kadish, Seven, Sharin, Sharna Olfman, Sharon Wise, Sheri Mead, Siobhan Mary Reid, Sonia Weaver, Sophie Faught, Stacco, Stacey Haines, Stefanie Baier, Stella Montour, Stella Voreas, Stephanie Pollack, Stephen Kessler, Steve Broadside, Steve Fenwick, Steve Morgan, Steve Rottinghaus, Steven Epperson, Summer Brooks, Sumner Bradley, Susan, Susan Blacker, Susan McKeown, Susan Schechter, Susie Meserve, Suzanne Beachy, Suzanne Richardson, Tamasin Knight, Tammy & Joe McCorkle, Taylor Schulte, Terramuggus, Terry Kupers, The Icarus Project, TIm maxrocknroll, Tim Scott, Tim Wise, Timothy, Toby Watson, Tomi Gomory, Tony, TR Tomkins, Tsuyoshi Matsuo, Vanessa Krasinski, Vara Adams, Veronica Rose, Victor Perera, Vikki Gilbert, Vinay Nair, Vivi Fragou, Wayne Lax, Wendy Dixon, William Stuart McDougall, Willians Valentin, Wilton Hall Jr., Yana Jacobs, Zach Summer, Zeya Kai

387

About Will Hall

WILL HALL, MA, DIPLPW is a counselor, teacher, writer, and community development worker. Active during the University of California anti-apartheid movement, he went on to work for the Santa Cruz Resource Center for Nonviolence and the Earth Island Institute. In his 20s he was forcibly committed to San Francisco's public mental health system, and, while in the locked unit at Langley Porter Psychiatric Institute, he was diagnosed with schizoaffective disorder schizophrenia and put on disability. He became a leading psychiatric survivor organizer, including host of *Madness Radio*, co-founder of Freedom Center and Portland Hearing Voices, and a co-coordinator of The Icarus Project, and he is author of the *Harm Reduction Guide to Coming Off Psychiatric Drugs*, translated into 15 languages. For his work Will has received the Judi Chamberlin Advocacy award, the Portland Oregon Open Minds award, and the Stavros Center for Independent Living Disability Advocacy award.

> *"When I was growing up, I wanted to be a magician. Then I wanted to be a biologist, then I wanted to be a psychologist, then I wanted to be a community organizer, then I wanted to be a philosopher. Now I'm sort of all of them."*
>
> — Will Hall interviewed in the *Portland Mercury* newspaper

CPSIA information can be obtained
at www.ICGtesting.com
Printed in the USA
FFOW01n1311080716
25754FF